Take Charge of Treatment for Your Child with Asperger's (ASD)

of related interest

The Autism Discussion Page on anxiety, behavior, school, and parenting strategies
A toolbox for helping children with autism feel safe, accepted, and competent
Bill Nason
ISBN 978 1 84905 995 4
eISBN 978 0 85700 943 2

Autism and the Stress Effect
A 4-step lifestyle approach to transform your child's health, happiness and vitality
Theresa Hamlin
Foreword by John Ratey and Temple Grandin
ISBN 978 1 84905 748 6
eISBN 978 1 78450 178 5

Parents Have the Power to Make Special Education Work
An Insider Guide
Judith Canty Graves and Carson Graves
ISBN 978 1 84905 970 1
eISBN 978 0 85700 878 7

When the School Says No...How to Get the Yes!
Securing Special Education Services for Your Child
Vaughn K. Lauer
ISBN 978 1 84905 917 6
eISBN 978 0 85700 664 6

Navigating the Medical Maze with a Child with Autism Spectrum Disorder
A Practical Guide for Parents
Edited by Sue X. Ming and Beth A. Pletcher
ISBN 978 1 84905 971 8
eISBN 978 0 85700 860 2

Take Charge of Treatment for Your Child with Asperger's (ASD)

Create a Personalized Guide to Success for Home, School, and the Community

Cornelia Pelzer Elwood and D. Scott McLeod

Foreword by Shonda Schilling

Jessica Kingsley *Publishers*
London and Philadelphia

First published in 2016
by Jessica Kingsley Publishers
73 Collier Street
London N1 9BE, UK
and
400 Market Street, Suite 400
Philadelphia, PA 19106, USA

www.jkp.com

Library of Congress Cataloging in Publication Data
Elwood, Cornelia Pelzer, author.
Take charge of treatment for your child with Asperger's (ASD)
: create a personalized guide to success for home,
school, and the community / Cornelia Pelzer Elwood and D. Scott McLeod.
pages cm
Includes bibliographical references and index.
ISBN 978-1-84905-723-3 (alk. paper)
1. Asperger's syndrome in children. 2. Children with autism spectrum disorders. 3. Parents of autistic children. I. McLeod, D. Scott, author. II. Title.
RJ506.A9E4446 2016
618.92'858832--dc23
2015028809

British Library Cataloguing in Publication Data
A CIP catalogue record for this book is available from the British Library

ISBN 978 1 84905 723 3
eISBN 978 1 78450 207 2

Printed and bound in the United States

We dedicate this book to Alexander Hines Elwood, who by being himself has inspired us to learn, grow, write, and help others.

Contents

Foreword

It is hard to imagine it has been eight years since our son Grant was diagnosed with Asperger's Syndrome. It was something I had never heard until that August morning. As his mother I had always known Grant was different from our other children. I watched him struggle with simple social cues and learned behaviors he seemed to miss, or if he did pick them up it was far later than other children. The diagnosis was a relief. He was different.

Then came the frightening unknown. How do I parent this child and be the mother that he needs when I only know how to be a regular mom? I could only read as time went on and try to incorporate what others learned into our new daily life. It took us years to help Grant find his "normal."

When I opened this book it immediately was recognizable! Here were my mental notes in print—from what doctors to see, to assistance from the school, to the transition from young man to an adult. To be able to have a resource of not just advice and experts, but from people who *know* what you are going through. The cliché "been there, done that" is crucial in this case.

Life with an Aspie can be lonely. Many people around you are like the person in the grocery store looking at the "bad kid" and thinking, "I wish they'd teach their kid better." It is a feeling every Aspie parent can identify with. This book takes you step by step on an amazing journey, slowly taking the fear of the unknown away. I was lucky to know these two special people on my journey.

My son is now a successful ninth-grader in school. He has friends and even a girlfriend. After putting so much time and resources into his life skills my husband and I laugh as he is the most mature, "ready for the world" child we have. That's something I wouldn't even have *tried* to think a few years ago. Read this, add your experiences, and share your discoveries. The saying "Once you meet one Aspie, well you've met one Aspie" will become the most sacred truth you could know. In the end you are going to realize God gave you an amazing gift, just a bit different wrapping paper! You will also realize you and your child do have a common language all your own.

SHONDA SCHILLING

Acknowledgments

Cornelia and Scott

Thank you to Jessica Kingsley Publishers and Rachel Menzies for allowing us this opportunity.

Thank you to Kristen Mellitt for helping us reach our vision. Collaborating with you has been a pleasure.

Thank you to Shonda Schilling for writing the Foreword and for providing encouragement from the beginning.

Thank you to Beth Kaufman for helping to lead us through this process. Your expertise, friendship, and investment of time and energy means so much.

Thank you to Jillian Hansbury Dyment for being such an exceptional special educator and for being a model of collaborating excellence. Thank you for playing such a significant role in helping us think about Alexander's needs and the needs of other students. We appreciate your many contributions of tools, time, and effort for this book.

Thank you to Elsa Abele and Beverly Montgomery for being such outstanding professors for autism spectrum disorders and advocates for individuals on the autism spectrum. We are very grateful that your final assignment at Antioch University led to the foundation of this book.

Thank you to the extraordinary professionals who have enhanced our lives and added tools to our book. We deeply value your input both as contributors to Alexander's team and to our project: Elizabeth Blumenfeld, Kathleen Capone, Michaelene Cronin, Lisa Guerra, Muniza Haq, Dr. Celia Oliver, Melissa Partridge, Dr. Deborah Pease, Maddalene Randall, Sharon Richardson, and Jennie Schofield.

Thank you to the readers of our early drafts and for the people who supported our project in various ways: Jennie Dunkley, Jennie Gooch, Richard Hines, Ellen Korin, Katie Leighton, Amey Lewis, Harriet McDougal, Selwyn Notelovitz, Cornelia Pelzer, Randy Pelzer, Meredith Roy, Amy Voorhes, and Marjorie Wentworth. Your assistance made a major difference to our project.

Thanks to Asperger/Autism Network (AANE) and Antioch University's Autism Spectrum Disorders program for being great resources for individuals on the autism spectrum and their families and to professionals.

Cornelia

Thank you to Michael for believing in me and championing my efforts in countless ways. Your continued support touches my heart.

Thank you to Will for enhancing my life. I appreciate all of the fun, humor, talents, interests, inspiration, and uniqueness that you offer our family. You are an incredibly important part of our family, and I adore you!

Thank you to our entire family for embracing our unique dynamic and for loving us through all of our successes and struggles. A special thank you to my mom for modeling true support, my brother for your daily connection, and my in-laws, including my sisters-in-law and brother-in-law, for doing so much for our family.

Thank you to my close friends and mentor, who have become my extended family and our community. I cherish our connection. The love you provide helps me raise Alexander. Your inspiration, wisdom, and talks positively impact everything I do, including this project.

Thank you to the supportive special educators, general educators, aides, service providers, and family friends who have formed the community that has helped Alexander and our family grow. A special thank you to Josh Croteau and Kevin Doherty, who have supported Alexander's growth. Your daily encouragement and support will have a lasting, positive impact.

Scott

Thank you to my family, Jeanne and Jessica McLeod, for allowing me the time to pursue projects such as this.

Thanks to my parents, sister, and extended family for years of support.

Thank you to Dr. Michael Cauley for extending the dream of Father Tom Panowitz and creating the programs from which Aspire grew. I am also grateful for the leadership of Peggy Carolan and Dr. Ward Cromer who were champions of our programs from the very beginning.

Thank you to Dot Lucci for the creativity and expertise that you regularly share.

Thank you to the leadership of the Lurie Center for ongoing support, especially Dr. Christopher McDougle and Dr. Ann Neumeyer.

Thank you to the current and former Aspire staff, Lindsey Bernard, Lori Hodgins Brazell, Dr. Michael J. Cauley, Francois Dalembert, Kate Garrity, Ann Giauque, Carrie Gross, Jen Kracof, Anna Kyritsis, Christina Lazdowsky, Kathy Lewiecki, Sylvia Lewinstein, Dot Lucci, Genna Lyons, Dr. Alyssa Milot, Dr. Brett Mulder, Leslie O'Brien, Colleen O'Loughlin, Rose Quinn, and Elise Wulff.

Thank you to my colleagues at The Lurie Center and Spaulding, especially Julie O'Brien, Michelle Alexander, Ellen Roth, and Suzanne Bloomer.

Thank you to colleagues and friends at AANE, especially Dania Jekel and Dan Rosenn.

Thank you to all of the participants and families that have been and are part of Aspire for helping us all learn how to help each other grow.

About the Authors

Cornelia Pelzer Elwood

My son, Alexander, is not like most children. He feels perplexed and overwhelmed in most environments including school, home, and the community, which can lead to meltdowns and distress for everyone involved. For example, right before he was diagnosed with Asperger's Syndrome (AS), he went through a series of interviews to determine which school he would attend for kindergarten. On the day of what I considered his most important interview, he and I walked into a charming neighborhood school that my husband and I had toured previously and identified as our top choice for him. He wore a button-down shirt tucked into pressed slacks with a belt and dress shoes. His strawberry blond hair was cleanly cropped and carefully brushed. He looked the part. I helped him navigate the waiting room with a group of four-year-olds and their parents, and he managed it nicely. A school staff member escorted Alexander and a group of ten to fifteen children into a classroom for a project. I watched him walk up the stairs with the group. All signs looked positive. I thought that maybe this school could be within our reach.

When I returned an hour later to pick him up, Alexander was not with his group. During the group interview, he had no interest in the project and had no reservations about displaying this lack of interest. He met each teacher request with a "NO!" He kept looking at the clock and asking when he could leave. When a teacher continued to encourage him gently, he got so frustrated that he ran out of the room and refused to return. When he saw me, he adamantly told me that he wanted to leave immediately. The school did not hide the fact that they were eager for him to depart as well. Needless to say, he did not attend that school.

Alexander is bright, funny, and honest, and offers a unique and valuable perspective to discussions. However, he interacts differently. This blend of gifts and talents commingled with social, communication, sensory, and limited interests challenges is the struggle many children with AS face.

I entered parenthood as a responsible mother with an open heart, willing to do anything for my child. I still found that our lives spiraled out of control even with my greatest effort. Although well meaning, I (and other people who interacted with my son) made many mistakes because we did not understand Alexander's presentation of AS. We inadvertently created chaos. I felt inadequate for too long in my ability to offer proper support or solutions. After years of tears, frustration, and self-judgment, I went back to school to learn more about autism spectrum disorders.

In graduate school, my professor assigned an "alien experience" project wherein students individually spent at least an hour in a completely unfamiliar location where we would feel out of sync and not know the confusing hidden rules. I chose to eat at an Ethiopian restaurant. I was unfamiliar with the food and unsure of how to proceed without utensils. This experience viscerally demonstrated to me the fear, feeling of being overwhelmed, and disorientation individuals with AS feel much of the time.

Special education and the Individualized Education Program (IEP) process started as alien experiences for me. I found the course of trying to figure out everything related to Alexander's school highly stressful. I felt that I often walked into situations in which everyone knew the rules except me. I recognized the importance of finding my way for Alexander, but felt helpless in my ignorance.

I desperately wanted and needed a book to tell me what to do. Of course, Alexander did not come with an owner's manual, so I made one in the form of a guide for home, school, and the community. My guide helps me collaborate with Alexander's school and community, educate others about his unique form of AS and the interventions that have supported him, and teach Alexander how to thrive as a family member, student, and community member. My guide organizes my parenting approach, informs Alexander about his AS, and strategically leads him to success and independence at home, at school, and in the community.

D. Scott McLeod

Dr. McLeod is a clinical psychologist who has dedicated his thirty-year career to supporting the needs of children exhibiting social, emotional, cognitive, and behavioral difficulties as well as their families, schools, and communities. His clinical interests include AS and other autism spectrum disorders (ASD). He has worked on the staff of Massachusetts General Hospital (MGH) since 1990. As the Executive Director of MGH Aspire, he transformed the program to provide cutting-edge services for individuals with ASD. He serves as a clinical instructor of Psychology for Harvard University Medical School. He has a long and distinguished record of advocacy through his role as educational consultant for over fifty schools supporting students with ASD in the classroom, school, and the community. Additionally, he maintains a private practice for individuals on the autism spectrum and their families. He served on the Board of Directors of the Asperger's Association of New England from 2001 to 2014. After multiple years of experience, he is regarded as an expert and esteemed leader in the field of ASD.

How collaborating about Alexander brought us together to write this book

Scott served as the educational consultant for Alexander's school at the time when I created my guide. I shared the tool with him and the staff when we worked together on a project to support Alexander. Scott and I agreed that the guide offered an effective collaborative tool that could help other families.

We recognized that parents often do not have sufficient support and preparation to navigate effectively through the special education universe at their child's school. Parents usually have great intentions, but do not always know all of the most important information to be successful in their collaboration and advocacy efforts. The essential tools, strategies, and knowledge that we believe parents need are not presented together in a single resource. That is why we decided to write *Take Charge of Treatment for Your Child with Asperger's (ASD).*

School districts and families have varying resources. Not all school districts are equal in terms of their ability to provide educational assistance for children on the spectrum. Not all parents can fund recommended programs outside school for their child with AS. Insurance and governmental resources do not cover the full spectrum of needs for AS families. One goal of this book is to contribute to this advocacy effort by reducing costs for families and schools and increasing efficiency to better address the needs of children with AS.

Supporting individuals with AS and their families is a passion for both of us. Our goal is to assist parents with one of their most important jobs—working with the school, community, and their child to help the child reach his or her potential. Success at home, at school, and in the community can positively impact his or her independence and life trajectory. We designed this book to make the process simple, practical, and successful.

A Note on Terminology

The 2013 edition of the *Diagnostic and Statistical Manual of Mental Disorders* (*DSM-5*) was published by the American Psychiatric Association. In this edition Asperger's Syndrome (AS) is no longer included as a separate diagnosis, but is subsumed under the broader category of Autism Spectrum Disorder (ASD). While this means that AS is no longer a formal diagnosis, the term continues to be widely used. It is generally accepted that many individuals may wish to retain their previous diagnosis because the label is considered part of their identity or may reflect a peer group with whom they identify. A clinician can indicate both the *DSM-5* diagnosis as well as the previous diagnosis, such as AS, in a person's clinical record.

For children who are being newly diagnosed, undoubtedly some who previously would have been given an Asperger's diagnosis will now receive an ASD diagnosis instead. Throughout this book, when we refer to AS, we are including children with ASD and related conditions, such as Pervasive Developmental Disorder—Not Otherwise Specified (PDD-NOS), High Functioning Autism (HFA), and Non-Verbal Learning Disorder (NVLD). Often parents, educators, and service providers who work with children who have these related diagnoses find information about AS helpful and have success with the same tools and strategies as used with children with AS.

For ease of reading, we have used "he" or "she" instead of "s/he" in the text. The examples and strategies listed are for boys and girls regardless of which pronoun is used.

Introduction

Like many people, and perhaps like many of you, I long dreamed of being a parent. When I gave birth to my son Alexander fourteen years ago, I entered motherhood with enthusiasm and an open heart. Even so (perhaps also like many of you), though I was willing, I was not prepared for the experience of parenting a child with special needs.

I do think that I have some qualities that are compatible with mothering a child with special needs. I have always welcomed a new experience as an interesting adventure. My own parents helped me understand social expectations while appreciating individuals who didn't conform. I feel deep compassion and empathy for people who suffer. I have always had the desire and capacity to nurture and give tremendous support to the people I love. These attributes helped a lot; however, my inexperience with parenting and working with school systems and lack of knowledge about autism and effective Asperger's Syndrome (AS) strategies proved to be obstacles.

I became a mother two weeks after leaving a job that I loved with an entrepreneurial search firm. In that job I understood what I needed to do, had a natural talent for it, and worked very hard. The nature of the position allowed me to feel the thrill of success and frequent reward. Acknowledgment was a huge incentive for me. While falling in love with my precious baby mesmerized me, the beginning of motherhood did not offer validation for a job well done or an achievement high. While I fully embraced my new role and chose to devote myself to being a stay-at-home mom, I mourned the end of my old life. I didn't discuss this or even admit it to myself because I didn't think I should feel this way. It was a complex transition.

One month after I gave birth, life was extremely different. I was hormonal and sleep deprived. Alexander suffered from severe colic. He cried in pain day and night, projectile vomited, and had diarrhea regularly. We visited the doctor's office at least once a week. My doctor advised me to take soy and dairy out of my diet to determine if the crying was allergy-related, because I was nursing. I was so hungry at times that I felt like I was starving.

Being hormonal, exhausted, and hungry was not a good combination, but I couldn't consider my needs at the time. Alexander's needs were all-consuming. I felt deep empathy for the amount of pain he was in. I was determined to do anything to help him feel better.

Alexander has also struggled with sleep since the day he was born. He did not sleep for a stretch through the night until he was seven months old. By that point, I was ragged. One of my best friends gave birth to her son one month after Alexander was born. I visited her house by myself for dinner one night in the early days, and I was shocked. I didn't hear screeching. Their house was peaceful! I thought she was a lucky exception. Only after I asked around did I realize that her experience was more the norm.

I needed to work hard to arrange situations in a very particular way for activities to be successful. For example, once a friend invited Alexander and me for an overnight play date. I really liked the other mom and child and accepted their invitation. I had been brought up to be an easy guest, to accept whatever the host offers with gratitude and without asking for more. However, I quickly realized that the transition to another home was difficult for my son. We stayed in a very bright room without any shades. I had to go against my upbringing and ask to tape tin foil on the windows to block the light. I feared that our hosts would think I was an annoying guest and that we wouldn't be invited back. I learned to advocate for Alexander's needs, but inside I felt uncomfortable and embarrassed that others had to accommodate us.

While my maternal love inspired great compassion for Alexander's suffering, our downstairs neighbors, who moved in one month before his birth, were not pleased. They resented the noise and chaos and acted out against us in increasingly serious and terrifying ways that made me fear for our safety. They cut our stroller and baby blanket with scissors, inked our clothes while in the common laundry, keyed our car, barged into our apartment, and told our babysitter that Alexander was a "bad baby."

Being a harmonizer, I worried every time Alexander cried. I apologized to the neighbors and tried desperately to appease them. They asked us not to go in our living room before 9:00am, because their bedroom was directly below. I agreed to living in only two-thirds of our already small space because I was scared of what they might do next. We lived in this situation for over two years. Towards the end, my body shook before entering the building.

As a result, I felt safer and more comfortable outside of our home. I established a daily routine and on most days left the house whenever possible. This strategy helped because I am naturally a social person. From early in Alexander's life, I coordinated almost daily play dates. I helped form a playgroup that included seventeen moms and their babies. From the beginning, I could tell that Alexander didn't enjoy that experience. He seemed to shut down, tried to escape the crowd, and often cried until we left. All the other babies had a wonderful time. Why didn't my son? Looking back, I couldn't see what is now so obvious with the benefit of fourteen years with Alexander. The room was very loud and visually chaotic. Children bumped him unexpectedly. The experience was an assault to his sensory system. At the time I didn't even know what a sensory system was!

When Alexander was a toddler, our life was filled with classes. I thought he would become more comfortable socially with more exposure, but it didn't work. Music and gymnastics classes were often just as overwhelming for him as a toddler as playgroup had been when he was a baby. During our first music class, an activity called for every child to mirror his or her parent. Alexander was the only child who wouldn't. This episode was another clue that his brain worked differently. I gradually began to register that maybe his struggles and preferences were not the sort that he would outgrow.

What worked in those early days? Reading. Alexander's favorite time of the day seemed to be when we read together alone. He would ask me to read book after book, and we regularly read for two hours at a time. On one long plane flight, I read to him for five hours straight. He was my first child, and I had no frame of reference for what was typical. I asked my friends if their children were interested in reading that much. None were. Alexander loved learning his letters from the moment I introduced him to letter blocks. At the playground his preferred activity was standing at a big letter board while I quizzed him where each letter was. Over time I began to recognize that reading was not just a passion for him—it was his way of self-regulating. To this day, reading to Alexander in a quiet space is the single best antidote for any upset.

As Alexander approached two years of age, his physical suffering abated, but I observed increasing signs that he was different from his peers. Interacting with other kids didn't interest him much. He struggled with physical activities involving balance and motor planning. He held his ears and winced in pain when he heard loud noises. He couldn't tolerate the sensation of walking on sand. As he got older, he pulled away from anyone that tried to hug or touch him. Clutter, people running around, and balls flying through the air overwhelmed him. Thunder terrified him.

As we'll talk more about later in the book, when Alexander was two, we moved to London for my husband's job. Shortly after arriving we enrolled him at a charming Montessori preschool, partially because during the interview they explained that Montessori embraced all children, even those who seem different or have challenges. Though I didn't know at the time that Alexander had AS, I had already recognized that he was unique and wanted a place that would accept him for who he was. Although a part of me felt like every other mom dropping off her child for the first time, another part of me was anxious because I had seen my son struggle with classes. I took him to school and hoped for the best.

Six weeks into the school year, the head of the school asked for a meeting with my husband and me. She told us that Alexander shut down regularly by staring into space and not interacting with his peers. Each morning upon arriving at school, students were required to shake hands and look the teacher in the eye. Having grown up in the South in the United States, I embraced the focus on good manners. But the interaction quickly overloaded Alexander's sensory system and triggered upsets, something we didn't understand at the time. Monday mornings were the worst. They began with a half-hour sing-along attended by parents and students. The event was loud and chaotic, and Alexander absolutely hated it. His struggles with transitions, change, and sensory overload (all topics we will discuss in depth in this book) were something I didn't yet grasp.

There were thirty-five children and seven teachers together in one classroom. The school had an international student population, which meant that Alexander encountered different languages, accents, and ways of dressing. The school had no outdoor playground, so the children were allowed to be active and rumbustious in the classroom, leaving no quiet refuge. Teachers set up activity stations from which the students could choose and move from station to station at their own pace. I can now see that the clutter, noise, unexpected touch, and visual disorganization caused Alexander to experience the environment as unpredictable and an attack on his senses. Like our home life when Alexander was a baby, our preschool experience had gotten off to a challenging start.

At around age three, Alexander communicated to us that he didn't want physical contact. Unexpected touch was most upsetting, but he had a hard time tolerating even holding hands or hugging. I felt a tremendous sense of loss that I could no longer physically express the love and nurturing I felt for him, but I came to understand Alexander's request as I learned more about his sensory struggles.

At around this time, Alexander also began having tantrums that lasted forty-five minutes or longer. His loud yelling jangled my nerves, and I just wanted to stop the screaming. I tried to talk him through it and soothe him, but this approach escalated him further. Time-outs on the stairs caused louder screaming. I felt at a complete loss. Our home life was chaotic despite our best efforts to be responsible and loving parents.

When Alexander was four years old, I decided to seek professional help, thinking that we needed to learn better parenting skills. Our psychologist offered some behavioral options, which were minimally effective. After six months of trial and error, she recommended that we consider a psychological assessment to try to understand Alexander's behavior. We worried that receiving a clinical diagnosis would label our son, but we went ahead with the assessment because we recognized that we really needed to find some strategies that worked for Alexander and our family.

At the testing center a developmental pediatrician interviewed my husband and me for about four hours, asking a lot of questions about Alexander's developmental history and our family backgrounds. A clinical psychologist tested Alexander in a separate room. At the end of a long day, we met with both women, who told us that Alexander undoubtedly had AS and explained how they had come to that conclusion. We had never heard of AS, but we were partly relieved to have a way to make sense of Alexander's behaviors. Right away we began to read books and search the internet to learn more about what Alexander's diagnosis meant for his future and for ours. It was strangely comforting to recognize Alexander in the various descriptions of AS.

Our psychologist helped my husband and me to navigate this new sea of information. The next thing she discussed with us was whether or not we would share Alexander's diagnosis with others and when we would share it with him. Together we decided that we would be open about it with others and with him. We agreed to treat the diagnosis as a fact about him: Alexander is tall, he has strawberry blond hair, and he has AS. We thought sharing the AS diagnosis made sense for our family, because we anticipated that people would treat him with less judgment and more respect and compassion when they understood. We also didn't want him to feel that we were ashamed of anything about him or that he should hide any part of himself.

After a month of educating myself about AS and speaking regularly with the psychologist, we decided we were ready to introduce AS to Alexander. Every night we read together for about thirty minutes before bed, typically a relaxing and enjoyable time for both of us. I started the discussion before reading one night. I began by talking about the positive aspects of AS, telling Alexander that many people with AS are very smart, creative, and interesting, and that they have the capacity to learn a tremendous amount about certain topics.

I then calmly and matter-of-factly told Alexander that he had AS. I gave examples from his preschool life of his intelligence, creativity, and ability to learn an incredible amount about the things that interested him. I let him know that these gifts enrich everyone in our family every day. I told him, for example, that his passion for learning letters and reading from a very young age inspired me. I let him know that his ability to take discarded boxes and cardboard toilet paper tubes and transform them into elaborate castles amazed me.

We were pleased and relieved that Alexander received the diagnosis as a matter of fact. He was open to talking about it and felt proud of his strengths. He loved hearing about famous people who reportedly have AS and enjoyed reading fiction with main characters who have AS. He occasionally asked questions. He embraced many strategies, such as visual tools, that we put in place to support him. By the end of second grade, he felt comfortable enough with his diagnosis that he wanted to share it with his class so that they could better understand him and his unexpected behavior.

I found telling others about Alexander's diagnosis more challenging. I was still processing the diagnosis myself and was unprepared to handle all of the different reactions people had to the news. Some were eager to share information and resources about AS, some refused to believe the diagnosis, some didn't know what to say, and some became very emotional. I both appreciated and was overwhelmed by the outpouring of love and support we received.

I was also unprepared for the rejection. A few families quietly withdrew, ultimately making it clear that they no longer wanted their children playing with Alexander. A school rescinded their acceptance based on his diagnosis. These reactions hurt. Were we going to have to accept rejection as part of our new reality? Would Alexander face such treatment based on a label for the rest of his life?

I will never forget what my mother said to me at that time. She told me about a family with a child with special needs who embrace and adore him. They are open about his diagnosis, celebrate his strengths, and help him with his struggles. She said that our family would rally to give Alexander all of our love and support. Her words encouraged and inspired me. I might not always be able to control others' reactions to Alexander and his AS, but I knew that I was going to give him the best that I possibly could.

After his diagnosis, we had Alexander assessed by an occupational therapist and a speech and language pathologist, and he began both occupational therapy and social pragmatic classes. We followed many of their suggestions, too. For example, we bought a mini-trampoline and a large therapy ball and practiced exercises that the occupational therapist recommended as part of a home program. Alexander began to use a therapeutic rubber seat cushion to help develop his core muscles.

Our psychologist referred us to an AS consultant who came to our house every week for about a year to coach us on transforming our home into an AS-friendly environment. She walked us through setting up Alexander's room, helping him manage his anger, and assisting him in dealing with his new baby brother, Will. She also taught us how to develop social communication skills such as not interrupting, establish a reward system, and make visual timetables. She helped the staff at Alexander's school create a more AS-friendly environment, and organized meetings between the school staff and my husband and me to work on collaboration.

Ultimately, getting Alexander's diagnosis was positive for me. It meant that there were resources and information available to us. I stopped judging myself so harshly as a mother. As I learned more about AS, I started to feel more capable of helping Alexander. The diagnosis provided a big-picture sketch, but I realized I needed to identify the nuances of his profile—the unique ways AS presented in him—in order to come up with specific strategies that would work for him and our family.

I began to wish frequently, and particularly when Alexander started school, that there was a handbook to help me support him. I wanted a mentor to teach me about interacting with Alexander's teachers and other professionals. I decided to try to find the answers myself. I realized that I needed to have a firm grasp on Alexander's unique profile and to become his case manager. The culmination of my efforts, in collaboration with Scott, resulted in this book.

Part I

What You Need to Know Before Using the Tools

Chapter 1

Embrace Your Case Manager Role

I came to realize that the best strategy for helping Alexander, his school, and our family was for me to assume the role of case manager. My purpose is to promote the most successful outcome for him in all the environments in which he participates—at home, at school, and in the community.

What is a case manager?

A case manager for a child with AS is a parent or guardian who plans, coordinates, monitors, and advocates for his care to address his unique, profile-related needs at home, at school, and in the community.

The case manager role

Whether you realize it or not, you became a case manager at the time you received your child's AS diagnosis. As parents, you are the only adults who have long-term knowledge of your child, work with all of his professional providers, and are in the position to monitor his day-to-day activities. You have the broadest knowledge to help his support network understand his profile.

The question "What works?" has motivated me since Alexander's birth. For years I could answer the question "What doesn't work?" much more easily. Over time, I noticed patterns in the situations and environments, which ultimately led me to understand what works and why. With this knowledge, I have embraced the case manager role. Case manager responsibilities include:

- understanding your child's unique AS profile
- educating your child and people interacting with him at home, at school, and in the community about his unique AS profile

- collaborating with your child's special educator, general educator, and professional team
- understanding your child's school and helping your child understand his school
- coordinating efforts between home, school, and outside providers
- communicating efficiently and comprehensively about your child's needs
- facilitating generalization of knowledge in different environments by sharing important information with all professionals
- advocating for services.

The information in this book will give you all of the resources you need to fill this role effectively.

Why parents assume the case manager role for their child with AS

Autism spectrum disorders are complex and affect every area in the life of the child with AS twenty-four hours a day, seven days a week. You, parents and guardians, are the only people who have continued access to every aspect of your child's life.

Throughout the course of development for a child with AS, he will likely see many providers. Ideally, he will be diagnosed within the first two to five years of his life. He will likely work with many professionals through early intervention, home-based Applied Behavior Analysis (ABA), preschool, and school. Additionally, he may receive therapeutic services from outside professionals. You are typically the only people who collaborate with and gather information from all of the providers. Therefore, you have the most knowledge about your child and can help his support network to understand his profile.

You will likely find that not all educators have a solid understanding of how to educate individuals with AS. In the early years when times got tough for Alexander at school, I looked to school staff for answers—and they looked right back to me. Not surprisingly, this approach failed. Even if you do encounter teachers and staff with significant AS knowledge, there are inevitable personnel changes at the end of the school year. In addition, with Alexander's complex profile, truly understanding his impairments and needs can take months even for experienced professionals new to his case. Counting on an AS-savvy educator each year who connected with my son was unrealistic. I needed to be able to take the lead.

How parents become effective case managers

You can become successful as a case manager through:

- understanding AS and your child's unique AS profile
- being organized and prepared
- remaining emotionally calm
- maintaining a sense of humor.

Understanding AS and your child's unique AS profile

You can benefit from identifying your child's unique profile because all children on the autism spectrum are different in terms of strengths, weaknesses, and performance. AS presents differently from individual to individual based on the intensity of the different aspects of the syndrome, and treatment strategies can vary significantly based on the needs of each individual with AS. Chapter 3 will help you to understand the characteristics associated with AS and to develop your child's unique profile guide.

Being organized and prepared

You need to be organized to keep track of the important interactions with your child's school and professional service providers. You will be most efficient and effective in your role when you have an easily accessible system for managing case management-related information. The following are some suggestions for staying organized:

1. Develop a filing system to organize all of your child's reports, reviews, and evaluations.
2. Use a notebook or computer to keep school meeting minutes and notes from significant discussions with teachers, school staff, educational consultants, and service providers. Archive any important e-mails from school or service providers.

3 Start a folder at the beginning of the year to keep all AS-related materials from teachers, such as daily notes about the child's day and other AS-related tools. Start a similar folder when your child begins services with new professionals such as occupational or speech therapists.

Remaining emotionally calm

Your emotional predictability is a key ingredient in building a successful environment for your child with AS. Parents can get very emotional due to fears about their child's struggles and desperate desire for him to thrive. Young children with AS are particularly reactive to changes in both their physical and emotional environments. They often do not have the filters to handle their parents' upset, anger, or fear. You will support your child when you model how to manage emotional struggles while maintaining an even keel.

You should respond calmly and rationally to outside professionals. Outbursts with professionals can compromise the effectiveness of your case manager role and can negatively impact parent/professional trust. You can achieve the greatest results when you consciously consider the professional's perspective and do not take situations personally. When this becomes difficult, you can benefit from talking about your struggles with someone you trust in order to cope with your emotions. We will talk more about this in Chapter 4.

Maintaining a sense of humor

Humor is another important element of case management because it does not always come naturally to children with AS. Some children with AS commonly ask why others find a certain situation, comment, or joke funny. They benefit from parents modeling and providing a running narrative about what they find amusing. You can promote a playful interchange with your child when you use humor. Everyone will have more fun.

Infusing humor into relations with professionals can help you not take things so seriously. Parents can get bogged down and overwhelmed by the problems they face when parenting a child with AS. Displaying a sense of humor can play a big role in helping people relax and communicate on a more human level. Again, we will discuss the role of humor more in Chapter 4.

How to gain confidence in the case manager role

Parents' time is a limited resource. You are juggling the demands of parenting a child with AS, potentially holding a job, and managing other adult roles and responsibilities. Parents go through a period of intense information-gathering after receiving their child's AS diagnosis. They obtain information through books, internet searches, conferences, professionals, and parent groups. This book helps parents channel their efforts efficiently.

Parents commonly worry that they do not have enough knowledge or confidence to successfully address the needs of their child with AS. It is important to remember that you can only do your best within your given situation. You can determine what is possible for you to do and act on it to the best of your ability. Remember that parents do not need to know everything about AS in order to provide solid support for their child. Their child is a person first, a person with AS second. When parents utilize the tools and information in this book in conjunction with having an understanding for what is realistically possible, they can become effective case managers for their child with AS.

Chapter 2

Our Approach

How to Use This Book

Having positive experiences at home, at school, and in the community benefits you, your child, your family, the teachers, school staff, service providers, and everyone who interacts with your child. Your support and advocacy efforts lead to these positive experiences and have a significant impact on your child's short- and long-term success. We realize that AS is complex, and you may be overwhelmed by the tremendous amount of information you need to grasp quickly. Our goal is to help you better understand AS and to make the process of taking charge of your child's treatment easy for you.

Create a guide—your case management tool

As described in Chapter 1, I have come to embrace the fact that my husband and I are Alexander's case managers. We are the two people who have seen him through every stage, know his history, have learned from all of his talented specialists, and will be with him into adulthood. We will always look to professionals for their specific expertise, but we were in the best position to develop a guide to provide people working with Alexander with essential information about him. Assuming the case manager role and creating and sharing this guide have given me the ability to help Alexander and collaborate with his support team most effectively.

I know better which strategies work for Alexander than professionals who are unfamiliar with his profile. If I had created the guide earlier in Alexander's school career and been able to preview important information with his teachers, we could perhaps have avoided some of the challenging incidents that occurred. For example, we could have prevented Alexander's traumatic meltdown when two teachers grabbed his arms to remove him from the classroom if we had shared with them Alexander's sensitivity to touch. I want you to feel as empowered as I did when I realized I could make a difference by becoming my child's case manager.

You will be able to offer each member of your child's team a comprehensive snapshot, based on your own experience, of what works. There will still be hiccups along the way, but you will always have a starting point for opening the lines of communication and sharing proven strategies. As you and your child's team collectively discover more successful tools and techniques, you will add them to your guide. My guide is a living, growing, and evolving document, and yours will be, too.

What is a guide?

Let's start by talking about exactly what a guide is. A guide is a parent-generated case management tool, individualized to your child's AS profile and life to maximize success at home, at school, and in the community. Your guide will serve as an instruction booklet for your child, a toolbox and teaching template for his teachers and support team, and a case management road map for you. The guide will teach your child, in a succinct, accessible, visual format, how to thrive in various environments. Professionals will receive important information about your child's AS profile and proven, AS-friendly tools to use with him. You will have a tactical, AS-specific plan for supporting your child and collaborating with his teachers and service providers. As we will discuss in more detail later in the chapter, you will create your guide by completing exercises for every chapter in the book. The exercises consist mainly of checklists, making completing your guide easy and straightforward.

Template checklists are available to download from www.jkp.com/go/elwoodandmcleod.

Why create a guide?

Your guide will help you take a comprehensive, whole person, positive approach to parenting your child with AS. You will grasp what your child needs and how to support your family, provide targeted strategies and interventions, and meet your child with AS with understanding, honesty, and compassion.

When you develop a plan, your parenting shifts from being unconscious and haphazard to conscious and strategic. Without a guide, even with best intentions, parents may end up reacting to situations and behaviors. With a guide, you can proactively address and purposefully respond to situations in a way that aligns with your family values and vision for your child. Your guide can help you and everyone who interacts with your child to respond calmly and effectively, rather than reacting rashly and feeling overwhelmed. Explosive or out-of-control atmospheres can transform to calmer and more orderly environments. An improved experience in any part of your child's world will lead to reduced stress levels in all areas of his or her life.

You can make a difference in your child's future independence and success by beginning your efforts as early as possible. Supporting your child with AS requires a coordinated effort between you, your child's school, and his or her community. Your individualized guide will help organize and orient you, enabling you to:

- understand and educate others about your child's unique profile
- collaborate and communicate effectively with your child's team
- establish routines and schedules
- delineate behavioral expectations for your child
- educate your child about important adults in his or her life
- manage crises and emotions
- facilitate smooth transitions
- promote your child's independence.

This book will teach you how to achieve these goals. Your guide will promote a consistent treatment approach and common language across environments. Teachers and service providers care very much about their students; however, they often have an entire class or caseload to figure out. Professionals cannot always tell from an IEP alone the level of support or differentiation (changes to the social and academic curriculum and school environment) a child will need. When you can provide information about your child's profile and keys to how he or she can succeed, everyone will benefit.

Benefits of a guide

As we mentioned above, the guide serves different purposes for you and your family, your child, and your child's teachers and support team. Let's look at the specific benefits everyone will derive from creating the guide and using it effectively.

Family

The guide will provide parents with a structure for home education. You will integrate AS-specific, therapeutic interventions into your household. Having a defined plan will enable you and your partner to be on the same page and take a unified approach to parenting. As your guide helps you to parent more effectively, you'll strengthen confidence in your parenting skills.

Alexander started to align his behavior with our parenting goals after I reviewed my guide with him. He better met our behavioral expectations such as dinner manners and hidden expectations such as family standards when he saw them explicitly presented in simple language and a clear format. He became more independent as I wrote straightforward instructions for daily living skills such as how to wash his hair and made checklists for his daily routines like how to clean his room. Our home went from feeling confusing and chaotic to becoming a more predictable safe haven as we used the same language and responded in a consistent way to his upsets.

It is common for children with AS and their typically developing siblings to experience conflict. Your guide will also help your other children gain useful tools and improve sibling relationships.

For example, Will and Alexander have very different interests, which often lead to turmoil in our home. Will is physically active and loves hosting play dates. Alexander often prefers having quiet time to explore his special interest. Before he understood Alexander's differences, Will often inadvertently triggered Alexander simply by being himself—laughing, running around, screaming with friends, or bouncing and throwing balls. After reviewing my guide, Will began to understand Alexander's struggles such as his sensory over-reactivity to noise. He started to think about how he could host play dates in a way that would work for Alexander. For example, instead of being near Alexander, he would deliberately bring his friends to other parts of our house. He would coach his friends about the importance of trying to be quiet around Alexander. Will's growing awareness about Alexander's struggles promotes creative solutions and empathy and decreases resentment and hurt feelings.

You may find, as we have, that the guide is also beneficial for your typically developing children. Will uses many of the tools in our guide. For example, he regularly checks our posted daily schedules. Knowing what will happen and when helps him feel grounded. He appreciates the direct instruction that the guide provides about things like how to host a play date or make phone calls to friends' homes. The result is a calmer, more harmonious home environment for everyone.

Your child with AS

Your guide will help your child become familiar with her unique profile (we will cover this topic in depth in Chapter 3). She will come to appreciate her strengths and learn to cope with her vulnerabilities. She will gain clarity about why certain situations are confusing or overwhelming to her and be able to use strategies to remain calmer. The guide will help teach behavioral expectations, and your child will gain confidence as she is able to meet these expectations. Using the tools in the guide, she will be able to participate more fully in all aspects of life—as a part of your family, as a student, and as a member of the community. Ultimately, she will internalize, become competent with, and perform skills independently to be able to advocate for herself.

The guide will help inspire AS-friendly treatment, profile understanding, and compassion for the struggles of the child with AS, and will often lead to less judgmental reactions to unexpected behaviors. This trend will help your child gain trust for the individuals working with her and the environments in which she interacts. Her conduct and relationships will improve.

Teachers and support team

The guide will give everyone who comes into contact with your child, from teachers to service providers to babysitters, with an AS-friendly, child-specific training tool. Everyone will have the same information, bringing a welcome consistency at home, at school, and in the community. Knowing your individual child will allow teachers and professionals to tailor curricula and environments specifically to him or her. They will be more confident and at ease working with your child, make the most of their time with him or her, and create a calmer teaching and learning environment, all of which will set the stage for mutual success.

Sharing your guide at school and in the community also provides the structure for productive communication. You will have a plan in place that will help you avoid misunderstandings and work together for your child's benefit. In turn, your child will have the chance to practice skills outlined in the guide in many different environments.

At the beginning of every school year, I call a meeting with Alexander's special educator. Using my "Beginning of the relationship meeting with special educators or service providers" tool (found in Chapter 4), I set up operating instructions for our collaboration. I find out if the special educator prefers calls, e-mails, or in-person meetings. We determine how often we will communicate, what the special educator would like to know from me on an ongoing basis, and vice versa. I review information about Alexander's profile, and we discuss how we can use the same tools at the same time to promote mastery of skills in different environments (skill generalization). I go through a similar process of establishing parameters for communication and a collaboration plan when we begin our work with any new service providers.

Special Educator's Perspective

Alexander's former special educator, Liz Blumenfeld, found receiving the guide very beneficial:

> In special education, when you get a new student the first thing you usually do is read his/her IEP. A legal document that provides certain critical pieces of information is, of course, helpful in terms of getting to know the child in a basic sense: the disability, how it affects the child in a school setting, strengths, needs, goals, and so on. To me, the IEP provides a snapshot. The guide that was shared with me about Alexander provided me with so much more invaluable information.
>
> Not all students with Asperger's present similarly in the classroom, so just having a base of knowledge about Asperger's could not have prepared me for working with Alexander. The guide details not only what social cognition is, but also exactly what Alexander's impairments in this area look like, sound like, feel like. I also felt that certain characteristics of his behavior and personality were not only described, but also explained. The guide provided me with critical information, such as strengths, likes, and dislikes. It helped me to better understand his abilities and perceptions in addition to why he had certain likes, dislikes, preferences, and perceptions. A lot of the guesswork of "figuring out" a student and why they do and say the things that they do was already explained. I think this time/energy saving allowed me to focus my efforts on making things work!
>
> Additionally, to have the information handed to me regarding what works in terms of social support, sensory support, educational integration, and so on—I felt like I started off with so much more information in my toolbox. After reading and absorbing the information in the guide, I felt like I had a better understanding of who Alexander is and what my approach with him should be. I also felt overwhelmed at the seeming

complexity of his profile, but encouraged by all of the support strategies and information that helped guide me in my work with him. Having this wealth of information not only helped me in my work with Alexander, but I'm sure it saved Alexander many moments of anger, frustration, or the feeling of being misunderstood.

Finally, it gave me an idea of what life with/for Alexander might be like. I know this perspective helped me in my communications with Alexander and his family.

Other adults caring for or socializing with the child

I share my guide with family members and friends who spend a lot of time with Alexander. For example, my mother knows exactly what I work on and interacts with Alexander using the same language and approaches. She has been able to forge a deep and important relationship with him because she integrates seamlessly into our family dynamic.

I will often provide some information from the guide to families we socialize with frequently. I find that if everyone knows what to expect and what works for Alexander, gatherings are more comfortable.

I also use the guide as a training tool for new babysitters. I've found that the babysitters who want to work with our family are often graduate students with an interest in AS, enrolled in special education, occupational therapy, or psychology programs. We are able to take a unified approach in caring for Alexander, and they get the added benefit that the guide and their experience with Alexander support their professional development.

Generalization

When I share my guide with Alexander's school, outside service providers, and people at home, I am able to maximize the benefits of everyone's treatment efforts. When we coordinate strategies and language, each environment makes more sense to Alexander, and he is able to generalize skills in multiple settings. The term "generalization" is an important concept when discussing children on the autism spectrum. Taking skills from one environment to another is challenging and often requires direct instruction. We discuss skill generalization in every chapter and provide a detailed description of it in Chapter 4.

How to use this book to create your guide

We designed this book to be flexible. You can adapt it to your own needs, preferences, and timeframe. If you are able, we recommend that you work through the whole book from beginning to end and complete your entire guide. But if you would rather, you can refer to chapters that cover specific topics about which you need immediate guidance and come back to the rest later.

Each chapter begins with a story about Alexander that illustrates something important about the subject of the chapter. The main text of each chapter will cover all of the information you need to learn and digest, using additional examples to help make clear any concepts that may be unfamiliar to you. Additional Boxes will provide more in-depth information about more complicated topics, such as "Pragmatics" in Chapter 3 and "The Hidden Curriculum" in Chapter 6.

Exercises

You will finish each chapter equipped with the knowledge you need to complete the exercises in the Parents Take Charge section of that chapter and create your guide.

When working on the exercises, which are available for your reference at the end of each chapter in print format and online at www.jkp.com/go/elwoodandmcleod to download in an interactive PDF format, remember to keep in mind:

- the information and examples from the chapter
- your own personal experiences and observations
- feedback from the child's school team and outside professionals
- information from books, classes, or conferences that has resonated about your child
- your child's feedback
- assessment information.

Also bear in mind that the examples given in the book are just for reference and that full lists can be found in the digital checklists.

Social Stories™

The Social Stories™ and notes found in the Parents Take Charge sections of the book are written for specific situations that may not apply to your child. We included them in the book to demonstrate the level of explicit detail necessary to help your child and the type of matters you can address such as schedule changes, behavioral expectations, strategies to manage crises and emotions, and transition previews. We did not include the Social Stories™ in the digital component given their highly individualized content, but you and/or your child's teacher can use the examples in the books as springboards to write notes or Social Stories™ for your child's similar yet unique situations. For example, the Parents Take Charge section in Chapter 5, Routines and Schedules, includes a note about a change in schedule due to a science electricity fair. Your child's school may not have a science electricity fair, but you could use it as a starting point to write a note about a special event that will impact his schedule.

Creating a guide is easy

We understand how busy and intense life can be with a child on the spectrum.

This book is meant to make your life easier and to help you become an effective case manager. With these objectives in mind, we designed our process to be simple and efficient. We have already done most of the work. We provide an entire toolbox with interventions and strategies that support children with AS ages five to fourteen. You only need to take a few easy steps to customize a comprehensive guide for your child.

Here is how the process works:

1 Sign onto the URL www.jkp.com/go/elwoodandmcleod to find our toolbox in an interactive PDF format.

2 Download the PDF and identify the tools (checklists) that will support your child.

3 Use the already-created tools as they are, or edit to reflect your child's profile and needs.

4 Add any tools of your own, not included in our toolbox, that have worked for your child.

5 Print your individualized guide and use it immediately as a teaching template, collaboration tool, and case management road map.

Who Will Use the Tools?

Different tools are designed to support different people. The exercise instructions will clarify who will benefit from the specific tools and how to use them. People and groups that can benefit from parts or all of the information contained in your guide are:

- mainstream teachers
- special education teachers
- ABA therapist
- classroom aide
- educational consultant
- family
- psychologist
- psychiatrist
- social worker
- coach
- speech and language pathologist
- occupational therapist
- camp staff
- babysitter
- tutor
- mentor
- any other person that interacts with the child regularly.

When you present the tools to your child, use visuals. We have provided examples for presenting the tools visually (see "Presenting Tools Visually" Box). Be sure to avoid visual overload by focusing on just one tool per page. Keep instructions simple, concrete, and explicit.

Presenting Tools Visually

How to take a shower

- ☐ Turn on water
- ☐ Use soap to wash your body
- ☐ Rinse your face

When you wash your hair:

- ☐ Wet all of your hair
- ☐ Put shampoo in your hand
- ☐ Lather all of your hair with shampoo
- ☐ Make sure to wash out all of the shampoo

How to clean up after the shower

- ☐ Put your dirty clothes in the hamper
- ☐ Hang your towel back on the rack

Keep in mind that all of the tools may not apply to every child. You can choose those that support your child at the time you're creating your guide and refer back to the book periodically for other recommendations that may be useful later. We said it before, but it is worth repeating: the guide is a dynamic document, which you can update as your child grows and changes.

We have included icons to identify for whom tools in the Parents Take Charge section at the end of each chapter and on the PDF are intended and who should create them. The idea is to make it easy for you to know who will use each tool and to help you get organized before you meet with teachers, special educators, or professionals in the community. You can look for the icons to find exercises that you will need to complete in collaboration with school staff or other members of your child's team so that you are prepared and able to use your time together efficiently. If an exercise doesn't have an icon indicating it needs to be completed with someone else, it means that parents can either use the tool as it is or customize it on their own to reflect their child's profile and needs. Table 2.1 explains what each of the five icons you will see throughout the book means and where you will find all instances of each.

Table 2.1 Icon Descriptions

Icon	Meaning	You can find
	Tools for Everyone: Child, home caregivers, school and community professionals	Parents Take Charge Chapters 3, 8
	Tools for Adults: Home caregivers, school and community professionals	Parents Take Charge Chapters 4, 5, 7–10
	Tools for the Child	Parents Take Charge Chapters 5–10
SCHOOL	Tools to Make with Special Educator or School Staff	Parents Take Charge Chapters 4–10
	Tools to Make with Professionals in the Community	Parents Take Charge Chapters 4, 5, 6, 8, 9

Part II

Tools

Chapter 3

Understanding Your Child's Unique Profile

"If you have met one person with Asperger's Syndrome (AS), you have met one person with AS."

STEPHEN SHORE, AUTISM EXPERT

In this chapter, we will introduce the general components and features of AS and what each means. But we begin with this quote from Stephen Shore because the most important message of the chapter is that every child with AS is unique. Just like a typically developing child, a child with AS has individual likes, dislikes, aspirations, and interests. For example, as we will discuss later, it is common for a child with AS to develop intense, sometimes consuming, interests. What these interests are varies from child to child and changes over time for the same child. For example, Alexander's first special interest was whales. He had a voracious appetite for a variety of whale books. He learned as many facts about whales as he could and educated everyone who would listen. He hung a poster and his own drawings of whales on his wall. His most cherished birthday present ever was a charitable gift of an adoptive whale in Alexander's name. He loved going on whale watches and adored Vineyard Vines shirts because of their whale logo. He had whale stuffed animals, puzzles, and paperweights. He raised money for the endangered Northern Right Whale by selling note cards printed with his drawings. To this day, when he signs a letter to someone very special to him, he draws a picture of a whale.

We want to help you learn to recognize the particular presentations of the elements of AS in your own child so that you can create his or her unique profile toolbox. As we explained in Chapter 1, you became a case manager at the moment your child received an AS diagnosis. Parents are the only adults who have long-term knowledge of their children, work with all of their professional providers, and are able to monitor their day-to-day activities. You are in the best position to help your child's support network understand his or her unique profile.

As we briefly discussed in Chapter 1, different disabilities require varying levels of parental understanding. For example, parents do not necessarily need to know the inner workings of a disorder such as dyslexia because the treatment protocol is to have the school provide special instruction. Although guided exercises at home can support instruction, parents typically do not have to be deeply involved in dyslexia management. The role of an AS parent, however, calls for active learning about the child's disability, support, and participation.

Before you can be a resource to others, you need to be completely familiar with your child's individual profile and the specific interventions (tools and strategies) that help him or her. What exactly do we mean by "your child's profile"? Each child on the autism spectrum has different strengths, weaknesses, and behaviors. AS varies from person to person based on the intensity of the different features, such as social impairments, communication deficits, and restricted patterns of behavior, interests, and activities. Other factors include each person's particular sensory, motor, cognitive, and emotional struggles. Treatment strategies can vary significantly based on the individual's needs. As we explain each component of AS, we will provide specific examples about Alexander that will demonstrate for you how we developed his unique profile toolbox. The combination of information and illustrative stories will give you the foundation you need to create your own child's profile toolbox in the Parents Take Charge section at the end of the chapter.

Before we discuss the various aspects of AS, we want to point out that even though your child's profile may not change over time, his or her most pressing challenges might. A young child's sensory issues at school may represent his or her most significant struggle, and interventions should focus on helping the child learn how to manage those issues. For example, a school-aged child might struggle with fluorescent lighting. The issue might be handled by changing to incandescent lighting or changing to a different type of fluorescent lighting that does not flicker. Though sensory issues often still impact adolescents, social issues often become more pressing. One of our goals is to make sure that you understand age-specific issues for your child with AS. You will then be able to take on the case manager role and highlight, communicate about, and treat your child's most important difficulties whenever and wherever they occur.

Diagnostic criteria associated with AS

Many clinicians identify three main areas requiring intervention for people with AS: social differences, communication differences, and restricted patterns of behavior, interests, and activities (see Figure 3.1). Let's take a closer look at each of these domains and help you identify how they factor into your child's profile.

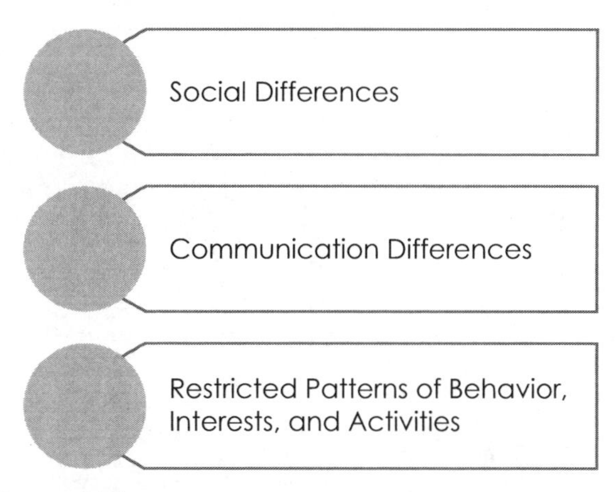

Figure 3.1 Features of AS

Social differences

People with AS struggle with *social cognition*, which is the intuitive ability to integrate one's own and others' thinking in the context of social interactions and communication. For example, imagine that you are getting ready for a job interview. Not only are you worried about the impression and signals you're sending to the interviewer, you are also concerned with reading his or her signals. How do you form an impression of this person? How do you determine what the other person's behavior means? Many people with AS have trouble with this kind of thinking.

The four components of social cognition that affect children with AS are theory of mind, central coherence, executive functioning, and non-verbal communication (see Figure 3.2).

Unlike typically developing children who intuitively understand many of the elements of social cognition, children with AS must be explicitly taught these social skills, similar to the way they are taught academic subjects.

Theory of Mind: The ability of an individual to think about the thoughts and feelings of another person.	**Central Coherence**: The ability to understand the big picture or main idea of a conversation, assignment, or context.
Executive Functioning: The ability to employ a series of strategies to stay on task to achieve a goal.	**Non-verbal Communication**: Communication without the use of spoken language, including through eye contact, reading non-verbal cues and facial expressions, gesturing, body posture, etc. Seventy percent of a communicative event occurs through non-verbal communication.

Social Cognition: The ability to have a hunch or intuition in the context of social interactions and communication by thinking of one's own and others' thinking.

Figure 3.2 Social Cognition Components

Like many people with AS, Alexander struggled socially. More often than not, interactions with peers did not go well. Once I learned about the social differences of individuals with AS, many of Alexander's social reactions and experiences made sense. I started recognizing his behaviors as predictable aspects of his unique profile rather than random, rude, or quirky conduct.

Theory of mind

When we lived in London, Alexander and I took a double-decker bus to school every day. One day we sat next to a very large man. Alexander looked at him and asked him why he was so fat. I was horrified, embarrassed, and furious. I felt inadequate as a mother. Why couldn't I teach him manners? Only later did I realize that his disability played a major role in his making comments like this, which he felt were simply honest and factual. He had a difficult time with theory of mind—taking the perspective of others—and did not realize that his comment could hurt the man's feelings.

Central coherence

Alexander was in art class one day, and his teacher was giving the students instruction. Alexander wanted to talk to his aide about a list that he was generating in class about a completely unrelated topic. His aide said to please wait until later because the teacher was talking. Alexander got furious at his aide for hushing him. He missed the big picture in that context. He was in art class to learn, and his job was to listen to instruction and complete the work assigned for the day. He could only see, in that moment, that he wanted his aide's attention and help, and she was being mean. He missed that he should be listening attentively to his teacher rather than talking to his aide and disrupting others.

Executive functioning

Alexander wrote a story about two cars and wanted to make it into a movie with his babysitter, who is an art therapist. The process involved multiple steps and activities. He had to paint the cars, build the backgrounds for all of the scenes, and film the sequences. He had a difficult time estimating how long the project would take. As he realized that it would take much longer than he anticipated, he felt distressed. His inability to step back and see the beginning, middle, and end of the project made him stressed and anxious. Every time he worked on it, he melted down in frustration. Even though this project was his passion, each work session became increasingly difficult until he aborted the whole project. Alexander's executive functioning difficulties kept him from participating in even his most preferred activities, and he struggled more when trying to accomplish non-preferred goals.

Non-verbal communication

Alexander often turns his body away from the person he's talking with, who then begins to think that he is uninterested or rude. Because Alexander is not facing the individual, and because he has trouble interpreting non-verbal cues anyway, he doesn't perceive the person's annoyance. The other person often gives up on the conversation, and Alexander wonders why it didn't go well. Given that approximately seventy percent of communication occurs through non-verbal expression, Alexander's social interactions are often negatively affected.

Communication differences

Having a conversation is such a natural, routine activity for most of us that we don't think about all of the elements involved, but there are many: introducing and maintaining a topic, turn-taking, choosing accurate words, adjusting to the listener's style, speaking intelligibly, and communicating non-verbally through proximity, posture, and facial expression (see Table 3.1). Typically developing children pick up these skills with little guidance, but many children with AS need explicit instruction to learn them. For example, Alexander often asks me to start telling a story that he would like to share with another person because he struggles with initiating conversation. Once I say the first sentence or two, he usually takes over. When he tries on his own to start a conversation, he often speaks so softly that the other person can't hear him. He gets frustrated because he thinks the other person is ignoring him, which sets the interaction off poorly. Like his social differences, Alexander's communication differences often make it challenging for him to interact successfully with his peers.

Pragmatics

Pragmatics is social language involving learning rules for interacting with others in a socially acceptable manner. Often speech and language pathologists (SLPs) deliver social skills assessments to children with AS at the first or second appointment. Sometimes, children with AS pass the test because they know the skill, but that doesn't necessarily mean that they can execute it. Even when responding accurately on the test about what is the "right" thing to do, the child may then, for example, talk too close, for too long, and in a manner that feels uncomfortably focused. Therefore, it is important for assessments of social pragmatics to include observing the child in real-life social situations.

Table 3.1 Communication differences: pragmatic language (Prutting and Kirchner 1987)

Managing topic	Select Introduce Maintain Change
Turn-taking	Initiate Respond Repair Pause Interrupt/overlap Feedback Add info to preceding topic Comments Quantity
Lexical selection	Cohesion Accuracy of words chosen
Stylistic variations	Ability to adjust style to listener
Para-linguistics	Intelligibility Vocal intensity Vocal quality Prosody (intonation and stress patterns) Fluency
Non-verbal aspects	Proximity Physical contacts Body posture Foot/leg, hand/arm movements Gestures Facial expression Eye gaze

Restricted patterns of behavior, interests, and activities

This category encompasses a number of behaviors associated with AS. For instance, a restricted pattern of activity could mean a repetitive use of objects, such as lining up toys, or a rigid adherence to a routine, such as insisting on taking the same exact route to school every day.

It also refers to restricted interests. As we mentioned at the beginning of the chapter, many individuals with AS develop special interests, which change over time. For example, Alexander's deep passion changed from whales to James Bond to actors. The child often becomes isolated because his interest is so intense that he wants all of his interpersonal interactions to revolve solely around that topic. When the child with AS realizes that conversations about his current interest sometimes last for a very short time and then sputter out, he may feel disappointed that not enough people share in his excitement. The child with AS often finds thinking about, writing about, and interacting with his special interest more fulfilling than interacting with peers because the social and communication differences we've discussed may make peer interactions uncomfortable and anxiety-provoking.

You can see how this might become a vicious cycle. The amount of time invested in special interests limits the amount of time spent on social interactions. Children with AS are bright and can learn social skills in pragmatics groups, but developing the skills requires practice. Without practice, peer interactions continue to be unsatisfying, and the child with AS continues to turn instead to his special interest to experience success and fulfillment. As individuals with AS follow this trajectory over time, they may fall further and further behind in their social development. Being aware of your child's unique AS profile and finding targeted strategies that work for him or her will help you break this cycle.

In addition, the description of restricted and repetitive patterns of behavior, interests, and activities for autism spectrum disorders in *DSM-5* includes hyper- and hypo-sensory responsivity or unusual interests in sensory elements of the environment as possible impacts. For example, an unusual interest in sensory aspects of the environment could include paying excessive attention to visual patterns or specific sounds. We cover hyper- and hypo-reactivity, over- or under-responsiveness to sensory stimuli, later in the chapter and in the Parents Take Charge section.

Associated features of AS

In addition to the components we've already covered, there are four associated features of AS that you should understand in order to select effective interventions for your child:

- sensory differences
- motor differences
- cognitive differences
- emotional vulnerability.

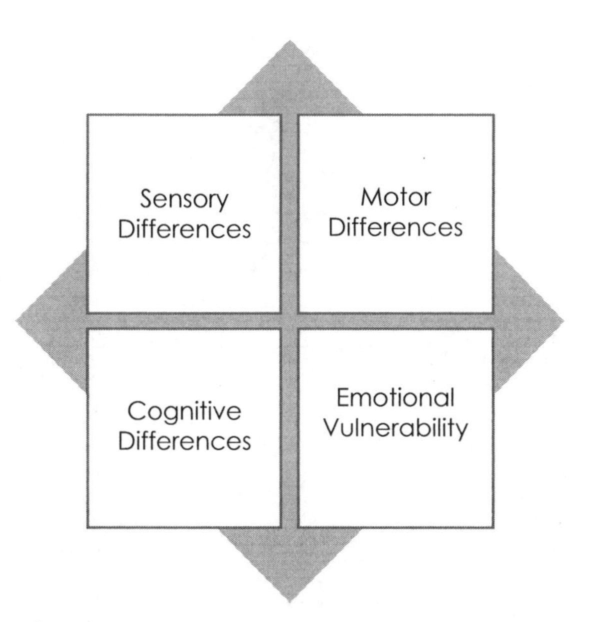

Figure 3.3 Associated features of AS

Let's take a closer look at each of these features.

Sensory differences

Simply put, a sensory processing disorder is a condition in which the brain has difficulty processing sensations in a "just right" manner. Seventy-eight percent of the autism population suffers from some type of sensory processing disorder (Miller 2006, p.281). Those with Sensory Modulation Disorder are over-reactive or under-reactive to sensory messages, or seek additional sensory input. For example, if a child refuses to eat, parents may want to consider that the child may be over-reactive to certain tastes or textures instead of blaming typical causes such as that he or she is full, engaging in a power struggle, or trying to hold out for sweets. Those with Sensory Discrimination Disorder have trouble discerning differences in how things look, sound, feel, taste, and smell (Miller 2006, pp.12–13). Those with Sensory-Based Motor Disorder struggle to get into and maintain a stable position (postural) or coordinate a sequence of movements (dyspraxia) (see Figure 3.4).

Your child may struggle with one or a combination of sensory issues, which can quickly deplete his or her energy. Responding to or managing sensory difficulties can require all of the attention of a child with AS, which can lead to meltdowns and trouble participating in the classroom or in social situations. If you suspect your child has a sensory processing disorder, you may want to see an occupational therapist for an assessment if you have not already done so.

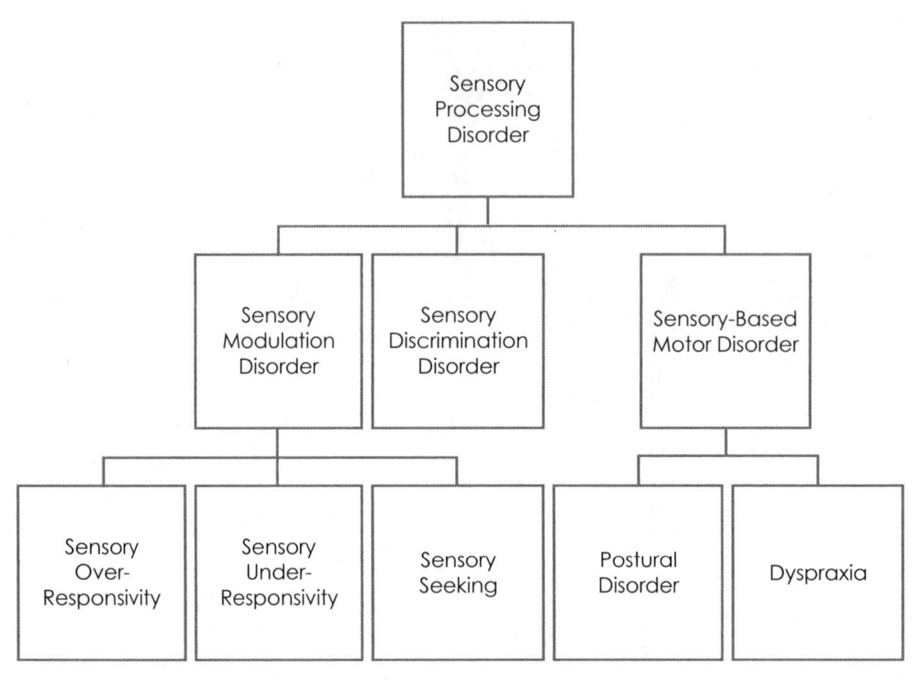

Figure 3.4 Sensory processing disorders (Kranowitz 2010, p.28)

Alexander has a complex sensory profile. He is over-reactive to touch, tastes, sights, and sounds, which is the source of a large portion of his anxiety. Loud noise, unexpected touch, and visual clutter are particularly troublesome for him. He struggles most days at home because the jarring sounds produced by ordinary activities such as turning on the garbage disposal, using the food processor, or running the lawn mower can escalate his responses.

Alexander also regularly struggles with sensory issues in the community and at school. He has no interest in going to amusement parks because of the noise, crowds, and frenetic activity. Sporting events are very unpleasant for similar reasons. The hallways at school overwhelm him, and eating in the cafeteria, with the loud chatter and banging of lunch trays, is out of the question. His over-reactive sensory system impacts a tremendous portion of his life.

Alexander also has an underdeveloped sense of balance and spatial orientation, or what is called an under-reactive vestibular system (see "More on Sensory Differences" Box), which results in low muscle tone and balance issues. His weak trunk and shoulder muscles impact his posture and handwriting. His weak postural control affects his ability to sit and focus for long periods of time, making sitting in a classroom and learning all day considerably more difficult. He was not confident riding a bike until he was eleven years old due to his balance struggles. Alexander confronts the consequences of his sensory profile on a daily basis.

More on Sensory Differences

The following is a list of the sensory systems that could be impacted if your child has sensory processing issues:

1 visual—seeing

2 tactile—touching

3 auditory—hearing

4 oral—tasting

5 olfactory—smelling

6 proprioceptive—"The sensory system that provides information received through your muscles about where your body parts are and what they are doing" (Kranowitz 2010, p.88)

7 vestibular—"The vestibular sense tells you where up and down are in relation to where you are. It tells you if you're lying down, balancing on one foot, spinning, falling, or bending to tie your shoes. It tells you if you are moving, in what direction, and how fast... Your vestibular sense keeps you upright and centered" (Kranowitz 2010, pp.9–10).

The following books are good resources about sensory differences and the variety of sensory profiles: *Sensational Kids: Hope and Help for Children with Sensory Processing Disorder* (Miller 2006); *The Goodenoughs Get in Sync: 5 Family Members Overcome Their Special Sensory Issues* (Kranowitz 2010); and *Building Bridges Through Sensory Integration: Therapy for Children with Autism and Other Pervasive Developmental Disorders* (Yack, Aquilla, and Sutton 2003).

Motor differences

Motor skills are movements accomplished when the brain, nervous system, and muscles function together. Fine motor skills are smaller motions that use the smaller muscles of the fingers, toes, wrist, lips, and tongue. Gross motor skills are bigger motions that employ the larger muscles of the arms, legs, torso, and feet. Individuals with AS often struggle with one or both types of motor skills.

As you probably recall from your own childhood, many social interactions with peers require at least average gross motor skills and fine motor control. Children with AS often feel awkward and behind in these situations. Playing soccer is a good example. Children with AS often have difficulties tracking the movement of a soccer ball and other children on the field and running to the ball simultaneously. To further complicate the situation, the ball doesn't go in the same direction all the time. Trying to do all these things at once takes so much thought that the movements of children with AS are often uncoordinated. They also can end up missing the other elements of the game, such as the rules and the social aspects. Children with AS must adjust constantly, which is often challenging and results in their being several steps behind their peers and persistently frustrated. Again, if you haven't already done so, you may want to see an occupational therapist or physical therapist for an evaluation if you suspect your child has motor issues.

Alexander's motor differences impact him at school both socially and academically. He struggles to navigate playgrounds because of motor planning difficulties. Motor planning is the brain's ability to actively plan ahead and complete unfamiliar activities. At recess, he resorts to walking around the perimeter of the playground by himself every day. This routine not only gives him a reprieve from social interaction but also allows him to avoid motor planning issues such as how to navigate a climbing structure.

Alexander grapples with activities that require fine motor skills as well. He has low muscle tone in his fingers, hands, and arms, which affects his control of fine hand and finger movements for tasks such as handwriting and cutting with scissors. His low muscle tone also affects the stability of his shoulder and neck muscles. In an attempt to control and stabilize himself when he writes, he grips his pencils with his fist rather than using the tripod grasp that children are taught in school. These issues delay his fine motor skill development and make handwriting tiring and difficult for him.

Cognitive differences

Like sensory profiles, cognitive differences can vary for individuals with AS. However, it is common for their profiles to be significantly uneven, usually with a considerable discrepancy between their verbal and performance skills. Verbal skills include the ability to express with spoken language a command of information and vocabulary; identify a common concept described by a series of clues; understand how to explain social rules or solve everyday problems; and identify similarities between words.

When we say "performance skills," we mean the child's ability to manipulate objects in his mind and respond non-verbally. For example, a child would use performance skills to determine what is missing from a picture of a scene or object, or to work a jigsaw puzzle.

Though it is not always the case, the verbal skills of individuals with AS are often much stronger than their performance skills. They often have good memories for vocabulary and factual information. These skills can make children with AS appear very bright and mask other cognitive struggles, so it is important to be aware of potential academic issues in fundamental areas of writing, reading, and math (see "Potential Academic Struggles for the Child with AS" Box).

Potential Academic Struggles for the Child with AS

The areas of typical concern for the student with AS include relatively weaker:

- organizational skills
- cognitive flexibility
- working memory—holding and sorting through information long enough to achieve the desired conduct or results
- visual-spatial skills—the mind's ability to manipulate two- or three-dimensional figures
- visual-motor skills—the visual ability to guide the body's movement
- gestalt thinking—understanding the big picture of a situation, story, or interaction
- processing speed—the speed at which the brain processes information.

Struggles in these areas often impact academic achievement. For example, writing assignments can be challenging because they require the student's organizational skills to manage the project, working memory skills to keep the topic in mind while generating the text, and visual-motor skills to physically write. Reading comprehension may be difficult for students with AS because they have trouble understanding the big picture of the story. Children with AS can have a hard time finishing their homework because they have difficulty with organization and multi-tasking (Braaten and Felopulos 2004).

Children with AS often start struggling with math in second or third grade when the curriculum begins to demand more abstract and flexible thinking. Parents and teachers are often surprised by this change. The student with AS usually excels in math before second grade because it requires rote skills. Having a better understanding of the child's cognitive profile can help parents and teachers plan for this change (Dyment, J.H., personal communication, 2013).

Cognitive differences can also negatively affect social interactions. As we've mentioned, individuals with AS are often good at memorizing facts and sharing information verbally. However, they may be several steps behind during a social interaction due to their slow processing speed. Many times the conversation has progressed to a new topic by the time the individual with AS is ready to respond. He may blurt out something that is appropriate to an earlier part of the conversation, but is irrelevant to the new subject of the discussion. The individual with AS thus often feels his social interactions are unsuccessful. After repeatedly experiencing this feeling of failure, individuals with AS may stop trying.

Like many children with AS, Alexander's cognitive profile is significantly uneven. For example, he scores on the high end of average in verbal comprehension and the low end of average for visual-spatial skills. His psychiatrist likened having this type of cognitive profile to running laps around a field with legs that have significantly different lengths. This analogy helped me understand how academically Alexander often stumbles, feels off balance, and becomes incredibly frustrated. He may make a few steps of progress, but often falls shortly after.

Alexander also has a very slow processing speed. Lessons, homework, and tasks around the house need to be broken down into manageable chunks to allow him to proceed one step at a time and avoid becoming overwhelmed. When given ample time to think, he is much more successful.

Emotional vulnerability

Emotional vulnerability is the last feature we will examine. Coping with the social, physical, and cognitive challenges we've discussed requires a tremendous amount of effort from children with AS. They often become fatigued, irritable, and stressed. Their valiant attempts at social and academic engagement are often met with failure, or the perception of failure, which can lead to depression. Some individuals with AS are clinically depressed, which adds a host of problems, including sleep disruption and trouble with concentration, to the many difficulties with which they are already struggling.

Most individuals with AS suffer from social anxiety because they don't know what to expect in many situations. They often wonder if they are acting appropriately or if they are going to embarrass themselves. As a result, individuals with AS often live in a persistent state of anxiety. Interestingly, objective measures such as heart rate and skin conductance may detect that anxiety, but the individual with AS may not have the ability to identify and report it himself.

Some individuals with AS have anxiety disorders such as generalized anxiety, post-traumatic stress disorder (PTSD), or obsessive-compulsive disorder (OCD). As you can imagine, having clinical depression or an anxiety disorder adds significantly to the complexity of the challenges that the child with AS faces.

Alexander suffers from OCD. He often struggles with intrusive thoughts. For example, at every meal his anxious mind insists that he eat from a particular fork and plate. His OCD requires that he retouch something if he inadvertently touches it. When he starts a creative project such as writing or drawing, he obsesses when he feels it isn't perfect. For example, he was distressed that a story he wrote was "not as good as Star Wars." He kept writing and revising, tearing up papers, and becoming increasingly distraught. Similarly, he frequently goes through dozens of sheets of paper, drawing the same image, before he feels comfortable with the result.

Taking the next step

You are now prepared to begin working on your own child's unique profile toolbox. As you work through each step, applying the information that's been presented, you may find it helpful to refer back to the descriptions and examples in the chapter.

As we've said repeatedly, AS presents differently in every person. It is helpful if teachers and service providers have prior experience working with individuals with AS, but it is not enough. Alexander's relationships with some teachers have inadvertently been damaged because they weren't aware of his profile. The mistakes sometimes took a long time to repair, and other times the relationships never recovered. Previewing your child's individualized profile information with all of the professionals in your lives sets the relationships up for success. The guides I created based on Alexander's profile have eliminated well-intentioned but counterproductive approaches such as trying to hug or touch him, placing him in a loud, chaotic environment, or changing a rule without talking to him about it first.

You can also use the unique profile toolbox you create to teach your child about himself so that he knows how to communicate about and advocate for himself. Children with AS are quite capable of learning about their unique profiles when parents share its components slowly over time.

My quest to grasp AS and Alexander's unique profile took years, but it was unquestionably worthwhile. His behaviors started to make sense, and I got better at figuring out from which part of his profile they stemmed. My understanding helps me celebrate his beauty, acknowledge his struggles, and target support. I can collaborate with his teachers and service providers and advocate for him from a more solid and confident place. The clarity I've gained releases judgment and unlocks deep compassion and admiration. We designed this chapter to help you identify your child's AS profile without having to spend years being confused.

Parents Take Charge

Creating Your Child's Unique Profile Toolbox

Follow the recommendations in this section to identify your child's unique profile and create your unique profile toolbox. We designed these recommendations for you to be able to complete by yourself. If you would like to explore any area further, see the table below to identify which professionals might be helpful resources.

	SLP	Psychologist/ Psychiatrist	OT	PT	Neuropsychologist
Social differences	X	X			
Communication differences	X	X			
Restricted patterns	X	X			
Sensory differences			X		
Motor differences			X	X	
Cognitive differences		X			X
Emotional vulnerability		X			X

Use the examples provided in this section as a springboard to think about each component of your child's unique profile. If you do not see an important part of your child's presentation, simply add it in the blank space provided in the template checklists you have downloaded.

Once you complete your unique profile toolbox, share it with all of the people who can benefit from the information—the child and anyone working with him or her at home, at school, and in the community. See p.40 for a complete list of specific individuals.

Your unique profile toolbox will support generalization in every environment. You and your child's support team can proceed with the same profile understanding, choose appropriate interventions based on this knowledge, and teach her about her profile using common language.

List your child's strengths

Examples of possible strengths

- ☐ Honesty
- ☐ Perseverance
- ☐ Intellectual curiosity, particularly with special interests
- ☐ Sense of humor
- ☐ Empathy
- ☐ Embraces routine and structure
- ☐ Concrete, literal thinking
- ☐ Logic oriented
- ☐ Verbal, expressive communication
- ☐ Creative and unique way of viewing the world
- ☐ Artistic
- ☐ Good rote memory
- ☐ Ability to imitate songs and movie lines well

(DYMENT, J.H., PERSONAL COMMUNICATION, 2013)

List your child's interests

Examples of possible interests

- ☐ Voice-over
- ☐ Gadgets
- ☐ Drawing
- ☐ Writing
- ☐ Dogs/animals
- ☐ Actors
- ☐ TV
- ☐ Movies
- ☐ Lego
- ☐ Dinosaurs
- ☐ Cars
- ☐ Skiing
- ☐ Math
- ☐ Maps
- ☐ Trains
- ☐ Cartoons
- ☐ Literature
- ☐ Video games
- ☐ Super heroes
- ☐ Nature
- ☐ Transportation
- ☐ Geography
- ☐ Tae Kwon Do or Karate
- ☐ Religion

(DYMENT, J.H., PERSONAL COMMUNICATION, 2013)

List your child's dislikes

Examples of possible dislikes

- ☐ Social injustice
- ☐ Transitions
- ☐ Changes
- ☐ Being wronged or bullied
- ☐ Being touched—especially unexpectedly
- ☐ Loud and/or unexpected noises
- ☐ Certain food textures
- ☐ Chaotic environments
- ☐ Sharing information about himself
- ☐ Bright light
- ☐ Certain smells
- ☐ Organized sports
- ☐ Busy environments (cafeteria or school assemblies)
- ☐ Being different
- ☐ Being outside the group
- ☐ Being in the spotlight
- ☐ Visual disorder
- ☐ Abstract concepts
- ☐ Jokes and riddles
- ☐ Sarcasm
- ☐ Clothing textures/tags
- ☐ Tactile sensations (such as glue, clay, finger paints)
- ☐ Recess
- ☐ Unstructured time
- ☐ Imaginative play
- ☐ Disorder

(DYMENT, J.H., PERSONAL COMMUNICATION, 2013)

List important information you would like to share with others about your child

Examples of possible important information to share with others

- ☐ Dietary restrictions such as gluten, dairy, soy, preservatives, or dyes
- ☐ Visual learner
- ☐ Comorbid diagnosis: anxiety (OCD, PTSD, general)
- ☐ Comorbid diagnosis: depression
- ☐ Comorbid diagnosis: ADHD
- ☐ Learning disabilities such as a non-verbal learning disability, reading, dyslexia, or math

(DYMENT, J.H., PERSONAL COMMUNICATION, 2013)

List how social differences related to theory of mind impact your child

Examples of possible impact based on theory of mind differences

Difficulty understanding:

- ☐ Unwritten rules of interacting socially
- ☐ Thoughts, feelings, and perspectives of others
- ☐ That other people's mental states may differ from theirs
- ☐ Need for providing background information for the listener

- ☐ White lies
- ☐ Idioms
- ☐ Deceit and persuasion
- ☐ Empathy
- ☐ Boundaries
- ☐ Motivation of others
- ☐ Purpose in a task or activity (showing work, explaining answers)
- ☐ The perspectives of characters in written material which makes reading comprehension difficult

(ABELE AND MONTGOMERY 2010)

List how social differences related to central coherence impact your child

Examples of possible impact based on central coherence differences

- ☐ Can misunderstand how to behave in different environments
- ☐ Can miss the main point of a conversation
- ☐ Can miss the point or goal of an assignment
- ☐ Focused on details versus the big picture: social, contextual, procedural
- ☐ Can mistake details for the big picture
- ☐ Can often feel that the environment is chaotic and overwhelming based on an inability to filter the details
- ☐ Can have trouble recognizing the big picture
- ☐ Can have a difficult time generalizing (generalizing skills means being able to use the same skill mastered in one environment just as effectively and fluidly in other environments)
- ☐ Can struggle with transitions, schedule changes, surprises, and word usage differences
- ☐ May need rules, routines, and rituals to experience order

(ABELE AND MONTGOMERY 2010)

List how social differences related to executive functioning impact your child

Examples of possible impact based on executive functioning differences

Includes trouble with:

- ☐ Flexible thinking—being able to shift tasks when reaching a goal calls for it
- ☐ Waiting to respond
- ☐ Knowing behavioral expectations of different environments
- ☐ Following or initiating multi-step directions or tasks to achieve a goal
- ☐ Impulsivity
- ☐ Planning
- ☐ Staying on topic or objective
- ☐ Organizing
- ☐ Observing self to assess performance in process of working towards and achieving a goal
- ☐ Working memory—holding and sorting through information long enough to achieve desired conduct

Affects:

- ☐ Completing homework
- ☐ Keeping track of things
- ☐ Managing large, long-term assignments
- ☐ Navigating open-ended questions
- ☐ Writing

(ABELE AND MONTGOMERY 2010)

List how social differences related to non-verbal communication impact your child

Examples of possible impact based on non-verbal communication differences

- ☐ Can be misunderstood as bored, not interested, inattentive, and rude
- ☐ Trouble recognizing and responding appropriately to non-verbal messages
- ☐ Trouble reading cues such as facial expressions and body language
- ☐ Can lead to being bullied because of misunderstanding the intent of others, usually communicated through body language or tone of voice

(ABELE AND MONTGOMERY 2010)

List the pragmatic language difficulties with which your child struggles

Examples of possible impact based on pragmatic communication differences

My child struggles with:

- ☐ Selecting a topic
- ☐ Introducing a topic
- ☐ Maintaining conversation about a topic
- ☐ Changing topics
- ☐ Initiating his turn when talking
- ☐ Responding when someone speaks
- ☐ Repairing the conversation
- ☐ Pausing when conversing
- ☐ Managing interruptions and overlaps in conversation
- ☐ Adding information to the preceding topic
- ☐ Knowing the right amount of information to share
- ☐ Cohesion of topic
- ☐ Choosing accurate words
- ☐ Adjusting to the listener's style
- ☐ Intelligibility
- ☐ Vocal intensity
- ☐ Vocal quality
- ☐ Intonation and stress patterns
- ☐ Fluency
- ☐ Proximity to speaker
- ☐ Physical contacts
- ☐ Body posture
- ☐ Foot, leg, hand, or arm movements
- ☐ Gestures
- ☐ Facial expressions
- ☐ Eye gaze

(PRUTTING AND KIRCHNER 1987)

List how restricted and repetitive patterns of behavior, interests, and activities impact your child

Examples of possible impact based on restricted and repetitive patterns of behavior, interests, and activities

- ☐ His knowledge is deep, and his preoccupation and passion is intense for his areas of interest. This can restrict his overall knowledge. My child's consuming interests are:
  - ☐ ____________________
- ☐ Stress can occur when transitioning from preferred activity.
- ☐ Engaging him in non-preferred activity can be difficult.
- ☐ He can experience stress during gap periods between special interests.
- ☐ These interests are not always age appropriate or socially appropriate (such as guns or body parts).

(FREEDMAN 2010)

List how sensory struggles impact your child

Examples of possible impact based on over-responsive sensory system

- ☐ Tactile defensiveness:
  - ☐ May avoid imposed touching such as hugs, kisses, and hand shakes
  - ☐ May have difficulty tolerating hair washing, hair combing, face washing, teeth brushing, or nail cutting
  - ☐ May be very protective of personal space
  - ☐ May be sensitive to temperature changes (food, water temperature, and weather)
  - ☐ May over-react to minor scrapes or bumps
- ☐ Auditory defensiveness:
  - ☐ May cover ears or use vocalizations (humming) in response to auditory stimuli
- ☐ Difficulty tolerating certain smells
- ☐ Troubles with certain tastes and textures
- ☐ Struggles with processing certain types of visual input
- ☐ Vestibular over-responsivity:
  - ☐ Motion sickness
  - ☐ Resistance to movement activities such as swinging or sliding in a playground
  - ☐ Prefers having head in upright position—dislikes diaper changes, washing hair
  - ☐ May not like having feet off the ground

- [ ] May become overwhelmed in multisensory environments (malls, theme parks, cafeterias, etc.)
- [ ] Struggles with modulating sensory input, which can result in dysregulation

(CAPONE, K., FROM DISCUSSION, 2013, USED WITH PERMISSION)

Examples of possible impact based on under-responsive sensory system

- [ ] Under-responsive vestibular and proprioceptive system:
    - [ ] Low muscle tone
    - [ ] Weak trunk and shoulder muscles impact posture and writing
    - [ ] Weak postural control impacts his ability to sit for long periods of time and focus
- [ ] Proprioceptive under-responsivity:
    - [ ] May not know amount of force he is using
    - [ ] May write with pencil either too lightly or too heavily
- [ ] Tactile under-responsivity:
    - [ ] May not notice that hands or face are dirty
    - [ ] May be messy eater
    - [ ] May bump into other kids
    - [ ] May not know when he is hurt—high pain tolerance
    - [ ] May not respond to temperature changes
- [ ] May not participate in games or social interactions
- [ ] May not be aware when he needs to use the bathroom or when he is hungry
- [ ] May have slow and sluggish responses
- [ ] Struggles with modulating sensory input, which can result in dysregulation

(CAPONE, K., FROM DISCUSSION, 2013, USED WITH PERMISSION)

Examples of possible impact based on sensory-seeking system

- [ ] Vestibular sensory seeking:
    - [ ] May seek movement to modulate sensory system
    - [ ] May struggle to sit still
    - [ ] May never get dizzy and seek spinning exercises
    - [ ] May never stand still—always moving
    - [ ] May be dangerous in their play in an attempt to get intense input: jumping from high places

- ☐ Proprioceptive sensory seeking:
  - ☐ May seek deep pressure to try to modulate their system
  - ☐ May constantly chew on things such as their shirt
  - ☐ May be dangerous in their play in an attempt to get intense input: crashing into people
- ☐ Tactile sensory seeking:
  - ☐ May frequently need to touch things on the table before they should
  - ☐ May irritate peers due to uninvited touch
  - ☐ May fidget
- ☐ Oral sensory seeking:
  - ☐ May overstuff mouth
  - ☐ May constantly put things in mouth—food and non-food items
- ☐ Olfactory sensory seeking:
  - ☐ May constantly smell things
- ☐ Auditory sensory seeking:
  - ☐ May make noises
  - ☐ May speak loudly
  - ☐ May seek out loud noises
- ☐ Visual sensory seeking:
  - ☐ May seek out bright lights or spinning objects
  - ☐ May flick fingers in visual field for visual input

(CAPONE, K., FROM DISCUSSION, 2013, USED WITH PERMISSION)

Examples of possible impact based on sensory discrimination disorder

- ☐ May not have the ability to take information from the environment and make sense of it
- ☐ Visual discrimination:
  - ☐ May have difficulty finding objects—especially in visually busy backgrounds (closet, drawer, backpack)
  - ☐ May have difficulty discriminating between similar objects or letters
- ☐ Auditory discrimination:
  - ☐ May have difficulty with attention, especially in places with significant auditory stimuli
  - ☐ May have difficulty discriminating words with similar sounds

- ☐ Tactile discrimination:
    - ☐ Receiving information from their sense of touch about size, shape, texture, and weight of objects may impact fine and gross motor skills
    - ☐ May frequently touch or fidget with objects
    - ☐ May not know where they have been touched
- ☐ Proprioceptive discrimination:
    - ☐ May need to visually monitor their movements to know where their body is, such as following the gym or yoga teacher, handwriting, and forming letter strokes
    - ☐ May have difficulty grading the amount of force they use
    - ☐ May seek out rough play
    - ☐ May have difficulty with body awareness and invade the personal space of others
- ☐ Vestibular discrimination:
    - ☐ May have difficulty with directionality—gets easily lost
    - ☐ May be uncoordinated
    - ☐ May have difficulty knowing their head and body position
- ☐ Oral discrimination:
    - ☐ May have difficulty discriminating foods of different tastes or textures
- ☐ Olfactory discrimination:
    - ☐ May not be able to discriminate smells or have a difficult time localizing from where a smell is coming

(CAPONE, K., FROM DISCUSSION, 2013, USED WITH PERMISSION)

Examples of possible impact based on postural disorder

- ☐ May have difficulty with ocular motor skills—being able to track a ball, shift gaze from one object to another, or converging or diverging eyes
- ☐ May have an open mouth posture and frequently drools
- ☐ May have difficulty with balance activities—may lean on desk or arm when sitting or hold onto a wall while walking
- ☐ May frequently trip or fall
- ☐ May have difficulty crossing their body midline, developing a dominant hand or using both hands together
- ☐ May tire easily and have poor endurance compared with peers

(CAPONE, K., FROM DISCUSSION, 2013, USED WITH PERMISSION)

Examples of possible impact based on dyspraxia

- ☐ May have difficulty:
  - ☐ Following multi-step directions
  - ☐ Initiating tasks
  - ☐ Learning new tasks
  - ☐ Maintaining/copying rhythms
  - ☐ Performing motor tasks with several steps
  - ☐ Expanding on play ideas
- ☐ Performance of tasks is slow and labored
- ☐ Poor task completion
- ☐ May be able to explain what they want to do, but struggles to execute the idea
- ☐ May prefer structure and have a difficult time with schedule changes
- ☐ May struggle with transitions

(CAPONE, K., FROM DISCUSSION, 2013, USED WITH PERMISSION)

List how motor struggles impact your child

Examples of possible impact based on motor struggles

- ☐ Motor planning difficulties can manifest as low frustration tolerance or avoidance
- ☐ Exhibits repetitive behaviors because he has limited motor plans from which to draw
- ☐ Limited motor plans exhibited at recess and during free time at home
- ☐ Fine motor skills not well developed; impacts writing and drawing ability
- ☐ May have difficulty collaborating with peers on different games because they have to motor plan what they want to do and what peer wants to do
- ☐ May have difficulty generating new ideas with peers or by themselves

(CAPONE, K., FROM DISCUSSION, 2013, USED WITH PERMISSION)

List how cognitive differences impact your child

Examples of possible impact based on cognitive differences

- ☐ Self-concept—even though he is bright, he can be easily confused
- ☐ Uneven range of cognitive skills:
  - ☐ Higher Verbal IQ than Performance IQ
  - ☐ Higher Performance IQ than Verbal IQ
- ☐ Solid factual knowledge—vocabulary and facts
- ☐ Strong rote memory skills

- ☐ Preference for literal reasoning over abstract thinking
- ☐ Literal thinking can lead to gullibility
- ☐ Difficulty with visual-spatial thinking
- ☐ Focused on details rather than the big picture—difficult time retaining the big picture, gestalt, of stories, social situations, new material, and so on
- ☐ Weak visual-motor skills
- ☐ Slow processing speed
- ☐ Difficulty changing activities quickly

List how emotional vulnerability impacts your child

Examples of possible impact based on emotional vulnerability

- ☐ Vulnerable to frustration and meltdowns
- ☐ Anxiety—exacerbated by sensory issues
- ☐ Obsessive-Compulsive Disorder
- ☐ Post-Traumatic Stress Disorder
- ☐ School refusal/reluctance
- ☐ Social anxiety
- ☐ Depression
- ☐ Dysthymia
- ☐ Anger
- ☐ Chronic stress

How to use the toolbox

Now that you have created your unique profile toolbox, you will be able to use your child's:

- strengths to help him or her build confidence
- interests to help him or her access the curriculum
- dislikes as a road map to help avoid meltdowns
- features and associated features to determine the most effective interventions and to promote empathy and understanding.

You will continue to put this information to use as you develop specific tools in the chapters to come.

Chapter 4

Collaboration and Communication

I have come to find over the past decade that collaborating well with Alexander's teachers and service providers is one of the most important contributions that I can make to his success and his support team's sense of harmony. Before I learned this valuable lesson, communication with educators and other professionals was often anxiety-producing. For example, as Alexander's behavior escalated, his preschool teacher Ms. Jones called me frequently when his day was not going well. It was Alexander's third year at the preschool following his AS diagnosis at the end of his second year, and this frequent calling was new. Ms. Jones's intentions were caring and supportive, but the calls made me feel increasingly alarmed. I worried that the school would perceive Alexander to be a disruption and ask him to leave. If I had established a plan with Ms. Jones up front to talk on the phone every day that Alexander escalated significantly, I would not have worried so much. Without an explicit agreement in place, each call made me wonder if we were headed towards expulsion.

In this chapter, we cover all of the steps you need to take to ensure effective collaboration, including determining agreed-upon methods and frequency of communication with your child's educators and other service providers. The Parents Take Charge section at the end of the chapter provides, and helps you customize, tools to maximize collaboration with your entire team.

The basics of effective collaboration

Using your guide

Research indicates that effective parent–teacher communication and collaboration has a strong bearing on the child's academic and social success (Stoner *et al.* 2005). Logistical preparation is essential to achieving this goal. My guide has been key for my situation. As we've mentioned in previous chapters, it provides me with a road map, Alexander with an instruction booklet, and his teachers and professionals with a toolbox. The guide enables our team to work as a unit to assist Alexander in reaching his potential. It also enables Alexander to take steps to help himself.

The importance of parental self-care

In addition to preparing logistically to collaborate with teachers and service providers, I prepare emotionally. I have worked hard to release the pain and upset I felt about Alexander and my parenting struggles during the early years. I know that my distress is not productive for me or anyone else, and I've committed to taking care of myself and working through my emotions with the help of talented professionals. I do a number of other things that you may already do or want to try yourself. I meditate and attend to my spiritual growth. I exercise almost every day to relieve stress. I plan events that I enjoy both with my friends and alone, such as going out to dinner, visiting a museum, seeing a movie or a play, listening to music, exploring a new city, or going to the beach. I read inspirational books and attend interesting talks. I recognize that if my tank is empty, then I have nothing to give. When I stay emotionally healthy, I am able to interact with Alexander's teachers and other professionals with a fresh and open perspective.

I encourage you to utilize and identify more of your own strategies for self-care. When you prioritize restoring yourself, everyone will benefit. As the flight attendants tell you on an airplane, you should put on your own oxygen mask before helping others with theirs. You will be better able to take care of others if you are taking care of yourself!

Giving your best effort

Being logistically and emotionally ready puts me in the position to give my best effort to collaboration. I consciously access the part of myself that works well with others. I warmly welcome and accept every one of Alexander's team members and am willing to do the work to interact effectively with them. I sincerely appreciate each professional's strengths and enjoy acknowledging what each does well. I also empathize with their struggles. I get pleasure from being part of a team and working towards a common goal. I don't always meet the standards I set for myself in this regard. I do, however, realize that bringing this positive energy and attitude improves the group dynamic and cohesiveness, which ultimately benefits my son, the team, and our family.

Collaborating well with your child's team

When you put your best effort into collaborating and communicating effectively, you will build successful relationships that support your child with AS. Parent–professional relationships have all of the potential pitfalls of any kind of relationship, such as personality or communication-style differences. Judgment and blame lead to communication breakdown, and compromised parent–teacher or parent–service provider relationships negatively impact the child with AS. Let's look at how to avoid these pitfalls and build positive relationships with every member of your team.

Building trust

Often children with AS struggle with transitions at the beginning of the school year. It is important for you as the parent and case manager to enter the relationship trusting that professionals are doing their best and that they are smart, committed people. This approach starts you off on the right foot for open communication, collaboration, and mutual respect. The assumption that the teacher or service provider is looking out for the best interest of your child with AS may be shaken at some point, but it helps to give professionals the benefit of the doubt at the beginning of your relationship. Most professionals in this field work very hard and want to succeed.

You can build trust by being open and honest about your child's issues and being mindful of the many demands on the professionals with whom you're collaborating. The first time you perceive a problem, address it directly with the professional rather than going over his or her head. And pick your battles. You could damage parent/professional trust if the teacher or service provider feels threatened that you will speak to his or her supervisor about every perceived glitch. You should elevate recurring issues or untenable situations only after you have exhausted all other avenues.

For example, one day Alexander came home from school distraught. When I asked what was wrong, he shouted that his teacher forced him to stay in a large closet for a long time and wouldn't talk to him because she was angry with him. The treatment sounded cruel, and I was furious. Once I calmed down, I contacted the teacher and shared how upset Alexander was and why. She, in turn, provided more details about the incident. She explained that Alexander became very angry during class due to unexpected cheering and started yelling. The teacher wanted to find a quiet space to help Alexander calm down. She chose the "closet" because it had wall coverings to help buffer school sounds. As a result of our discussion, I was able to explain to Alexander why the teacher took him to that location when he was upset. After that incident, the teacher created a visual tool to preview with Alexander, simply and explicitly detailing the plan for any future upsets. In this case, I believe that communicating with Alexander's teacher, rather than elevating this situation to the teacher's supervisor, helped Alexander, the teacher, and our collaborative relationship.

Communicating effectively

Communication frequency and preferences

At the start of your professional relationship, you and your point person need to agree on how you will interact as you work together to support your child. The amount and style of communication between parents and professionals can vary. You will want to determine with each teacher and service provider what form and frequency of communication makes sense in general. People respond differently to handwritten notes, e-mails, phone calls, and face-to-face visits. You should ask directly what method of communication each professional prefers, as well as make clear what type of communication you would like him or her to use in a crisis. (Making a crisis response plan will be discussed in more detail in Chapter 8.)

When communicating with teachers and service providers, try always to keep in mind that they often have heavy caseloads and a number of responsibilities. For example, when writing an e-mail, use short bulleted lists that highlight important points rather than long narratives. Write just one e-mail per day with a number of points listed rather than a series of separate shorter e-mails that will clog up the professional's inbox. One strategy is to start an e-mail draft in the morning to which you can add issues that arise over the course of the day. Some professionals may want to receive an early morning note if the child has struggled at home, to prepare them for how the child might show up and help them plan how to proceed with the day's schedule. Professionals may also want to have advance notice about incidents and special occasions—for example, trips, a traveling parent, houseguests, a sibling struggle, or difficulty with an extra-curricular activity—so that they can anticipate and better understand the child's behavior. Try not to overwork your special educator by relying on him or her for general information such as when the next school dance is scheduled or when the school will send release forms for an upcoming field trip. Keep communications focused on the needs of your child with AS.

Communication parameters

It is also important at the start of the relationship to develop ground rules and boundaries. For example, you can ask professionals to let you know if you inadvertently step into their territory. Basing your feedback on your expertise about your child and not telling teachers and service providers how to teach or do their jobs demonstrates respect for their experience and knowledge. Similarly, you can communicate that you will let them know if they tell you something about your child that doesn't ring true to you.

We realize it may not be easy when your child's wellbeing is at stake, but make every effort to respond calmly and rationally to professionals at school and in the community. When you assume the role of case manager, you are stepping partially out of your traditional parenting role in order to be the professional expert on the needs of your child with AS. Managing your emotions and keeping them out of communications and interactions with teachers and service providers as much as possible will help you excel in this role. Having outbursts can damage trust and impair communication. Again, we recognize that this may sometimes be difficult, but we have found from experience that we get the best results when we consciously consider the professional's perspective and don't take situations personally. You aren't, however, expected to behave like a robot. Humor can be an effective tool in your relationships with educators and service providers. Displaying a sense of humor can play a big part in helping people relax and communicate on a more human level.

I sometimes like to share funny anecdotes about Alexander at school meetings to lighten the mood. Alexander's actions and words can be unexpected, which can simultaneously mortify and amuse people interacting with him. School staff regularly experience this with Alexander. In response to an incident that a teacher shares, I might tell a story, for example, about a time when Alexander visited my in-laws in Alabama. My sister-in-law took him on a special outing to an art supply store. They both love art, and she wanted to help further his interest. She tried to sell him on many of the products, which she generously planned to buy for him. All Alexander wanted was a simple, black ballpoint pen. When she enthusiastically went on and on about different items, Alexander was unimpressed and finally said, "You don't work here, you know. Can we go?" The contrast between my sister-in-law's Southern effervescence and Alexander's blunt honesty struck me as funny.

I find that if I take a light-hearted approach, the person interacting with Alexander is more likely to see the beauty of his honesty rather than take his comments too seriously or feel offended. We can bond over a shared laugh.

Given that AS-related struggles can lead to many intense situations, a little humor can go a long way in keeping relationships pleasant and open.

It is common for parents of children with AS to feel stressed, bogged down, and overwhelmed by the problems they face when parenting a child with AS. You may find it helpful to work through your emotions and stress with the aid of a therapist, friends, or family members so that you can focus communications on supporting your child's education and goals.

Professionals may fear the ramifications of mistakes

Parents can foster positive communication with professionals by acknowledging that mistakes will occur when working with their child and responding openly and gracefully when they do. Like parents, professionals experience a rollercoaster of feelings based on the child's successes and failures. When a child struggles significantly under their care, they may feel their sense of competence is on the line. They may hesitate to inform parents of mistakes because they fear blame or even a lawsuit. If you aren't getting access to potentially important information, you won't be able to collaborate most effectively with your child's team. Parents frequently have experience addressing similar situations at home. Collaboration will be most effective when parents are understanding rather than judgmental of the professionals on their child's team.

A teacher might be reluctant to share that a child had a meltdown at school as a result of something he or she did, such as touching the child unexpectedly or losing his or her temper. One time, a teacher who was new to Alexander and didn't yet understand his profile saw him trying to pick a lock with a paperclip in the hall. She didn't know that Alexander had an agreement with his teacher that he was allowed to do this, and she asked him what he was doing. He told her that it was none of her business. She told him that he needed to stop and sent him back to his classroom.

Alexander was furious. He decided that this teacher was mean and that he didn't like her. This was unfortunate because she had already been chosen as his homeroom teacher for the following year. Alexander's feelings were blatantly obvious to this teacher and to most other people. The situation must have been embarrassing for her, but she chose to be open and honest about what had happened and work with us to fix it. With Scott's guidance and my knowledge of how to approach Alexander, we worked together to improve the situation. As part of our strategy to repair the relationship, she came to our house twice. Once, she brought her dog because we shared that Alexander loves dogs. Another time, she came to look at vacation pictures of one of Alexander's favorite places in the world, a lake in Alabama. We worked at home, at school, and with Alexander's psychologist to help him release his anger and move past the incident.

Getting to know your point person

Understanding your point person's moods, learning styles, communication habits, strengths, and weaknesses can also lead to more effective collaboration. For example, it is helpful for you to understand that when a child goes through a bumpy stretch at school, many teachers worry that they will be held responsible, and their egos may be fragile. They feel vulnerable. You can collaborate most effectively during these times by ensuring that the conversation about the situation is open and not perceived as judgmental. Just like students, teachers have varying learning styles, which you may begin to recognize over time. Teachers' learning styles can influence the form of communication they prefer or how you can best present information to them when you meet. You may see that certain teachers project confidence, while others seem tentative. Some may express frustration, and some may seem anxious. Becoming familiar with your point person can help you figure out when to push issues and when to give him or her space.

Importance of solid parent–teacher collaboration

The purpose of collaborating is to meet the needs of the child with AS, which will help create a teaching environment that is most successful for the child, other students, the teacher, and parents. Solid parent–teacher communication is important because children with AS do not typically express themselves in either predictable or easily understandable ways. It takes joint, ongoing coordination between home and school to figure out and share the most successful practices and interventions for the changing needs of your child. When everyone is using proven strategies consistently, the child better accesses the curriculum and his social world. As a result, he will be calmer in all environments, which benefits the child, the teacher, the classroom, and the family.

Ongoing collaboration is critical because a variety of surprising presentations are possible with children with AS. The child with AS may look like he is fitting in, getting along, and progressing successfully, but he may not be accessing the curriculum or the social world. He will often miss signals about the "hidden curriculum," a term coined by Brenda Smith Myles to describe the unspoken rules in everyday social interactions. For instance, a PE class tolerates yelling, but the same behavior is unacceptable in art class. This distinction is rarely verbalized; students are expected to notice and act accordingly.

It may surprise the teacher to find out that the child is severely stressed because, in addition to the child not understanding the hidden curriculum, children with AS are often not giving clear, expected non-verbal signals about what they are experiencing internally. Many children can get through their school day successfully and then have colossal meltdowns after school because they have worked so hard to behave in expected ways and to manage their anxiety and their sensory systems. They may look like they are doing fine at school, but their day depletes them. You and your child's teachers can better understand your child's needs and develop more informed interventions when you routinely update each other about his presentation in your respective environments.

You know your elementary school-age child far better than your child's teachers do. With solid parent–teacher communication, you can explain the meaning of your child's specific behaviors and suggest ways to address anxious reactions. For example, children can indicate stress by becoming more or less animated or energetic, using harsh words or curse words, or making certain facial expressions like grimacing. These communication keys help teachers understand what the student is experiencing and, therefore, how to modify the demands to support overall success. You can also offer strategies that you know are effective, such as moving out of your child's line of vision, helping him move to a quiet area, or reading to him.

Use collaboration to help your child with AS generalize skills

As we briefly discussed in the previous two chapters, generalizing skills means being able to use the same skill mastered in one environment just as effectively and fluidly in other environments, which is particularly difficult for most individuals with AS. Often when a child learns a skill in one environment, she may not realize that she can and should use the same skill in another environment. Adults need to clarify this connection explicitly for the child. Generalization of skills is most successful for individuals with AS when the same skills are practiced regularly in multiple environments.

When Alexander took social pragmatics classes, his group leader taught Michelle Garcia Winner's Social Thinking® concepts to the participants and followed up with a summary of what she covered to the parents. With permission, I forwarded the e-mails to Alexander's special educator. I also shared the focus points with his psychologist. This unified approach allowed us to work on key concepts simultaneously using the same language. For example, one concept that the leader taught was Winner's whole-body listening approach, which explains in detail how we use our eyes, ears, mouth, hands, feet, brains, body, and heart to listen. Alexander's special educator, psychologist, and I used this same concept and language in interactions with Alexander while his social pragmatics class was practicing whole-body listening. Our coordinated effort helped Alexander generalize that skill in multiple environments.

Skill generalization can be challenging because individuals with AS often do not understand what various contexts require of them without explicit instruction. Teaching a child about eye contact is a good example. Training someone to make more eye contact is not always the right guidance. There are some situations in which greater eye contact makes sense, such as when a child is having a conversation with his parents or listening to a friend tell him a story. Other times, such as when classmates are working together as lab partners in science, too much eye contact feels uncomfortable to the other student. Adults need to explain clearly the social and behavioral expectations called for in varying contexts and environments in order for the individual with AS to generalize skills.

You and your child's teachers or service providers can work together to help your child with AS make huge strides in skills generalization by focusing on the same skills at home, at school, and in the community. Speaking a common language in all environments plays a major role in supporting these goals. For example, when addressing struggles with eye contact, the teacher might suggest that the child look at the bridge of someone's nose to avoid sensory overload. If a parent advises the child to look at someone's forehead instead, the subtle difference in advice could unnecessarily cause confusion. Consistent language helps the child understand that the exact same issue is being addressed in multiple environments.

As another example, Alexander's psychologist worked on using "I-statements" with Alexander to support self-regulation and self-advocacy. For example, she taught Alexander that rather than reacting in frustration when a babysitter arrived late without notice, he could say, "I feel very upset when you arrive late unexpectedly." This conversation helped his babysitter to better understand his needs and both parties felt good after the conversation. His psychologist enrolled me in generalizing this skill at home. I acknowledged his "I-statements" and pointed out when I made "I-statements." Using the same language in both environments helped Alexander generalize the skill. I in turn shared this strategy with Alexander's school so that they could work with the same tool using the same terminology.

I've found that collaboration is most effective when Alexander's special educator and I have open, daily communication and organize home and school efforts to maximize skills generalization. I send e-mails when Alexander struggles significantly at home. I share the nature of his issues and any recommendations based on prior experience with the same type of problem. Teachers send home a daily communication log (see the Parents Take Charge section), which tells me if there were any changes to the regular school routine, how the morning and afternoon went, what specials Alexander attended, any notable sensory behavior, and comments from school. If issues occur during the day, teachers often share the strategy they used, which I then reinforce at home.

Alexander is most successful when teachers prepare and plan for each day by creating and using tools that support him and the other students in his class. For example, if a visitor comes to the classroom, the special educator might print an information sheet with the visitor's name, the purpose of the visit, and the behavioral expectations of the class. The special educator previews the tool at school before the visit and sends it home so I can support the message. Similarly, teachers might create tools to teach rules such as safe body expectations (see the Parents Take Charge section of Chapter 6). They introduce the tools and send them to me, and Alexander and I work on the same skill simultaneously at home and in the community.

Sharing information: what works

Now that we have covered how to approach collaboration with your child's teachers and support team, we will discuss some ideas for practical strategies that you can use in different environments. The Parents Take Charge section of this chapter will offer specific tools for you to pick and choose depending on your child's unique AS profile.

Overview

This list highlights the most important, big-picture components of an AS-friendly environment. You can put these points into practice at home and share them with the professionals with whom your child interacts. See the "An Overview of What Works" Box for more detailed information about each of these items.

- Build a trusting relationship.
- Honor and celebrate the strengths and interests of the child with AS.
- Provide positive reinforcement.
- Approach mistakes and struggles educationally; not punitively.
- Collaborate to ensure the child has opportunities to practice skills in different environments.
- Provide slower pacing.
- Incorporate daily living skills into overall programming to promote independence.
- Organize environments to support greater inner organization.
- Preview.

(FREEDMAN 2010)

An Overview of What Works

1 *Building a trusting relationship* with the child with AS is a key ingredient to setting up environments that work. When the child trusts an adult, he has less general anxiety in the setting because he understands that someone cares and will be there for him. The child is more likely to accept feedback about a potentially skewed perspective from a person he trusts. Essential factors in building trust with a child with AS include being blunt and honest in a sensitive and non-judgmental manner and providing a predictable environment and an emotionally stable atmosphere.

2 *Honoring and celebrating the strengths and interests* of a child with AS helps him feel appreciated and valued. This type of acknowledgment assists the child with AS in opening himself to an interpersonal connection. The child can also engage academically and socially through his interests.

3 *Taking a positive, educational approach rather than a punitive one* with a child with AS helps keep him primed for learning. Children with AS regularly receive negative feedback for their social mistakes. Because they do not often make the connection between their

behavior and consequences, these patterns can keep repeating. In an educational environment, success is possible when the child with AS receives positive feedback for the things he does well and explicit, non-judgmental education about what he needs to improve and how to correct the behavior.

4 *Practicing skills in different environments* supports generalization. As we mentioned earlier, a child with AS does not necessarily have mastery over a skill when he can perform it in one environment. He must learn the skills across many settings, which requires parents to facilitate communication with the school and external service providers.

5 *Providing slower pacing* accommodates for the fact that many children with AS have slower processing in general or slower auditory processing specifically. Because children with AS must read non-verbal cues and recognize the hidden curriculum through the thinking part of their brains, they are processing more than most people. Slowing down the pace is always useful, even when it appears that the child is integrating information at a faster rate.

6 *Incorporating daily living skills and focusing on independence* helps prepare the child for adjusting to the increasing demands that come with aging and maturing. Children with AS do not learn daily living skills automatically; parents, teachers, and group leaders must explicitly teach them. Children with AS must practice these skills and come to understand the value of these skills to their lives.

7 *Creating organized environments* helps counteract the inherent feeling of inner chaos that the student likely experiences.

8 *Previewing* helps children with AS deal with unexpected and expected transitions. Because the attention of children with AS is commonly focused on the recent past, the present, and the near future, previewing organizes and orients them, which supports access to their academic and social worlds and promotes calm.

Visual aids

Visual supports are very useful because of the way that individuals with AS process information. Children with AS can use visual supports in the form of pictures more efficiently than words. Interpreting language requires a number of steps that can be challenging for children with AS. They have to translate the words into mental images and then insert themselves into these mental images. Pictures, on the other hand, can enable children with AS to identify themselves in situations instantaneously and provide quick insight into what they are supposed to do. For example, teachers can take a picture of a child in a classroom behaving in an expected way. The photograph would help the child skip several cognitive steps and immediately understand what he needs to do. Furthermore, children with AS can read visuals at their own pace and refer back to them if needed.

Typically developing children also benefit from the use of visual supports. For example, when students in a new class are asked to introduce themselves by answering a set of questions, they feel less anxious when they have access to visual prompts. The visual aid helps them organize their thoughts and maintain the progression of their responses.

Educational interventions

Educational interventions are modifications or accommodations made at school and in the classroom that help level the academic playing field for children with AS. They help provide children with AS with access to learning that otherwise wouldn't be possible and allow children with AS to participate in the classroom as important, contributing members of an inclusive community.

As your child's case manager, you can provide special educators with information about her unique presentation. The profile of her individual development, strengths, and impairments will help special educators make strategic choices about educational interventions. Neuropsychological and occupational therapy reports can provide useful information about your child to help determine which tools will best support her in the classroom. In addition, you can let special educators know which educational interventions you have used successfully in the past. While teachers ultimately choose the educational interventions, your input is essential because teachers typically change every year and have varying levels of AS knowledge.

As a case manager, you can benefit from familiarizing yourself with the universe of educational tools and why they are chosen. With this knowledge, you can communicate and brainstorm with teachers more effectively. The Parents Take Charge section of this chapter offers an extensive list of tools organized by impairment.

Social skills supports

Social skills supports help address issues that arise at different times in the development of a child with AS. However, you cannot implement all of the strategies at the same time. The key is for you to become familiar with the options so you have tools available when you need them (see the Parents Take Charge section of this chapter for a wide selection). For example, you can role-play when you need to preview a situation with your child with AS such as initiating a conversation. Video modeling serves a similar purpose and can be highly effective because two dimensions can be simpler for a child with AS to process than three. Parents, teachers, or professionals can record themselves modeling a behavior or an activity. You can also record your child with AS role-playing so that he can watch the video, see himself in action trying different techniques, and figure out what works best.

Parents, teachers, and service providers can use *The Incredible 5-Point Scale* by Kari Dunn Buron and Mitzi Curtis (2003) to help a child with AS understand perspective taking and the impact of his behavior. For example, if a classmate accidentally brushes him in the hallway at school, he might react in a loud and explosive manner. After the child calms down, an adult can ask how he felt on a scale of one to five. He may say that the situation felt like a five because it upset his sense of touch, grated on him, and felt like an attack. The adult can acknowledge the child's sensitivity to touch, but explain that people expect that a light touch will elicit a Level 1 response. People typically do not notice and keep moving. The goal is for the child to take the perspective that, even though he may experience something toxic, his Level 5 reaction is more extreme than others would expect by several orders of magnitude.

Social Stories™ (see "Social Stories™" Box) also help to clarify situations, skills, and concepts. For example, part of being a student is occasionally going on field trips. Field trips have different expectations and hidden curriculum rules from other school activities. Not only do the students interact with new people such as field guides and bus drivers, they may also witness people behaving in unfamiliar ways. For safety reasons, teachers may be stricter on a field trip. For example, following directions the first time might be much more important at the Museum of Science than in the classroom. Adults should explicitly define these differences, and the resulting expectations and rules, prior to a field trip to give students with AS the best chance for success. Social Stories™ are an effective tool to explain the plan, timeline, and expectations of the student with AS.

Social Stories™

A Social Story™ is a tool developed by Carol Gray and has been used successfully with many children with AS. The purpose of the tool is to share accurate social information in a way that is reassuring and easy for the child to understand. The story explains situations, skills, or concepts and provides information about expected responses, the perspective of others, and social cues. Gray designed this tool with a specific style and format, which parents, special educators, and service providers can learn and use with their children with AS (see www.CarolGraySocialStories.com).

We refer to Social Stories™ often throughout the book and provide examples of social stories that Alexander's special educators created for him.

Gray's website is a great resource. In addition, she has written books including *The New Social Stories Book* (2010) and *My Social Stories Book* (2002), which provide Social Stories™ for common topics with which children with AS need support.

It is important to remember that many social concepts can take years for a child with AS to understand fully. Flexible thinking is an example of a concept that takes a long time to grasp, practice, and master. Speech and language pathologists, Social Thinking® professionals, and parents can periodically re-evaluate how to teach this and other difficult concepts over the course of the child's development.

Restricted and repetitive patterns

We discussed issues related to restricted and repetitive patterns and your child's unique profile in Chapter 3. Children with AS can experience significant stress from change, particularly when transitioning from a preferred activity. Their special interests are often so intense that they have trouble engaging in non-preferred activities. They often find activities related to their special interests more satisfying than social experiences and can miss out on the opportunity to practice social skills. These struggles occur in every environment in which the child with AS interacts.

The Parents Take Charge section provides a tool to help your child cope with this stress and offers strategies for helping him engage in non-preferred activities. You will learn to use your child's special interest to help him calm down and make social connections. When a child develops the skills to cope with the impact of this aspect of his AS profile, he can broaden his life, experience fewer upsets, and be more flexible.

Sensory support

We discussed sensory issues and your child's unique sensory profile at length in Chapter 3. In the Parents Take Charge section, you will be able to select tools from a wide variety of options, depending on your child's particular needs. To aid with collaboration, a private occupational therapist can evaluate your child with AS and write a report for the school detailing information about his sensory profile. An occupational therapist can also recommend an activity plan, or sensory diet (we will discuss this more thoroughly and offer related tools in Chapter 8), to support your child's unique sensory struggles, teach him how to make his body calm, and help him cope with his day. For example, if a child is highly sensitive to loud noises, the occupational therapist may suggest that teachers allow him to wear earplugs or earphones at certain times of the day and preview fire alarms and construction noises.

Once the occupational therapist completes the report, provide a copy to his special educator and school occupational therapist (if your child works with a school OT). They can use the information to build supports into your child's school day to help him remain calm and be able to access his academic and social curricula.

You are now ready to complete the exercises in the Parents Take Charge section to develop your own collaboration toolbox.

Parents Take Charge

Creating Your Child's Collaboration and Communication Toolbox

Certain tools support every environment in which the child interacts. You can collaborate effectively by sharing the following tools with the professionals working with your child and using them at home. This strategy will allow his support team to share a common language and consistent approach, which will increase clarity for your child.

Beginning of the relationship meeting with special educators or service providers

Either before or soon after school starts or when a new professional relationship begins with an outside service provider, set up and use the example of the Beginning of the Relationship Meeting checklist below to help you prepare for a meeting with your child's special educator or service provider. The purpose of the meeting is to establish collaboration preferences, tactfully identify the professional's AS understanding and knowledge, share information about your child's unique AS profile, and set up a follow-up meeting to collaborate on your child's guide. Given that initial interactions with a child with AS can set the tone for the year, proactive communication and preparation are worthwhile investments.

Develop a collaboration agreement with your child's new special educators and professionals in the community.

Example of a checklist for beginning of the relationship meeting with special educators or service providers:

- ☐ Establish the professional's preferred communication style(s): e-mails, phone calls, face-to-face visits:
  - ☐ ______________________________
- ☐ Determine frequency of communication:
  - ☐ ______________________________
- ☐ Identify what the professional would like to know on an ongoing basis. Possibilities could include:

- ☐ Note to prepare staff for how the child might show up
  - ☐ Information about special occasions and incidents
- ☐ Provide the professional with information about what you would like to know on an ongoing basis. Possibilities could include:
  - ☐ Schedule changes
  - ☐ Behavioral expectations for each context in which the child interacts
  - ☐ Is the child happy?
  - ☐ How is the child interacting with peers?
  - ☐ Was the child upset during the day? If so, what caused the upset?
  - ☐ Is the child accessing his social and academic curriculum?
  - ☐ How can parents support the teachers at home?
- ☐ Ask questions about the professional's AS knowledge and experience. Questions could include:
  - ☐ Strengths
  - ☐ Weaknesses
- ☐ Share presentation:
  - ☐ Child's unique profile—generated in the Parents Take Charge section of Chapter 3
  - ☐ Already-created tools from this chapter that are pertinent for the child
  - ☐ Tools that have been successful in the past
- ☐ Support skill generalization:
  - ☐ Ask if the professional would be willing to share tools he/she uses with your child
  - ☐ Discuss the importance of having a common language between home and school and community
  - ☐ Share what the family is currently working on with the child
- ☐ Set follow-up meeting to develop the special educator or service provider tools for the child's guide

An overview of what works

- ☐ Build a trusting relationship
- ☐ Honor and celebrate the strengths and interests of the child
- ☐ Provide positive reinforcement
- ☐ Approach mistakes and struggles educationally; not punitively
- ☐ Collaborate to ensure the child has opportunities to practice skills in different environments
- ☐ Provide slower pacing
- ☐ Incorporate daily living skills into overall programming to promote independence
- ☐ Organize environments to support greater inner organization
- ☐ Preview

(FREEDMAN 2010)

Visual aids to support comprehension of auditory material

You can put these into practice at home and share with the professionals with whom your child interacts.

- ☐ Written instructions
- ☐ Visual timers and visual schedules for time management
- ☐ Calendar
- ☐ Activity charts
- ☐ Overhead projector with notes provided
- ☐ Support with change: preview and visual indicator
- ☐ Visual instructions for how to interact with a group
- ☐ Classroom or activity etiquette—expectations of each environment or activity spelled out visually and explicitly; chart or note to continually remind

(CRONIN 2011)

Educational interventions organized by impairment

You can put selected interventions into practice at home and share them with the professionals with whom your child interacts.

Executive functioning impairment tools

- ☐ Visual schedules
- ☐ Planners
- ☐ Task boards
- ☐ Written and/or visual pacing process for assignments
- ☐ A written or drawn explanation of how to break down an assignment by explicitly teaching the child what to do when
- ☐ Written instructions
- ☐ Checklists
- ☐ Simple and intuitive rubrics
- ☐ Explicit descriptions of the expectations for an assignment or project and the steps necessary to complete it successfully
- ☐ Overhead projectors or SmartBoards
- ☐ Technology: laptop, tablet, organizational software
- ☐ Pictures of how the result should look (this bullet provided by Dyment, J.H., used with permission)

Visual input impairment tools

- ☐ Adapted/modified texts
- ☐ Text-to-speech software
- ☐ Books on tape
- ☐ Less on a page
- ☐ Visual copies of presentations
- ☐ Graphic organizer: a visual tool comprised of graphics used to help organize a child's thoughts for either writing or understanding something he read

Motor output impairment tools

- ☐ Scribe: a person who writes the answers that the child verbally provides to alleviate motor challenges
- ☐ Voice recognition software for dictation

Missing the hidden curriculum impairment tools

- ☐ Rules handbook
- ☐ Written expectations
- ☐ Social Stories™: a tool in the form of a brief story (developed by Carol Gray) to educate children about social skills
- ☐ Direct instruction
- ☐ Video modeling: a tool that involves having children watch a video to learn skills that are demonstrated

Central coherence impairment tools

- ☐ Explain the big picture upfront
- ☐ Use visuals and graphic organizers to present the big picture and the smaller parts (this bullet provided by Dyment, J.H., used with permission)

Perspective-taking impairment tool

- ☐ Comic strip conversations: a tool developed by Carol Gray to show all levels of communication and to make the abstract elements of conversations such as what people are thinking and how they are feeling more concrete by showing it visually through pictures of people with thought and word bubbles. The tool breaks down social interactions into short, drawn sequences.

Processing speed impairment tools

- ☐ Slower pace
- ☐ Reduced homework assignments
- ☐ Alternative assessments
- ☐ Previewing (this bullet provided by Dyment, J.H., used with permission)

Engaging in non-preferred projects impairment tools

- ☐ Use special interests
- ☐ Incorporate the child's strengths
- ☐ Be clear about the length of time they are expected to engage and why (this bullet provided by Dyment, J.H., used with permission)

Interpersonal communication impairment tools

- ☐ Provide scripts for certain group-work activities:
  - ☐ Give the child the language he can use when interacting
- ☐ Assign specific jobs when working in groups (this bullet provided by Dyment, J.H., used with permission)

Anxiety and presenting poorly to peers tools

- ☐ Pre-teach curriculum
- ☐ Use special interests to introduce challenging curriculum (this bullet provided by Dyment, J.H., used with permission)

Skill generalization impairment tools

- ☐ Re-teach curriculum
- ☐ Home–school communication to work on the same skills in multiple environments
- ☐ Connect new learning to child's prior knowledge

Social skills supports

You can put these into practice at home and share with the professionals with whom your child interacts. Sometimes techniques work well in combination.

- ☐ Social Stories™—Carol Gray developed this tool, which uses stories to teach social skills and "share accurate social information" (www.CarolGraySocialStories.com)
- ☐ Role playing—structured practice of specific social situations
- ☐ Video modeling—a tool used to teach desired social behavior by reviewing TV shows or video clips with a clinician to identify typical social behavior or problems with social behavior for the purpose of imitating the typical behavior and avoiding the problem behavior
- ☐ Directly teach conversation skills: how to initiate, maintain, end
- ☐ Non-verbal communication coaching
- ☐ Comic strip conversations
- ☐ Pictures or videos to identify emotions—the DVD *Mind Reading: An Interactive Guide* by Simon Baron-Cohen is a recommended resource
- ☐ Prime and/or prompt social behavior—strategies used to promote a particular social behavior by preparing the child before or reminding the child during a particular social interaction
- ☐ 5-point scales—*The Incredible 5-Point Scale* by Kari Dunn Buron and Mitzi Curtis helps educate children with AS about social and emotional concepts by breaking them down into a 5-point system

- ☐ Games: conversation and cooperative games; teach gaming skills for increased social interaction
- ☐ Thought bubble activities for perspective-taking
- ☐ Recess—adult facilitation for increased social interaction
- ☐ Teach Social Thinking® in addition to social skills. Michelle Garcia Winner explains Social Thinking® concepts including:
    - ☐ That our behavior impacts others, which ultimately affects us
    - ☐ Using our eyes to think
    - ☐ Keeping our brains in versus out of the group
    - ☐ Expected versus unexpected behavior
    - ☐ How to show others that we are listening

Restricted and repetitive patterns of behavior, interests, and activities support

You can put these into practice at home and share with the professionals with whom your child interacts.

- ☐ Let the child know how long he must participate in the non-preferred activity
- ☐ Tell the child why he is participating in a non-preferred activity and how it will benefit him
- ☐ Use his special interests to engage him in activities
- ☐ These preferred interests can be calming and grounding and can be used to make social connections
- ☐ Educate the child about what people are thinking when he engages in the interests in certain environments
- ☐ Try providing a schedule for special interest time. For example, you can have an hour of this interest at home, but not at school.

Sensory support organized by impairment

The sensory support checklists below include much detail about a number of different strategies for sensory processing disorders. If your child struggles with sensory issues, identify the sensory tools that best support your child's sensory profile. You can identify the strategies that will address the areas of greatest concern on your own by reviewing the descriptions below, or you can include your child's occupational therapist in this process.

You can put these strategies into practice at home and share with the professionals with whom your child interacts.

Over-reactive sensory system

Visual support for over-reactive sensory system

- ☐ Avoid visual surprises—lights turning on suddenly, balls flying
- ☐ Use incandescent lighting
- ☐ Organize space—no clutter
- ☐ Choose soft room colors
- ☐ Use partition to block visual input (Capone, K., used with permission)
- ☐ Use sunglasses or brimmed hats (Capone, K., used with permission)

Tactile support for over-reactive sensory system

- ☐ Provide comfortable textures—bedding and clothing
- ☐ Provide deep touch pressure to release endorphins that are calming to the system—use a heavy blanket, wrap child tightly in sheet, massage, roll a therapy ball over the child. Always follow the child's lead to make sure it is working for him or her.
- ☐ Allow the child to use tools or wear gloves for messy play (Capone, K., used with permission)
- ☐ Touch with deep pressure, not light touch (Capone, K., used with permission)

Auditory support for over-reactive sensory system

- ☐ Prepare for noise surprises—fire alarm, vacuum, fireworks, school bell
- ☐ Reduce sensory stimuli—close window
- ☐ Alert the child of volume changes and interruptions
- ☐ Speak with quiet voices
- ☐ Raise hand to speak in classroom
- ☐ Sit in quietest area
- ☐ Use sound-cancelling devices: headphones, earplugs, white noise

Olfactory support for over-reactive sensory system

- ☐ Avoid strong scents/smells such as perfume, lotions, or smoke
- ☐ Teach the child how to block smells

Proprioceptive support for over-reactive sensory system

- ☐ Heavy work such as jungle gym and jumping on trampoline
- ☐ Weighted vest
- ☐ Weighted backpack
- ☐ Weighted blanket or lap blanket
- ☐ Thera-Bands®

Vestibular support for over-reactive sensory system

- ☐ Slow, rhythmic movement—boat swing or rocking chair
- ☐ Adapt movement activities to the child's comfort level (Capone, K., used with permission)

General support for over-reactive sensory system

- ☐ Create exit plan for when the child becomes over-stimulated
- ☐ Prepare the child for what to expect in extremely stimulating environments

Self-calming strategy for over-reactive sensory system

- ☐ Identify a safe haven for calming activities

Under-reactive sensory system

Visual support for under-reactive sensory system

- ☐ Eye contact from the child before talking or engaging in activity
- ☐ Colorful rooms
- ☐ Bright lights
- ☐ Busy wall design
- ☐ Hanging displays
- ☐ Color overlays for worksheets or reading (Capone, K., used with permission)

Auditory support for under-reactive sensory system

- ☐ Classroom—creating a spontaneous, rather than predictable, environment
- ☐ Seating—near active, social people
- ☐ Seating—near sources of sound
- ☐ Changing background sounds

Olfactory support for under-reactive sensory system

- ☐ Expose the child to strong smells

Tactile support for under-reactive sensory system

- ☐ Direct tactile stimulation—different seating and clothing textures, dry vigorously, tickle
- ☐ Encourage participation in various tactile mediums such as paint, sand, and shaving cream (Capone, K., used with permission)

Proprioceptive support for under-reactive sensory system

- ☐ Heavy work such as jungle gym and jumping on trampoline
- ☐ Weighted vest
- ☐ Weighted backpack
- ☐ Weighted blanket or lap blanket
- ☐ Thera-Bands®

Vestibular support for under-reactive sensory system

- ☐ Fast movement
- ☐ Rotary movement
- ☐ Spinning
- ☐ Swing
- ☐ Mini-trampoline
- ☐ Movement with many starts and stops (Capone, K., used with permission)
- ☐ Varying speeds or directions of movement (Capone, K., used with permission)

Oral support for under-reactive sensory system

- ☐ Strong-tasting foods:
  - ☐ Bitter juice
  - ☐ Sour fruits
  - ☐ Spicy food
  - ☐ Hot sauce

General support for under-reactive sensory system

- ☐ Take outings involving sensory stimulation—amusement parks, malls, restaurants
- ☐ Participate in activities with sensory stimulation—bike riding, running, jumping
- ☐ Move at least every hour at school
- ☐ Take sports that force the child to move and be alert—karate, taekwondo dance class

(SCHOFIELD, J. DIRECT COMMUNICATION)

Self-alerting strategies for under-reactive sensory system

- ☐ Gum
- ☐ Sour candy
- ☐ Bottle with straw
- ☐ Therapy ball chair

Sensory-seeking system

Visual support for sensory-seeking system

- ☐ Ordered environment with labels
- ☐ Organization—no clutter
- ☐ Predictable environment
- ☐ Muted colors
- ☐ Soft lighting

Auditory support for sensory-seeking system

- ☐ Soft background music or sound
- ☐ Music in background with rhythmic beat (Capone, K., used with permission)

Tactile support for sensory-seeking system

- ☐ Fidgets (toys designed to keep fingers and feet busy, mind focused, and body relaxed such as a sensory stress ball)
- ☐ Different textured materials

Proprioceptive support for sensory-seeking system

- ☐ Therapy ball as chair
- ☐ Heavy work at chair—child puts his hands on the side of chair, lifts leg by pushing hands down into the chair
- ☐ Heavy work activities before a sit-down activity (Capone, K., used with permission)

(SCHOFIELD, J. DIRECT COMMUNICATION)

Vestibular support for sensory-seeking system

- ☐ Movement combined with organized response—swing and kick target
- ☐ Movement breaks before quiet activity (Capone, K., used with permission)

Oral support for sensory-seeking system

- ☐ Strongly flavored foods
- ☐ Chewy and crunchy foods (Capone, K., used with permission)
- ☐ Sucking milk shakes through a straw (Capone, K., used with permission)

General support for sensory-seeking system

- ☐ Change environments frequently—move furniture around
- ☐ Activities with vigorous continuous movement—trampoline jumping, rock climbing (Schofield, J. direct conversation)
- ☐ Strategies for movement when the child is acting out—run around the house five times
- ☐ Chores with physical activity—moving furniture, carrying shopping
- ☐ Activities available when the child finishes task early
- ☐ Sit on moving surface such as ball or cushion when concentration is necessary
- ☐ Prepare for tasks requiring concentration with vestibular and proprioceptive input

Self-calming strategy for sensory-seeking system

- ☐ Place for retreat when over-stimulated—with heavy work sensory tools

Sensory discrimination disorder

Visual support for sensory discrimination disorder

- ☐ Use colored overlays
- ☐ Block out extraneous visual stimuli in books or worksheets

(CAPONE, K., USED WITH PERMISSION)

Tactile support for sensory discrimination disorder

- ☐ Provide an opportunity to play in a variety of mediums such as sand, shaving cream, and play dough
- ☐ Work on writing with sandpaper
- ☐ Use needlepoint grids to increase feedback about where hand is
- ☐ Use electric toothbrush
- ☐ Use massagers or different types of vibrations

(CAPONE, K., USED WITH PERMISSION)

Auditory support for sensory discrimination disorder

- ☐ Use simple words and phrases
- ☐ Decrease background noise

(CAPONE, K., USED WITH PERMISSION)

Proprioceptive support for sensory discrimination disorder

- ☐ Heavy work such as jungle gym or jumping on trampoline
- ☐ Obstacle course, which involves crawling under, over, and around different objects
- ☐ Use of massagers or different types of vibration
- ☐ Electric toothbrush

(CAPONE, K., USED WITH PERMISSION)

Vestibular support for sensory discrimination disorder

- ☐ Heavy work such as jungle gym or jumping on trampoline
- ☐ Obstacle course, which involves crawling under, over, and around different objects

(CAPONE, K., USED WITH PERMISSION)

Postural disorder

General support for postural disorder

- ☐ Allow opportunities to change positions while doing table work (standing versus sitting)
- ☐ Provide opportunities to improve postural control through gross motor activities
- ☐ Provide alternate seating choices (bean bag chair, seat cushions, therapy ball)

(CAPONE, K., USED WITH PERMISSION)

Dyspraxia

Tactile support for dyspraxia

- ☐ Deep pressure before motor challenges

Proprioceptive support for dyspraxia

- ☐ Pressure to joints and muscles prior to motor challenges:
  - ☐ Pushes
  - ☐ Pulls
  - ☐ Lifting
  - ☐ Jumping Jacks

Fine motor support for dyspraxia

- ☐ Practice typing and navigating computers early

Organizational support for dyspraxia

- ☐ Assist with maintaining order in the child's personal space—desk, backpack, closet, dresser
- ☐ Develop routines
- ☐ Aid the child with managing homework materials

- ☐ Provide schedules
- ☐ Supply explicit checklists

Room support for dyspraxia

- ☐ Maximum open space in rooms—few obstructions
- ☐ Simple, easy-to-use fixtures such as light switches, cupboard handles, and bin lids
- ☐ Desk in quieter part of the room, with easy access to most-used locations

General support for dyspraxia

- ☐ Support the child in cafeteria and at recess
- ☐ Help familiarize the child with community settings by visiting regularly—playground, public library (Shaw, K., personal communication)
- ☐ Participate in activities that require minimal motor skills—for example, movies
- ☐ Allow more time for the child to move between classes and through areas needing motor skills, such as assembly and cafeteria
- ☐ Provide verbal alternative to assignments if fine motor requirements are too difficult

For more examples of strategies for supporting children with Sensory Processing difficulties, refer to Lucy Jane Miller's book, *Sensational Kids: Hope and Help for Children with Sensory Processing Disorder (SPD)*.

Special educators can use the communication log template below to provide you with daily information about your child's school day. You can customize this tool if you would like your school contact to provide different information about your child's school day than this template will offer.

Communication log

Child's name: **Date:**

Any changes to regular school routine?

Aide out Teacher out Substitute Other

Kind of morning

Excellent Good Average Difficult

Kind of afternoon

Excellent Good Average Difficult

Specials today

Lunch group Art Music PE Health

Notable sensory behavior

____

____

____

____

____

Comments from school

____

____

____

____

____

How to use the toolbox

Now that you have created your collaboration and communication toolbox, you will be able to:

- establish communication and collaboration parameters with your child's special educator and service providers using the Beginning of the Relationship Meeting tool
- integrate into your home and educate your child's special educator and service providers about big picture AS-friendly strategies and tools such as what works in general and visual aids
- implement at home and help your child's special educator and service providers address your child's unique profile-related differences by offering AS-friendly educational, social, restricted and repetitive patterns, and sensory interventions
- help your child generalize skills by using the same strategies in multiple environments.

Chapter 5

Routines and Schedules

We learned the hard way that Alexander needs routines and schedules to function well. For example, when my husband's work transferred us to London, creating a schedule on moving day did not cross my mind. When our moving truck arrived at our new home, the day was filled with men moving furniture in and out of our home. It was chaotic and loud. My husband had to work that day, so I managed the move alone. I tried to care for Alexander, answer questions, and direct the movers about furniture placement. Nothing was predictable. As the day progressed, Alexander's stress level escalated increasingly. By the end of the day, he was screaming at me and at the movers. I was embarrassed and overwhelmed. My son was two years and four months old, and he was out of control.

Fortunately, our home life in London was at first significantly less social than our previous experience in Boston, which supported overall stability. In retrospect, I recognize that the balance of downtime worked better for him. Once the new house, culture, people, and schedule became familiar and routine for Alexander, he felt settled. By this point, I recognized that structure supported him. I developed a consistent weekly schedule of classes and playgroup to help him navigate all of the changes.

A recurring issue we encountered was that my husband and I embrace schedules differently. I like an organized schedule; he feels hemmed in by a schedule and prefers to let life happen spontaneously. We have learned how to work it out between ourselves by taking turns being scheduled and spontaneous. However, that unpredictability did not work for Alexander, and many tantrums occurred as a result. Saturday "Daddy Days Out" were incredibly fun, but often ended in upset because they did not follow a consistent pattern. For example, Alexander was used to having daily naps during the week at 1:00pm. On Saturdays, he might not even get home until four o'clock. Tensions ran high. As we learned about what supports individuals with AS, we became more united in our approach. We both committed to making daily schedules and previewing schedule changes.

Our move back to the U.S. from London three-and-a-half years later was much more peaceful. A consultant guided our process. We had to move out of our home in mid-June and could not move into our new place in the States until the beginning of August. We stayed with family for six weeks and moved between three homes. Typically, this would be a recipe for disaster. The factors that made all the difference were that we created a schedule for every day and explained to Alexander behavioral expectations for every situation. Though this took more preparation time, it saved multiple hours of upset and increased family harmony significantly.

Parents' role in managing routines and schedules

As a case manager, your role as it relates to routines and schedules is to:

- implement and preview routines and schedules at home
- make sure that your child's teacher or special educator (your point person at school) understands that your child works best with schedules and routines written out and previewed
- advocate for schedules and previews to be used with your child in the community.

This chapter and your guide will facilitate this process.

Routines and schedules in every environment

As we learned to do, you can take control of arranging your child's environments to reduce stress. An important contribution parents can make to their child's sense of harmony is to provide structure without being too rigid. Households with children with AS call for significantly more planning, previewing, and using visual supports than households with typically developing children. In school and community environments, as well as at home, children with AS experience greater success when they can anticipate activities, understand what is expected of them, and know how to accomplish tasks. Parents can assist their children by creating schedules and explicitly, simply, and visually listing the steps of their daily routines.

While potentially overwhelming to parents, the child's support system and schedule must be in place all of the time, including weekends and vacations, in order for life to go smoothly for him and the entire family. Though it is an extreme comparison, parents wouldn't turn off a child's ventilator for a few days and expect that the child would be fine. Routines and schedules are a form of life support for a child with AS.

Assess your child's needs

You and your child's team will need to assess your child's needs in every environment. His needs will likely be different at home, at school, and in the community. For example, he might need intense support with routines and schedules at school and in the community and moderate support at home based on the difference in anxiety levels he experiences in each environment.

Children with AS have varying needs when it comes to schedules. For example, at school a first grader may need a written daily schedule and written activity schedules at his desk for every chunk of time throughout the day. He may also need a visual timer that has a red disc that disappears as the time passes, to help him know where he is within each activity chunk. On the other hand, a sixth grader may still use a written daily schedule at his desk, but he may be starting to develop the skills to manage with class schedules posted on the board for the entire class. This child would likely still need support with the transitions between classes and might need teachers to zoom in and out of the level of support, depending on the part of the day. A different sixth grader might do best with someone verbally explaining the schedule and having a backup written schedule. Make sure to meet your child with the level of support that he needs.

When your child struggles and exhibits challenging behavior, you can look at all of the types of issues that a child that age and with that profile might encounter. The key is to be a "detective" about what is causing the difficulty. For example, if you notice that mornings are troublesome for your child, you might look at his sleep and his nutrition, as well as how the morning is structured. If you determine that his sleep and nutrition are fine, but that time in the morning lacks structure, then you may want to implement routines and schedules. Unstructured time is one of the most common challenges for children with AS.

Create visual schedules

Written routines and schedules make home, school, and community life run more smoothly and encourage independence. At home, parents can establish morning, after-school, and night-time routines, which include a list of responsibilities for children with AS. They can also create visual schedules for every day of the week, including weekends. When you create daily and weekly schedules, include every activity. Remember to include time for transitions, too. Transitions from a preferred activity to a less preferred activity are particularly important. You will also want to schedule breaks. Many children with AS take different types of breaks such as walking breaks, computer breaks, or breaks to work on special interests (you will want to be specific about how the break will be spent). Having a thorough and detailed schedule enables children with AS to know what to expect and when. This clarity helps the children emotionally, and it serves to logistically organize their time. Understanding what they need to do will help them follow through with less dependence on their parents.

When parents and professionals at school and in the community create schedules, they can indicate different levels of precision depending on the circumstances. For example, parents may want to list dinner as "five-ish" if they cannot guarantee that everything will be ready at exactly five o'clock. This alerts the child that dinner could be served anywhere from 4:45 to 5:30pm and, therefore, relieves stress if the timing is not exact. In contrast, parents might want to use a specific time where they can exercise more control such as the end time of computer time. This facilitates an easier transition to the next activity.

One day I told Alexander that we needed to leave at 4:05 to drive to his appointment with his psychologist. I had a friend at my house and was not able to leave at 4:05 on the dot. The friend and I finished our conversation, and we walked out the door closer to 4:15. Alexander became increasingly anxious and angry as the minutes passed. Every minute, he reminded me that we were late. I felt stressed because I was simultaneously trying to be polite to my friend and to leave. Both of our nerves were jangled by the time we got into the car. This did not set up his appointment with his psychologist for success. I wish I had told Alexander that we would leave at 4:05ish and explained that means any time between 4:00 and 4:20 depending on when I finished visiting with my friend. That strategy would have saved unnecessary stress on everyone.

Alternatively, there are instances when I want to be more precise with the time. When Alexander is on the computer, I will preview with him, for example, that at 4:30pm he needs to get off the computer. I will set a timer to help me stick to my word. I will give him a warning like this at 4:27: "Alexander, I just want to remind you that you have three more minutes on the computer. Please start to wrap up whatever you are doing." At 4:29, I'll follow up with, "Alexander, you have one more minute." At 4:30, I will say, "Okay, Alexander. It is time to get off."

Create visual routines

In addition to creating and reviewing the schedule, you will want to write down the steps that the child will take every time he goes through the routine. As an example, every day when your child arrives at school, she might hang her backpack on her hook, put her coat on the hook, remove her lunch and homework folder from her backpack, put lunch on the top of her cubby, put her homework in the homework box, and put her folder in the tray. Make these steps available to her in visual form until she integrates them and masters the process. You will find that it is helpful to create visual routines for activities at home and in the community as well as at school.

Preview schedules and routines

Children with AS often do best when adults at home, at school, and in the community preview their schedules with them. For example, Alexander's aide previews his daily schedule at the beginning of every day. This process orients him.

Changes in schedules distress many individuals with AS, including Alexander. While some schedule changes aren't anticipated, adults know about other changes in advance. Children with AS can cope with the changes much better when adults preview them. For example, when there is going to be a major change in the schedule, such as Alexander's aide going out of town or a planned evacuation drill, his teachers proactively address this stressor by providing previews. They write a Social Story™ for every change, send the Social Story™ home for me to read to Alexander the night before the change, and then review it with him on the day of the change.

Support executive functioning skills

Individuals with AS often have difficulty estimating time. Schedules provide practice and start to teach children what time segments feel like. For example, they will know what a time span of 45 minutes feels like because that is the time they spend in their classes. They will start to understand what 10 minutes feels like because that is the time they use to transition.

Positively reinforce your child regarding routines and schedules

Children with AS regularly receive negative feedback for mistakes they make in their lives. They benefit from adults teaching them what behaviors worked, did not work, and why. At home, at school, and in the community, your child will learn how to use routines and schedules effectively when he receives positive feedback for the things he does well. You and other adults can help your child grasp what did not work and why by providing explicit, non-judgmental education about what he is doing ineffectively and how to put the correction in place.

Positive reinforcement can help teach a skill (see "Using Positive Reinforcement to Teach Skills" Box). For example, if you want to teach a child how to use a clock to navigate schedules and he does not see the value and purpose, you can both explicitly teach the value and purpose and positively reinforce him to use it. Adults might establish a reward system for correct clock usage.

The idea is that with time the child will see the benefit of using the strategy. When the child sees the connection between the use of the skill and positive outcomes, the process becomes self-perpetuating. For example, Alexander now sees how helpful and organizing schedules are for him, and he recognizes that he feels less anxious when he has a schedule in place. This recognition positively reinforces the process.

Positive reinforcement is not appropriate to use in all situations. For example, you would not want to use positive reinforcement to attempt to modify behavioral responses to an unexpected fire alarm, which could deeply impact the child's sensory system and send him into fight or flight mode. Based on the response to alarms for some children with AS with over-reactive sensory systems, asking them to modify their behavior would be unrealistic and unfair. However, adults can help a child in this type of situation by previewing the alarm, possibly providing headphones to decrease the impact of the noise, or allowing the child to leave the building before the alarm rings.

Using Positive Reinforcement to Teach Skills

Positive reinforcement is a basic behavioral principle that is used to encourage behaviors by providing an immediate reinforcement after the behavior occurs. Positive reinforcement works best for children with AS when the system is presented in a visual format with a simple, concrete explanation. The concept is to:

- notice the child using the desired behavior as quickly as possible and initially provide a tangible reward and verbal praise every time the child uses the behavior; you can do this either verbally or visually by checking boxes, drawing or showing smiley faces, or holding up a green card when the child does well

- provide tangible rewards that make sense for the child and the situation
- systematically fade tangible reinforcers and ultimately move from tangible reinforcements to verbal praise.

Routines and schedules at home

Though many elements of creating routines and schedules are the same across environments, certain aspects are different. This section will help you build in time for you, manage screen time, deal with boredom, and structure play dates.

Taking care of yourself

Parents can implement a number of strategies to support the household. When parents need a break, one option is to arrange support from other people. Additionally, parents can build free time into the child's plan for the day. Creating a visual list of free-time options helps the child choose how to fill this time. We provide a few possibilities in the Parents Take Charge section of this chapter and many in the downloadable template. When parents align the child's free time with their time off, the schedule can meet everyone's needs. For example, parents can take a break during the child's computer time. The Academy of American Pediatricians advises less than two hours of screen time per day, but occasionally exceeding that limit for overall household peace can serve families well.

Managing screen time

Time on the computer, television, and phone (screen time) can quickly become a preferred activity. Usage can spiral out of control for many children with AS because it is enjoyable and doesn't require navigating an unpredictable and complex social world, unlike interacting with humans. Additionally, screen time can often provide immediate access to information about their special interests.

However, many issues can arise from extensive computer use, such as computer addiction, sleep interruptions, legal issues, and safety problems.

For example, legal issues can arise from a number of behaviors, including finding pornography when seeking information about sex. Because children with AS are prone to misreading the intentions of others, they can encounter safety problems. Their lack of perspective-taking makes them less likely to be suspicious of others' intentions. If their own motives for exploring a particular topic are innocent, they may assume that everyone's are. They probably won't read between the lines if someone is e-mailing them messages that contain sexual innuendo, which makes them vulnerable. As with typically developing children, the best approach for protecting children with AS is direct instruction. See the "Internet Safety for Your Child with AS" Box for more guidance about keeping your child with AS safe on the internet.

Parents can proactively manage screen time by setting clear limits from a very young age. They can define for the child that screen time means anything with a screen, including television, gaming system, computer, smartphone, and so on. Specific limits per time segment, such as per day or per week, can help manage usage. Screen time can also be paired with other types of activities. For example, if the child with AS watches 30 minutes of television, then the next 60 minutes involve no screen time. Best results occur when parents establish a schedule and deal with power struggles about screen time as early in the child's life as possible.

Internet Safety for Your AS Child

- Keep your computer in a public space and make sure you can see the screen. Start this practice when your child is young so that it is natural from the beginning.
- Model appropriate computer usage in terms of the amount of time you spend on the computer.
- Instruct your child directly that the internet is designed for people of all ages and has sexual and violent content that is not suited for children. As such, parents and children should learn how to put parameters around usage:
  - Use child-protection software.
  - Teach your child how to understand the parameters. This instruction can connect to a family values conversation. You can tell your child that there is a lot of content on the internet that doesn't mesh

with your family's values. If they see something that doesn't match these values, they need to tell you about it.

  » Tell your child to talk with a trusted adult if he sees something on the internet that is confusing or makes him feel uncomfortable.

- Educate your child from a young age about stranger danger and who is safe. You do not need to list all of the things that could go wrong. However, you can mention during the course of your safety instruction discussions that some individuals try to lure kids, take money, or figure out social security numbers. Most people with AS will automatically answer when someone asks them a question. You need to instruct your child not to share personal information by teaching them to think of the context in which it is being asked. For example, someone on the internet may be trying to use your personal information to steal money. The key is to emphasize to your child to talk with a trusted adult if there is any question.
- An excellent book for parents that discusses legal and safety issues for individuals with AS regarding the internet is *The Autism Spectrum, Sexuality and the Law: What Every Parent and Professional Needs to Know* (Attwood, Henault, and Dubin 2014). This book includes a true story about an individual with AS who got in trouble with the law by accessing child pornography on the internet, his parents' perspective, a psychologist's (AS expert) view, and a sex therapist's guidance.

Handling boredom

As we mentioned earlier in the chapter, unstructured time is one of the most common challenges for children with AS. Home life can be less structured than other environments. Parents can utilize strategies at home to minimize boredom and promote independence. For example, they can create an activity list that their child with AS can reference when he needs to find something to do. When parents make activity options feel fresh, they can engage their child with AS more successfully. Parents can rotate games and activities that are available for their child. For example, a UNO deck can be left out for a few weeks and then put away and replaced by checkers. The idea is to accommodate the child when he is younger and teach him to utilize similar strategies by himself when he is older.

Weekends have always been toughest for us because there is more unstructured time. We have greatest success when we create and preview Alexander's schedule. We start by writing down the activities that are planned and non-negotiable, such as his occupational therapy appointment every Saturday morning at 9:45. We then use our activity list to schedule the remaining activities for his day.

At this point, if we forget to create a schedule one day, Alexander is likely to say that he wants to create a schedule for himself with me. He sees the value, knows it is a tool that works, and is taking more ownership over the process. He has not reached independence with it yet, but he is making progress.

Children with AS will invariably experience times when they feel bored in different environments as well. Parents can teach children with AS skills to develop resiliency and find solutions for managing boredom. For example, in preparation for sitting in the waiting room before a dentist appointment, parents can recommend that their child with AS bring a book to read or paper and pens to write or draw with. Many parents prepare a special bag that the child with AS can use only when there is not much else to do, such as at doctors' offices or on long car trips. These bags should otherwise be off limits, in order to keep the contents interesting and special. It also wouldn't hurt for parents to suggest to the child on occasion that he sit quietly and wait, because that is a life skill everyone needs to develop.

Structuring play dates

Parents can best support their child's social education and growth at home by creating social opportunities in conjunction with explicit, visual tools to educate and guide them about how to interact. Tools can include a schedule, written behavioral expectations, or possibly a video-modeling clip to preview how to handle specific interactions. Parents can also integrate social concepts that the child is practicing in outside social groups or at school.

Play dates hosted in homes with children with AS require a significantly greater level of structure, social support, and adult attention than those in homes with typically developing children. Most elementary-age children with AS are unable to manage a play date on their own. The hosting parent can help the child with AS and his friend create a schedule by providing a list of possible activities and letting them take turns choosing until there are enough activities to fill the time. The parent can write down the choices in schedule form and bring the list to every activity, checking them off as they work through the list (see the tool in the Parents Take Charge section of this chapter). A timer or verbal countdown can help everyone keep track of the time and know when to transition. Should a social issue arise between the children, the adult can help resolve it. Play dates work best when the parents of both children understand that the parent of the child with AS will be occupied with overseeing the play date rather than socializing.

One of the most important aspects of supporting a play date is doing your best to ensure it ends successfully. Children with AS usually remember what happens last and not necessarily what happens during the play date. For example, if a two-hour play date went well with the exception of the last ten minutes, a child with AS will probably recall it as a failed experience. The end of the play date is a transition and needs as much attention and guidance as transitions between activities. For younger children, ending with an inexpensive, tiny gift for both children helps the play date end well and memorably.

Routines and schedules at school

Routines and schedules will help minimize your child's anxiety and maximize his clarity at school. Schools are usually very structured and have many types of schedules including yearly schedules, weekly schedules, daily schedules, and schedules for activities during the day. Best practice calls for teachers of individual classes such as science, social studies, and math to post their schedules each day for the benefit of all students. The key is to have every schedule written out and to preview both the schedules and any changes to the schedules with your child with AS.

You and/or your child's teacher should start with the longest-range schedule, the annual schedule, and work your way down to the schedules for each activity during the day. When your child uses a schedule and understands what to expect, he can navigate his school days more calmly and independently and better access the social and academic curricula. The exercises in the Parents Take Charge section of this chapter will guide you through developing the longest-range through the shortest-range schedules and routines, as well as help you prepare for common schedule changes that occur at school.

Routines and schedules in the community

You will likely have less control over your child's routines and schedules in the community than you have at home and school. At home, you have complete control over them. At school, you can have quite a bit of control if you develop a positive relationship with your child's teachers and focus on communicating your child's needs. In the community, you can advocate for routines and schedules, but they are not always guaranteed.

The key factors for you to determine when developing routines and schedules for your child's community activities are:

- which professional or adult to collaborate with to develop the schedule
- how experienced the professional or adult is in developing schedules
- who will develop the schedule—you or the professional
- how structured and predictable the activity is
- how much schedule-related information the professional or adult can provide.

If the professional regularly uses visual schedules with the client population and has the ability to structure the activity, then she might want to be in charge of creating the schedule. For example, Alexander started going to an occupational therapist before he could read. After several sessions ended with Alexander getting stressed, I told his therapist that Alexander does best with schedules. Fortunately, the occupational therapist had pre-existing materials to provide a schedule for the children with whom she works and could accommodate him. After our talk, his therapist brought a large laminated paper with Velcro tabs placed at intervals. She had created laminated pictures of different rooms and OT tools for him to stick to the paper. She guided him to create a schedule by having him look at the pictures and choose his first activity. She had some input about activity choices as well. Within five minutes, they had created an entire schedule for their 45-minute session together. This activity was Alexander's preview. As they completed each activity, they removed the corresponding image from the laminated paper. This system helped him understand how much he had completed and how much he had left to do before they ended the session and led to a much more peaceful and productive session.

Similarly, Alexander went to a neuropsychologist for the first time after his fourth-grade year. I was very concerned about how he would do, because fourth grade was particularly tough for him. Additionally, his school had tested him in second grade and the process was horrible for everyone. I knew that I needed to do everything that I could do to help set this round of testing up for success. I told his neuropsychologist about his history and mentioned that he does best with previews and schedules. The neuropsychologist kindly offered to let him come to our parent session, which took place before Alexander's testing sessions began. During his preview visit, Alexander spent time in the office, toured all of the rooms, and previewed his first testing session's schedule. The doctor answered all of Alexander's questions. With this support and the doctor's knowledge and manner, the experience was very successful for Alexander.

In other cases, adults within the community may have little experience with creating schedules, but can provide a moderate amount of information about the activity. For example, I often hosted play dates at my house, but on the rare occasion that Alexander went to a friend's house I kept the timeframe short and casually asked about the plan for the play date. I always explained about Alexander having AS and that he is most successful when he knows what to expect. After the parent shared the plan, I would write it down and preview it with Alexander before he went to play.

In some environments the adults don't usually create schedules for the children participating in their activities, but can provide a moderate amount of information. For example, Alexander took an improvisation class one summer. His sensory struggles with loud, unexpected noises such as clapping and issues with unexpected changes in the schedule based on the nature of improvisation made the experience difficult for him to tolerate. The theater group was extremely willing to do anything they could to help him. The teacher provided us with a big picture idea of the schedule for each day, which we wrote down and previewed with Alexander. We also previewed that there would be changes in the schedule. Without the support of the schedule and preview of potential changes, I don't think he would have even been able to stay in the room.

Some professionals or adults have no experience with developing schedules for children and cannot offer much schedule-related information. For example, baseball coaches do not always have a plan. Sometimes they may change a plan in the middle of practice to accommodate the needs of the team members. If the kids on his team continue to drop fly balls, then he might decide mid-practice that the team will work on fielding pop-ups. In this type of situation, you can talk with the coach to get as much information as you can, such as the start and end time of practice, and share this information with your child. You can also preview that baseball practice is different than more structured environments and create a Social Story™ explaining why no concrete schedule can be provided and strategies for coping with this unpredictability.

My experience is that making routines and schedules for activities within the community is not a given, but most people will do their best to help if they understand Alexander's struggles and why he needs them. I try to make fulfilling my request as easy for them as possible. Many times I offer to create the tools if the adult in the community is willing to provide the information. If he or she follows through, I am tremendously grateful and make sure that they know it. I also feel relieved that the relationship is off to a good start.

Generalizing skills

As you have seen throughout this chapter, the process for utilizing routines and schedules is the same for every environment in which the child with AS interacts:

- Assess your child's needs.
- Create visual schedules.
- Create visual routines.
- Preview schedules and routines.
- Support executive functioning skills.
- Positively reinforce your child regarding routines and schedules.

You can support generalization by educating your child about routines and schedules and communicating with his support team to make sure that the language used is consistent in every environment.

You can provide direct instruction about how the strategies work. For example, you can coach your child that schedules and routines help him be more successful because:

- they help him stay organized
- when he is more organized, he will feel less anxiety
- when he has less anxiety, he will perform better.

Your child can internalize the sequence and generalize the skill when he uses the strategies and receives this straightforward communication in every environment.

For example, Alexander's occupational therapist went on maternity leave this year. The new occupational therapist did not provide a schedule for Alexander when they first started working together. After a few difficult sessions, Alexander asked his new occupational therapist if they could use a schedule. The occupational therapist developed a written schedule with Alexander at the beginning of each session, and Alexander was able to be much more successful both with the therapy and with his therapist. He generalized that schedules work for him in all environments.

The Parents Take Charge section of this chapter will help you develop visual routines and schedules for you to use at home and to share with your child's educators at school and with professionals and other adults in the community.

Parents Take Charge

Creating Your Child's Routines and Schedules Toolbox

These workbook examples help you break down into manageable parts a number of common routines and schedules that your child will encounter at home, at school, and in the community. Each breakdown provides necessary structure for a given situation and can be used to preview and to use in the moment. We also include examples that can help your child handle possible changes to his schedules and routines. These tools work as a simple guide for your child and a teaching template and collaboration toolbox for you and the professionals that support him.

Routines and schedules: Every environment

Strategies for creating routines and schedules in every environment

Create routines and schedules at home and coordinate with your child's support team to use the same strategy in every setting:

- ☐ Assess your child's needs as they relate to routines and schedules
- ☐ Create visual schedules
- ☐ Create visual routines
- ☐ Preview schedules and routines
- ☐ Preview schedule changes
- ☐ Support executive functioning skills

Coach your child that schedules and routines help him be more successful because:

- ☐ They help him stay organized
- ☐ When he is more organized, he will feel less anxiety
- ☐ When he has less anxiety, he will perform better

Routines and schedules: Home

The goal is to define clearly the routines and schedules that structure your home and family life—daily, weekly, free time, weekend, screen time, and play dates. These routines and schedules will vary from family to family. These exercises will help you to understand and articulate the routines and schedules in your home. Note these routines and schedules in your guide.

- Use the list and examples provided in this section as a springboard to think about routines and schedules that would support your child at home. If you do not see a routine or schedule that is important to your family, simply create one using these examples as models.
- Once you create routines and schedules unique to your child's needs and situation, preview them with your child and have a copy available for review in each situation and environment until he integrates the routines and schedules and demonstrates mastery.
- Once you create home routines and schedules unique to your child's needs and situation, parents, babysitters, and anyone else in a home care role can use these tools to approach routines and schedules consistently.
- Routines and schedules should be introduced one at a time as part of home education.
- Remember to preview changes to routines and schedules with your child.
- When you create your routines and schedules toolbox, put one per page in a succinct, simple, accessible format. Less writing on each page helps the child with AS avoid visual overload.

Home routines may include:

☐ Morning routine
☐ After-school routine
☐ Night routine
☐ Homework routine
☐ Sunday night routine

Home schedules may include:

☐ Daily schedules
☐ Screen time schedule
☐ Weekly schedule at a glance
☐ Play date schedule
☐ Whole family schedule

Build schedules by structuring unstructured time; this may include:

☐ Free-time options
☐ Activity bag
☐ Weekend activity list

Examples: Home routines

The lists below serve as examples of home routines and schedules, which you can consider a springboard to making your own lists. Feel free to:

- use the space provided in the template checklists you have downloaded to add points to the routines or schedules
- or create entirely new routines and schedules that would support your child.

Morning routine

- ☐ Get dressed
- ☐ Clean room
- ☐ Sensory gym
- ☐ Eat breakfast/take pills
- ☐ Rinse plates and utensils and put in dishwasher
- ☐ Brush teeth
- ☐ Brush hair
- ☐ Put on shoes, coat, and gloves or sunscreen (depending on the weather)
- ☐ Get backpack and anything else you need for school

Night routine

- ☐ Dinner—5ish
- ☐ Read independently for at least 30 minutes
- ☐ Shower
- ☐ Put on pajamas
- ☐ Bring towel back to bathroom and put on rack
- ☐ Brush teeth
- ☐ Floss teeth
- ☐ Use mouthwash
- ☐ Choice: reading or art
- ☐ Breathing—8:15
- ☐ Bed—8:30

Sunday night routine

If one night of the week has a different routine, customize this list by checking points that pertain to your child and adding others that are not included:

- ☐ Dinner—5ish
- ☐ Read independently for at least 30 minutes
- ☐ Shower
- ☐ Put on pajamas
- ☐ Bring towel back to bathroom and put on rack
- ☐ Brush teeth
- ☐ Floss teeth
- ☐ Use mouthwash
- ☐ Watch movie
- ☐ Breathing—8:15
- ☐ Bed—8:30

After-school routine

- ☐ Hang up coat
- ☐ Put hat and gloves on the shelf in the cubby
- ☐ Place shoes in cubby
- ☐ Take out homework, lunch box, and water bottles and bring to kitchen
- ☐ Place backpack in cubby

Homework routine

- ☐ Go to desk and review assignment instructions with an adult
- ☐ Begin work independently
- ☐ If you need help, ask an adult
- ☐ When homework is complete, put in homework folder
- ☐ Put homework folder in backpack

Daily schedule

The following is an example of a weekday and a weekend schedule, but the child will benefit most when they have schedules for every day. For each day, you can customize the blank schedule template provided in the template checklist you have downloaded.

Weekday

- ☐ Morning routine
- ☐ School
- ☐ TV until 3:30
- ☐ Homework
- ☐ Exercise
- ☐ Free time
- ☐ Dinner—5ish
- ☐ Independent reading
- ☐ Night routine

Weekend

- ☐ Morning routine
- ☐ Occupational therapy
- ☐ Free time (30 minutes)
- ☐ Activity
- ☐ Lunch
- ☐ Activity
- ☐ Free time (one hour)
- ☐ Dinner—5ish
- ☐ Night routine

Weekly schedule

Customize your child's weekly routine by filling in the table in the template checklists you have downloaded with all of your child's activities. Include transition times.

Weekly schedule

Monday	Tuesday	Wednesday	Thursday	Friday	Saturday	Sunday

Whole family schedule

Week of ________	Monday	Tuesday	Wednesday	Thursday	Friday	Saturday	Sunday
Mother							
Father							
Child							
Child							

Screen time schedule

Schedule screen time. Fill in the screen time chart indicating:

- when it is allowed
- how much time per day, week, or month is permitted
- specific times for use
- activities paired with screen time.

Customize the table in the template checklists you have downloaded to reflect your child's weekly screen time (television, computer, gaming system, tablet, etc.) schedule. Parents, babysitters, or other adults providing childcare can preview this checklist in the morning so the child knows what to expect in his day. Change to reflect any schedule changes.

When it is allowed	How much time per day, week, or month	Specific hours	Activity pair
Monday			
Tuesday			
Wednesday			
Thursday			
Friday			
Saturday			
Sunday			

Play date schedule

Create a play date schedule to support your child's social interactions at home. First list activity options for play date:

☐ Snack

- ☐ Craft (list options):
    - ☐ Paper-mache
    - ☐ Drawing
    - ☐ Shrinky dinks
- ☐ Soccer
- ☐ Board game (list options):
    - ☐ Checkers
    - ☐ Monopoly
    - ☐ Apples to apples
    - ☐ Sorry!
- ☐ Bake cookies
- ☐ Make lemonade slushy
- ☐ Trampoline
- ☐ Basketball
- ☐ Movie
- ☐ Video game (list options):
    - ☐ Wii
    - ☐ Mindcraft
- ☐ Sensory game
- ☐ Trip to ice-cream shop

Let children take turns choosing their activities and build the play date schedule:

Child	Time	Activity
James	3:00–3:15	Snack
Alexander	3:15–3:45	Board game—Checkers
James	3:45–4:15	Trampoline
Alexander	4:15–4:45	Bake cookies
	4:45–5:00	Eat cookies and prepare for James to leave

Examples: Structuring unstructured time

Create a list of free-time options and weekend activity options to help your child structure his free time. Customize the following list by checking points that pertain to your child and adding others that are not included.

Parents, babysitters, or other adults providing childcare can refer the child to this list to help him choose free-time activities.

Free-time options

The following are just a few examples. The full list can be found in the template checklists you have downloaded.

- ☐ Read
- ☐ Exercise
- ☐ Play a game
- ☐ Bake or cook
- ☐ Hang out with someone and talk
- ☐ Listen to music

Weekend activity options

The following are just a few examples. The full lists can be found in the template checklists you have downloaded.

- ☐ Walk
- ☐ Bike
- ☐ Play in sensory gym
- ☐ Go outside
- ☐ Play a game
- ☐ Puzzles

Take an outing to:

- ☐ Aquarium
- ☐ Museum
- ☐ Park
- ☐ Zoo
- ☐ Movie theater
- ☐ Climbing gym

Activity bag

Create an activity bag to keep the child engaged on outings such as doctor's appointments and trips. List the items for the bag. Customize the list below to reflect contents of an activity bag that would keep your child engaged and entertained by checking the points that pertain and adding those not included. Parents, babysitters, or other adults providing childcare can fill a bag with the contents on the list and bring the bag on outings where the child may have to wait or have unstructured time such as to a doctor's office or on a trip.

Possible contents:

- ☐ Book—special book of fiction or non-fiction
- ☐ Activity book—coloring book, mazes, word search, math puzzles, crossword, sudoku
- ☐ Paper
- ☐ Pens
- ☐ Crayons
- ☐ Cards
- ☐ Special Lego set
- ☐ Chess—travel set
- ☐ Gum or other non-perishable food

Routines and schedules: School

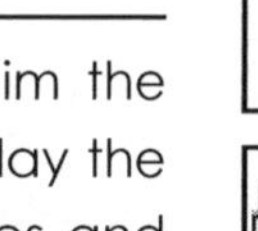

Your child will be most successful when you explicitly teach him the routines and schedules of the school. You and the teachers will lay the foundation for success at school when you define these routines and schedules for your child.

Teachers may discuss some of their expectations for routines and schedules during the school day, and may assume that students are already aware of others. Regardless of whether teachers talk about the routines and schedules, you should cover them in an explicit, visual format in order to ensure that your child with AS understands.

- Talk to teachers about classroom routines and schedules.
- Use the list and examples provided in this section as a springboard to think about routines and schedules that would support your child at school.
- Once you create school routines and schedules unique to your child's needs and situation, preview them with your child. Have a copy available for review in each situation and environment until she integrates the routines and schedules and demonstrates mastery.
- Collaborate with school professionals to preview schedule changes with your child.
- When you create your routines and schedules toolbox, put one expectation per page with succinct, simple, accessible instructions. Less writing per page helps the child with AS avoid visual overload.

School routines:

- ☐ Arrival routine
- ☐ Morning routine
- ☐ Closing routine

School schedules:

- ☐ Daily schedule
- ☐ Weekly schedule
- ☐ Schedules for particular classes
- ☐ Change in schedule plan:
    - ☐ Evacuation drill
    - ☐ Field trip

☐ Aide out of town

☐ Testing

☐ Special programs

Examples: School routines

The lists and explanations below serve as examples of school routines and schedules, which you can consider a springboard to making your own lists. Work with your child's special educator and/or teachers to define routines and schedules for your child's school day. Feel free to:

- use the space provided in the template checklists you have downloaded to add points to the routines or schedules
- or create entirely new routines or schedules that would support your child.

Arrival routine

☐ Arrive at school between 7:40 and 7:50

  ☐ Meet ________ (teacher) at the door and walk to classroom

  ☐ If ________ (teacher) is not at school, I meet ________ (another teacher)

☐ Hang backpack on hook

☐ Put coat on hook

☐ Remove lunch and blue folder from backpack

☐ Put lunch on top of my cubby

☐ Pass in homework and put blue folder in tray

☐ Say "hi" to teachers

☐ Go to Safe Spot and begin morning routine

(BLUMENFELD, E., PERSONAL COMMUNICATION, 2011)

The ____________________ (class) morning routine

My name is ________ and I am a student in _______ grade.

Each day when students get to school, they follow a morning routine. This includes:

☐ Hanging up coat and backpack

☐ Turning in homework

☐ Putting down chair

☐ Reading the morning message

☐ Checking the schedule for the day

I am good at the morning routine. Each morning, I hang my backpack and coat, take down my chair, and go over the schedule for the day. Doing the morning routine is important because it helps students prepare for the day.

Starting tomorrow, I am going to try adding one thing to my morning routine. I will read the morning message to myself after I take my chair down. Reading the morning message before morning meeting is a job for all students to do.

My teachers know that I can add reading the message to my morning routine and they will feel proud of me for trying it! (Blumenfeld, E., personal communication, 2011)

Closing routine

- ☐ Go to break
- ☐ Get lunchbox and homework folder together
- ☐ Put lunchbox and homework folder in backpack
- ☐ Bring packed backpack to read aloud
- ☐ Sit in meeting area

(BLUMENFELD, E., PERSONAL COMMUNICATION, 2011)

Examples: School schedules

The following is an example of a schedule for one day, but the child will benefit most when he has schedules for every day. For each day, you can customize the blank schedule template provided in the template checklists you have downloaded.

Daily schedule

- ☐ Check in preview with aide or special educator
- ☐ Math—in class
- ☐ Math—in learning center
- ☐ Walk with Mr. C.
- ☐ Special interest
- ☐ Academic preview social studies
- ☐ Art
- ☐ Social studies
- ☐ Break
- ☐ Social studies
- ☐ Lunch
- ☐ Special interest
- ☐ Academic preview English Language Arts (ELA)
- ☐ ELA
- ☐ Break
- ☐ ELA
- ☐ Conservatory
- ☐ Special interest
- ☐ Homework/check-out

(HAQ, M., USED WITH PERMISSION)

Weekly schedule

- ☐ Double periods: On Mondays you will have a double ELA class and a double social studies class. On Fridays you have a double science class. This means that the class goes for about one and a half hours. This is different from sixth grade. This is one way seventh graders learn. You will have a break built into this class.
- ☐ Advisory: In seventh grade, morning meeting is not scheduled every day. Instead, students go to advisory twice a week. Advisory is a 40-minute block. During this block we talk about topics that are important to us and to our teachers. We might also play games, like we did in morning meeting.
- ☐ Every morning I will meet with _____ (aide) or _____ (special educator) to review my schedule and preview the day.
- ☐ Monday
    - ☐ Even day (heavy morning and heavy afternoon)
    - ☐ Double social studies and ELA
    - ☐ Art
    - ☐ Conservatory
- ☐ Tuesday
    - ☐ Heavy morning and light afternoon
    - ☐ Community service
    - ☐ Conservatory
- ☐ Wednesday
    - ☐ Heavy morning and light afternoon
    - ☐ Double science
    - ☐ Lunch with a friend
    - ☐ Advisory
- ☐ Thursday
    - ☐ Heavy morning and light afternoon
    - ☐ Double ELA
    - ☐ PE
    - ☐ Communication tip
- ☐ Friday
    - ☐ Even day (heavy morning and heavy afternoon)
    - ☐ Double science
    - ☐ PE
    - ☐ Advisory

(HAQ, M., USED WITH PERMISSION)

Tomorrow at school (detailed schedule for a day at the beginning of a school year)

I am a smart, hardworking, friendly ___________ grade student who wants to do well at school.

Tomorrow morning, I will have a morning meeting. I will sit in a circle with my friends and I will share something I did this weekend. If I don't share, that is fine too. I will say, "Pass."

I have ELA, in the morning. In ELA, _________ (teacher) will show his website to the class. After we check out _________ (teacher)'s website, I will organize my binder with _________ (aide) and ________ (special educator). Once I have organized my binder, I will have time to myself.

After ELA, I have math in the morning. There will be an activity in math. I will have to think and wonder about things in the room. _______ (special educator) will help me.

After lunch, I will go to _________ (teacher)'s room for social studies. I will try to follow the activity.

After recess, I am going to do a writing activity with ________ (aide) for 30 minutes.

After the writing activity, I will have time to myself.

In the afternoon, I will go to ___________ (teacher)'s room for science.

Any time I want to take a break, I can ask my teachers or my teachers will give me a choice to go to my Break Spot. There will be activities in the Safe Spot for me to help me calm down. I can read to myself, have _________ (aide) read to me, sit on the thera-ball, or draw for five minutes.

I am going to have a great day and I will be proud of myself!

(HAQ, M., USED WITH PERMISSION)

Changes in schedule

Evacuation drill

Sometimes at school, we have to practice leaving the building safely as a whole school. This is important for everyone at school to practice, so that we all know how to leave safely when we need to evacuate (leave the building).

Some of the times we need to do this are during fire drills and during evacuation drills. During an evacuation drill, we need to leave the school building and leave the school grounds.

When we have an evacuation drill, an adult will come on the loudspeaker and let everyone know that we need to evacuate.

When that announcement is made, it is your job to stop what you are doing and follow the teacher's directions.

If you are in your classroom during the announcement, you will stop what you are doing and line up with __________ (aide) and the class. We will walk out of the building calmly and quietly.

When we get outside, everyone will walk out of the school ground and walk together to a church. It is important that you stay with your class.

When we get to the church, it is your job to follow the teacher's directions and sit on a bench until it is time to go. You will know it is time to walk back to school when your teacher tells you it is time.

It is important that you stand in line calmly and quietly with your class until we get back into the classroom.

(HAQ, M., USED WITH PERMISSION)

Note home regarding a change in schedule

Hi ____________,

I hope you are having a relaxing evening. I wanted to give you a heads up that because we have an evacuation drill tomorrow we will not be going to ________ (class) for ______________. You and I will take any of the remaining time to ________________.

Thanks, __________ (child's name)

See you in the morning!

(GUERRA, L.A., USED WITH PERMISSION)

Testing—change in schedule

This year as a grade _________ student, I will be doing some testing with different teachers. I will start with ____________ (teacher) tomorrow. If another learning center teacher is out, _____________ (teacher) may need to cover for that teacher so that my testing session with her will happen the next day. My work with __________ (teacher) will focus on _____________ (subject). _______________ (teacher) will be working with me all this week on the days I have ____________ (subject) on ___________ (day), _________ (day), and ___________ (day). She will write it into my schedule in the morning so I know. When I am doing this work with __________ (teacher), my ___________ (subject) and special interest time will be switched so that I do my testing first and then I will have my special interest time.

Just like my other testing, I will go down to ___________ room because it is a quiet room, and I am familiar with that room. I will be working for about _____ (number) minutes, and I can take a _____ (number) minute break about mid-way through. For my break, I can take a walk with __________ (aide) or take a walk by myself. __________ (aide) will not be staying in the room during my testing, but will come back mid-way for a walking break.

This is a ___________ (grade) expectation for me so I will try my best.

(GUERRA, L.A., USED WITH PERMISSION)

Science Electricity Fair

Tomorrow, in the ____________ (room), grade _____ is going to have an Electricity Fair. All grade _________ (number) students are expected to participate and share their hard work with other students and teachers. The fair will start around ___________ (time). Below is how the fair will run in the ___________ (room).

From _________ – ___________ (times), grade 4 and grade 8 classes will visit us with a teacher. Around _______ (time), grade 5 and another grade 8 class will come with ___________ (teacher) and __________ (teacher). They will be there for about fifteen minutes. Around __________ish (time), __________ (teacher) will come with his class. Again they will visit the _____________ (room) for about fifteen minutes. Also, around __________ish (time) grade 1 and grade 2 will walk in. They will preview the circuits for about fifteen minutes. Around ___________ish (time) grade 3 will visit. The last group will visit the ___________ (room) around ___________ish (time).

I will walk with _________ (aide) to the __________ (room) around _________ (time) to make sure I'm ready and organized before students and teachers come to visit my project. I will have my circuit board in place on a table near the door. I will share the table with ________ (classmate) and _________ (classmate).

I know there will be students, teachers, and parents coming to the electricity fair, which means that the __________ (room) might get a little loud or noisy. If it gets too loud and noisy, I will let __________ (aide) know and ask for a break. I will walk and come back to the __________ (room).

(HAQ, M., USED WITH PERMISSION)

Aide going out of town

__________ (aide) is going to __________ for a friend's wedding. He will be out from __________, __________ (date) to __________ (date). While __________ (aide) is out, my schedule will remain unchanged. __________ (special educator) and __________ (speech and language pathologist) will help me. If I want, __________ (special educator) can walk with me to all the classes just like __________ (aide) does, or I can go by myself. When I have to take a five-minute break, I can take a timer from __________ (special educator) and come back to class. My teachers trust that I will do a good job while __________ (aide) is away because I have shown independence in class when __________ (aide) has been out sick.

(HAQ, M., USED WITH PERMISSION)

Routines and schedules: Community

Your child will be most successful when you explicitly teach her the routines and schedules for various contexts in the community. Be sure to note the routines and schedules in your guide.

Professionals with whom your child interacts may discuss some of their expectations for routines and schedules. Some places you visit may have routines and schedules posted. In some situations, neither of these things will happen. You should be sure to go over routines and schedules in an explicit, visual format in order to ensure that your child with AS understands.

- You can define some community routines and schedules on your own.
- Others, such as routines and schedules for camp, you will want to develop in conjunction with individuals who support your child in the community.
- Use the list and examples provided in this section as a springboard to think about routines and schedules that would support your child in every context in which she participates in the community.
- Once you create community routines and schedules unique to your child's needs and situation, preview them with your child and have a copy available for review in each situation and environment until she integrates the routines and schedules and demonstrates mastery.

- Collaborate with adults in the community to preview schedule changes with your child.
- When you create your routines and schedules toolbox, put one routine or schedule per page with succinct, simple, accessible instructions. Less writing per page helps the child with AS avoid visual overload.

Activities in the community may include:

- ☐ Extra-curricular activities:
  - ☐ Sports
  - ☐ Drama class
  - ☐ Music class
- ☐ Working with AS professionals (at their office):
  - ☐ Psychologist
  - ☐ Psychiatrist
  - ☐ Neuropsychologist
  - ☐ Social worker
  - ☐ Coach
  - ☐ Social pragmatics specialist
  - ☐ Occupational therapist
  - ☐ Executive functioning specialist
  - ☐ ABA specialist
- ☐ Camp (explain rules for various environments and activities)

(LIST DEVELOPED WITH DYMENT, J.H.)

The lists and explanations below serve as examples of routines and schedules, which you can consider a springboard for making your own lists. Feel free to:

- use the space provided in the template checklists you have downloaded to add points to the routines or schedules
- or create entirely new routines or schedules that would support your child.

Daily camp schedule

The following is an example of a schedule for one day, but the child will benefit most when he has schedules for every day. For each day, you can customize the blank schedule template provided in the template checklists you have downloaded.

Monday

Times	Activities
9:00–9:15	Arrivals/greetings
9:15–10:00	Bus to camp outdoor camp ground
10:00–10:10	Transition
10:10–10:55	Social thinking group
10:55–11:10	Transition
11:10–11:55	Boats
11:55–12:10	Buddy lunch—boating area
12:10–12:30	Group meeting
12:30–1:10	Group leader choice
1:10–1:15	Transition
1:15–2:00	Swim
2:00–2:30	Transition/departures Bus back to main campus
3:00	Pickup

Psychologist: Session schedule

- ☐ Mood check-in (2–3 minutes)
- ☐ Homework review (3 minutes)
- ☐ Agenda setting (2 minutes)
- ☐ Session content (20–25 minutes)
- ☐ Homework assignment
- ☐ Client feedback

(FRIEDBERG AND MCCLURE 2002)

Occupational therapist: Session schedule

- ☐ ______________ (child's name)'s choice—10 minutes
    - ☐ ______________ (activity name such as helicopter swing)

- ☐ ______________ (occupational therapist's name)'s choice—10 minutes
  - ☐ ______________ (activity name such as astronaut board)
- ☐ ______________ (child's name)'s and ______________ (occupational therapist's name)'s choice—10 minutes
  - ☐ ______________ (activity name such as bolster hang)

(SCHOFIELD, J., USED WITH PERMISSION)

Social pragmatics: Session schedule

- ☐ Greeting
  - ☐ Check-in
  - ☐ Share
  - ☐ Review schedule
- ☐ Topic lesson
  - ☐ Discussion, worksheet, activity practice or role-playing activity
- ☐ Group activity
  - ☐ Activity, related to lesson
- ☐ Relaxation/reflection activity
- ☐ Clean-up and goodbye

(EXAMPLE FROM MGH ASPIRE)

How to use the toolbox

Now that you have created your routines and schedules toolbox, you will be able to:

- decrease stress and confusion for your child by clarifying expected routines and schedules in every environment in which he or she interacts
- implement structure for home and have guidelines for a unified approach to parenting
- nurture more productive and pleasant relationships between your child and their teachers and service providers now that expected routines and schedules in their environments are explicit
- help your child generalize skills by using the same strategies in multiple environments.

Chapter 6

Behavioral Expectations

Like most children with AS, Alexander has struggled with intuitively understanding expectations from an early age, which has affected his relationships and sometimes mine, too. People have often judged us both. For example, Alexander has always had trouble with the motor planning and coordination necessary to cut his food into bite-size pieces. For a long time we didn't force him to cut his food because it was such a painful process—I would just cut it for him. During dinner on a trip when Alexander was ten years old, Alexander put huge chunks of meat on his fork and ripped bites off of the meat with his teeth. It was clear that the other people at the table were horrified. I'm sure to them Alexander looked like a caveman, and that they figured that Michael and I just had not taught him proper table manners. Alexander had no idea that the way he was eating was offensive until I explained the behavioral expectation to him.

At school, Alexander frequently misunderstood how to be a student. Over the course of the school day, he wasn't able to adapt his behavior to the different expectations of the various activities and environments. For example, in one classroom a teacher might be okay with students calling out answers, while in another the teacher might insist that students raise their hands. Alexander needed instruction about appropriate behavior in every situation, including how to sit at his table spot, interact with visitors, and listen to presentations.

Before I understood his diagnosis, his teachers reported that he "misbehaved" regularly, and they struggled when working with him. His confusion about what was expected of him and how to interact with teachers, staff members, and the principal often led to angry outbursts, when he would yell things like: "You are rude," "I am not going to do what you say," "Get away from me," "This project is stupid," "I don't like you," and "I'm out of here." Sometimes he would then leave the room without permission.

Until they became familiar with Alexander's profile, Alexander's educators and fellow students often viewed these reactions as bad behavior rather than the result of confusion and frustration. They judged him negatively.

Teachers imposed consequences, and peers sometimes avoided him. Without knowing it, Alexander sabotaged himself and his relationships at school. He picked up on the negative responses to him and the feedback snowballed, sparking more bad behavior and reinforcing a negative self-image. Once we gave Alexander explicit education about how to behave in every environment, he knew how to act in the way that was expected. Instead of being confused and frustrated, he was empowered. School became a much more positive experience for him.

Setting behavioral expectations in every environment: rules as tools

As we discussed in Chapter 3, on the whole people diagnosed with AS have social differences relating to social cognition, including the ability to comprehend naturally the thoughts and feelings of another person (perspective-taking); to understand the big picture of a situation or the main idea of a conversation (central coherence); to use a series of strategies to stay on task to achieve a goal (executive functioning); and to interpret non-verbal communication. Most children with AS cannot draw on a built-in sense of perspective to modify their behavior according to the situation.

Without these intuitive abilities, children with AS need explicit rules. Teaching your child specific rules of behavior for home, school, and community is a simple and fundamental way to give your child the tools he or she will need to navigate daily interactions successfully.

What are behavioral expectations?

Behavioral expectations are rules that are made explicit, as well as rules that are assumed or unspoken (also called the "hidden curriculum" by Brenda Smith Myles—see "The Hidden Curriculum" Box), in various situations and contexts at home, at school, and in the community.

In this book, the term behavioral expectations applies to:

- family standards
- manners
- school rules that appear in the school handbook
- teacher and classroom, or special room (for example, the library or gym), rules

- rules for navigating daily situations or public environments
- rules for successful meetings with professionals and service providers.

Both explicit and unspoken rules must be presented clearly to your child to lay the foundation for success in all environments. At home, some manners are examples of explicit rules. Most parents articulate these expectations to their children: "No elbows on the table," "Shake hands and say 'hello' when you greet a visitor," or "Say 'please' when you ask for something," for instance. Family standards such as "Live with integrity" and "Operate with excellence" are examples of hidden rules. Many families do not talk about their standards, but assume their children know them.

The Hidden Curriculum

As we mentioned in Chapter 4, the term "hidden curriculum" was coined by AS authority Brenda Smith Myles. It refers to the unstated, implicit lessons, values, and perspectives that children are meant to pick up in their everyday interactions at home, at school, and in the community. The hidden curriculum concept arises from the assumption that children will recognize and absorb behavioral expectations at school that may not be part of the formal course of study—for example, how they should interact with peers, teachers, and other adults; how they should perceive different races, groups, or classes of people; or what ideas and behaviors are considered acceptable or unacceptable.

Children with AS often do not pick up the hidden curriculum intuitively and must be taught explicitly. At school, the handbook defines explicit rules outlining behavioral expectations, but teachers often assume that students know hidden rules such as how to follow directions, how to sit and do work at a desk or table spot, and bathroom etiquette. A child with AS will likely need these expectations clearly spelled out for them and will need to practice them in order to learn and master them.

Brenda Smith Myles has written a number of helpful books and articles about the hidden curriculum, including "Understanding the hidden curriculum: an essential social skill for children and youth with Asperger Syndrome (Myles and Simpson 2001) and *The Hidden Curriculum: Practical Solutions for Understanding Unstated Rules in Social Situations* (Myles, Trautman, and Schelvan 2004).

The term "behavioral expectations" also encompasses the kinds of information you need to spell out to help your child navigate daily situations.

At home this might mean hosting a play date, eating with family, playing with a sibling, or listening to a babysitter. Children with AS also do best when parents think through their everyday lives and habits, and identify what is expected in public places they visit regularly such as restaurants, toy stores, parks, libraries, or beaches, as well as what is expected when they work with other professionals and service providers. The Parents Take Charge section of this chapter will help you develop tools for establishing behavioral expectations for all of the situations and contexts that apply to your child with AS and your family.

The social fake

As we've seen in previous chapters, children with AS often lack perspective-taking, which prevents them from recognizing that their blunt honesty might hurt someone's feelings. One technique that adults can teach them to help them meet behavioral expectations and avoid offending others is the "social fake." The social fake is a concept developed by Michelle Garcia Winner and means responding in a socially kind way rather than with total candor (Winner 2007). For example, when Alexander is hosting a play date he is not particularly excited about, we have taught him how to pretend to be neutral about seeing his friend rather than saying, "I really don't want you to be here. Can you go home?" Your child might need instruction about how to be gracious about a gift she receives that she doesn't like. We might teach Alexander to say "Thank you. I appreciate it" rather than "I hate this book."

Interestingly, for many individuals with AS, the social fake cannot be a lie. Being dishonest, even if it is something most would consider a harmless "little white lie" meant to protect someone's feelings, might make a child with AS very uncomfortable. Therefore, you may need to teach more oblique social fakes like "It was nice of you to think of me" rather than expecting them to say "I love this book" when they really don't. In the Parents Take Charge exercises at the end of this chapter, we note specific situations that may call for using the social fake.

The benefits of setting behavioral expectations

You will make your child's life much easier and less stressful if you think about and clarify for him the specific rules and expectations that govern your household and family, as well as his classroom, school, and community. As we explained in Chapter 3, many people with AS, both children and adults, suffer from social anxiety because they are constantly worried about whether they are getting it right or behaving inappropriately.

The anxiety of children with AS decreases and their performance improves when they know how to act and complex demands are broken down into manageable parts. In the Parents Take Charge section, we help you break down a variety of common situations and interactions into a series of steps to use as a guide for your child and a teaching template and collaboration tool for you, your child's educators and caregivers, and professionals working with your child in the community.

In addition to decreasing stress for your child with AS, behavioral expectations will give clarity to confusing or overwhelming situations, help him align his behavior more consistently with expectations, which builds confidence, and enable him to participate more purposefully in all aspects of life.

Setting behavioral expectations also offers opportunities for positive reinforcement. An effective way to positively reinforce your child is to observe his behavior and acknowledge him immediately when he behaves in an expected way, which will help you avoid the cycle of constantly identifying behavioral transgressions. As a guideline, try to have eight to twelve positive statements paired with one critical statement. In addition, try to avoid always using your child's name when you redirect him, because you run the risk that he will start to associate his name with a negative reaction.

The rest of your family will also benefit from clear behavioral expectations. Rules provide structure for home education and offer guidelines for a unified approach to parenting. Before we developed a consistent set of rules, Alexander would be confused when I enforced one set of rules and my husband, babysitter, or extended family members enforced another. Often he would end up yelling at whomever was enforcing the stricter rule. We inadvertently sabotaged each other's efforts by not being on the same page. The ensuing disharmony was unnecessary and avoidable. Once we established a uniform set of behavioral expectations—which were also helpful to our typically developing son—our home environment became calmer and more pleasant. My husband and I were able to parent more effectively, which built our confidence.

Finally, you and your child's educators and service providers will collaborate to help your child generalize some behavioral expectations across environments. For example, the expectation of chewing with your mouth closed is the same in multiple environments. However, a child with AS may think that he only needs to chew with his mouth closed at home if he is only taught the rule at home and no one provides direct instruction to follow the expectation in a variety of contexts. A child will need to be taught explicitly that chewing with your mouth closed is a behavioral expectation whether you are in a restaurant, at the dinner table with your family, or in the school cafeteria. Adults in every environment can help the child generalize the skill by reinforcing this message. Of course, the child will want to know if there are circumstances when chewing with an open mouth could be acceptable. Some parents (like me) wouldn't want to give the child permission to chew with an open mouth while alone, but doing so would convey a consistent message that certain behaviors are acceptable in certain environments.

The tools in the Parents Take Charge section will address a multitude of situations at home, at school, and in the community.

Creating Your Child's Behavioral Expectations Toolbox

These workbook exercises help you break down a number of common situations and interactions that your child will encounter at home, at school, and in the community into manageable parts. Each breakdown provides instruction for behavior in a given situation, and works as a simple guide for your child and a teaching template and collaboration toolbox for you and the professionals that support him.

Behavioral expectations: Every environment

As we've discussed previously, children with AS often have struggles that impact all the environments in which they interact. Generalizing a behavioral expectation such as whole-body listening can lead to greater success in every context.

- Using the list below and examples in this section as a starting point, work with your child's special educator and/or teacher(s) and people who support him in the community to determine the behavioral expectations that he needs to master first. If you don't see a behavioral expectation that is important for your child, simply create one using the examples as models.
- Introduce behavior expectation topics one at a time in a coordinated effort across contexts.
- Use the same language in every setting when introducing the tool.
- Preview the behavioral expectation with your child before use in each environment.
- Have a copy available for review in each situation and environment until your child integrates the expectation and demonstrates mastery of it.

- Once the child becomes competent with one behavior expectation topic, continue practicing it and simultaneously start teaching another behavior expectation in every environment.
- When you create your expectations toolbox, put one expectation per page with succinct, simple, accessible instructions. Less writing per page helps the child with AS avoid visual overload.

Aspects of behavioral expectations in every environment

- ☐ Safe body expectations
- ☐ Expectations for when someone says "hi" to you
- ☐ Whole-body listening expectations
- ☐ Integrity: My words make a difference
- ☐ Volume-o-meter
- ☐ Group effort expectations
- ☐ Expectations for disagreeing
- ☐ Expectations for working with someone who is hard to work with

Examples: Behavioral expectations in every environment

The lists below serve as examples of behavioral expectations used in multiple environments, which you can consider a springboard to making your own lists. Feel free to:

- use the space provided in the template checklists you have downloaded to add points to the expectations
- or create entirely new behavioral expectations that would support your child using these tools as models
- include both explicit behavioral expectations and those that are unstated.

Safe body expectations

Keeping a safe body means:

- ☐ Keeping myself safe
    - ☐ Only eat food that is safe for me
    - ☐ Take breaks when I need them
    - ☐ Take care of my body

- ☐ Keeping others safe
    - ☐ Keep my arms, legs, feet, hands, and so on to myself
    - ☐ Take breaks when I need them
    - ☐ Be gentle when closing doors, so I do not startle people
- ☐ Keeping school property safe
    - ☐ Wash the tables if I make marks on them
    - ☐ Take care of school books
    - ☐ Keep artwork and other hallway decorations on the walls
    - ☐ Clean things up, especially if I left them there

Keeping a safe body is my responsibility. I do not get any reminders for keeping a safe body.

(DYMENT, J.H., USED WITH PERMISSION)

Expectations for when someone says "hi" to you

- ☐ Try to acknowledge others by saying "hi" when they say "hi" to you
- ☐ *Expected* and considered polite:
    - ☐ If someone says, "Hi. How are you?" you say "I'm well. How are you?"
- ☐ *Unexpected* and considered rude:
    - ☐ Ignore someone who says "hi" to you

Whole-body listening expectations

Whole-body listening means that I am paying attention to the speaker with my whole body:

- ☐ My body is facing the speaker
- ☐ My eyes are looking at the speaker
- ☐ My mouth is silent
- ☐ My body is mostly still

Why do I use whole-body listening?

- ☐ I can get the most information
- ☐ I show that I am polite
- ☐ I will be able to participate better
- ☐ I will not distract others
- ☐ It is expected and makes others feel comfortable

(DYMENT, J.H., MODIFIED FROM WINNER 2005, USED WITH PERMISSION)

Integrity: My words make a difference

This 5-point scale teaches children with AS about words and how words can impact others, as well as the speaker. Use this scale when your child with AS is calm to talk with her about the words she uses. I had this scale posted in my house and would refer to it when either of my children used kind words or harsh words to help them learn about their impact.

Level	Examples of these words	What people think/what could happen
5	☐ "I will kill you"	☐ People will be extremely frightened
	☐ "I will hurt you"	☐ People will think I am a violent person
	☐ Other threats	☐ When I get older, the police will not tolerate this
		☐ I will lose friends because people will be afraid of me
		☐ I will need to fix it
4	☐ Swear words	☐ People could be frightened of me
	☐ "I hate"	☐ These words will hurt people's feelings
	☐ Insults	☐ People could think I am mean
		☐ I will need to fix it
3	☐ "I don't like"	☐ People might learn more about me
	☐ "I don't prefer"	☐ They might be disappointed that I do not like something, but they probably will not be hurt
2	☐ "I like..."	☐ People will feel good
	☐ "This is fun"	☐ They will want to be around me
	☐ "I am happy about..."	☐ People will like me
		☐ People will know I am safe
1	☐ Compliments/kind words	☐ People will want to be around me
		☐ People will want to be my friend
		☐ People will feel safe near me
		☐ People will think I am kind and friendly

(DYMENT, J.H., INSPIRED BY BURON AND CURTIS 2003, USED WITH PERMISSION)

The Volume-o-meter tool provides your child with explicit information about the voice volume expectations in various environments. You will have best results if you preview this tool when your child is calm.

Volume-o-meter

Level	Type of voice	Where and when is it expected?	How does this make people feel?
5	SCREAMING voice	☐ Outside ☐ Calling for help	☐ Jittery ☐ Scared ☐ Mad
4	VERY LOUD voice	☐ Gymnasium ☐ In the auditorium (on stage) ☐ Outside playing ☐ Calling for a dog	*In an expected place:* ☐ Happy they can hear *In an unexpected place:* ☐ Bad ☐ Jittery ☐ Confused
3	Sharing voice	☐ At home, if you are calling someone in a different room ☐ In the classroom when you want everyone to hear you ☐ Teachers use sharing voices during meetings	*In an expected place:* ☐ Like I can hear the person talking ☐ Like I know what to do *In an unexpected place:* ☐ Upset ☐ Frustrated ☐ Annoyed
2	Conversation voice	☐ Talking to family ☐ At the dinner table ☐ On the phone ☐ Meetings ☐ Class ☐ Indoor recess ☐ Snack	☐ Happy ☐ Neutral
1	Whisper voice	☐ In the library ☐ If other people are working ☐ At a museum ☐ When you re-enter the classroom ☐ When something is private	☐ Helps me concentrate ☐ Calm ☐ Relaxed ☐ Safe ☐ Like I can do my best work ☐ Helps me and others know what to do
0	Silent	☐ Movie theater ☐ Performance ☐ Independent reading ☐ Independent work times ☐ When listening	☐ Good ☐ I can concentrate ☐ Calm ☐ Cozy ☐ Tired

(DYMENT, J.H., MODIFIED FROM BURON AND CURTIS 2003, USED WITH PERMISSION)

Group effort expectations

The "Group effort expectations" tool explains explicitly how your child can participate in group projects or activities.

Definitions:

Effort = Trying hard

Group effort = Working together to accomplish a goal

Group expectations:

- ☐ Include everyone—make sure everyone has the same amount of work
- ☐ Take turns
- ☐ Split up jobs and make a plan
- ☐ Try to agree
- ☐ If someone does not like the job, do not force them to do it
- ☐ Make sure everyone gets a fair part

Things to think about:

- ☐ Am I doing enough work?
- ☐ Am I doing my job?
- ☐ Am I hogging attention?
- ☐ Am I helping?
- ☐ Am I cooperating?
- ☐ Am I being fair?
- ☐ Am I helping the group move along?
- ☐ Am I being flexible?

In the end:

- ☐ If you are fair, everyone will probably be happy
- ☐ Everyone has pitched in
- ☐ The whole group is responsible for the outcome

(DYMENT, J.H., USED WITH PERMISSION)

Expectations for disagreeing

How to disagree:

- ☐ Talk softly (Level 2)
- ☐ Raise hand quietly
- ☐ Start with "I think..." or "I was thinking..."
- ☐ Try to compromise
- ☐ Use safe, kind words

What *not* to do when you disagree:

- ☐ Call out
- ☐ Use unkind or unsafe words
- ☐ Interrupt
- ☐ Use unkind or loud tone
- ☐ Roll your eyes

(DYMENT, J.H., USED WITH PERMISSION)

Expectations for working with someone who is hard to work with

- ☐ First, try to work together
- ☐ Do *not* say, "I don't want to be your partner." The person might get upset

- [ ] If you cannot work together, ask an adult to help you figure it out

(BLUMENFELD, E., USED WITH PERMISSION)

Behavioral expectations: Home

The goal is to define clearly the behavioral expectations that govern your home and family life—family standards, manners, and rules for interacting with parents, siblings, babysitters, and others. These rules vary greatly from family to family. These exercises will help you to understand and articulate the rules in your home. Note these expectations in your guide.

As we've noted, children with AS understand expectations best when concepts that may seem obvious are broken down and explained. For example, parents can clarify that "kindness" means being friendly to others in actions and words. Actions include being tolerant and patient and responding when others talk. Kind words are those that make people feel good, help people, and do not insult them, put them down, or make them feel uncomfortable or scared. Examples of kind words are: "You did a great job," "Thank you," "Please," "I think you are a good person," "I enjoy playing with you," and "I can help you." This level of detail helps children with AS understand family expectations.

- Use the list and examples provided in this section as a springboard to think about behavioral expectations that would support your child at home. If you do not see a behavioral expectation that is important to your family, simply create one using these examples as models.
- Once you create expectations unique to your child's needs and situation, preview them with your child and have a copy available for review in each situation and environment until he integrates the expectation and demonstrates mastery.
- Once you create home expectations unique to your child's needs and situation, parents, babysitters, and anyone else in a home care role can use these tools to teach your child how to master each behavioral expectation.
- Behavior expectation topics should be introduced one at a time as part of home education.

- Once the child becomes competent with one behavior expectation topic, continue practicing it and start teaching another behavior expectation.
- When you create your expectations toolbox, put one expectation per page with succinct, simple, accessible instructions. Less writing on each page helps the child with AS avoid visual overload.

Family standards may include:

- ☐ Have integrity
- ☐ Operate with a standard of excellence
- ☐ Have nice manners
- ☐ Honor religious or spiritual beliefs/faithfulness
- ☐ Give back (community service)
- ☐ Be generous
- ☐ Be honest
- ☐ Be tolerant
- ☐ Achieve academically
- ☐ Practice patience
- ☐ Embrace diversity
- ☐ Practice openmindedness
- ☐ Work hard
- ☐ Persevere
- ☐ Be active
- ☐ Embrace culture (arts, music)
- ☐ Treat others with respect
- ☐ Reach out to others
- ☐ Practice environmental responsibility

(LIST DEVELOPED WITH DYMENT, J.H.)

Specific contexts at home may include:

- ☐ Hosting a play date
- ☐ Eating with family or guests
- ☐ Interacting with sister or brother
- ☐ When your brother or sister is upset
- ☐ General table manners
- ☐ Specific table manners:
  - ☐ Eating rolls
  - ☐ Food in teeth
  - ☐ If you do not like the food
  - ☐ If you spill a drink or food
- ☐ General everyday manners
- ☐ Specific everyday manners:
  - ☐ When meeting people

- ☐ When you receive a gift
- ☐ Say "Excuse me" when...
- ☐ With elderly people

Examples: Family standards

The lists below serve as examples of home behavioral expectations, which you can consider a springboard to making your own lists. Feel free to:

- use the space provided in the template checklists you have downloaded to add points to the expectations
- or create entirely new behavioral expectations that would support your child
- include both explicit behavioral expectations and those that are unstated.

Integrity

To live with integrity:

- ☐ Be honest:
    - ☐ Do your own work
    - ☐ Do not claim others' work as your own
    - ☐ Admit your mistakes
    - ☐ Do not blame others
    - ☐ Turn in lost items when you find them
- ☐ Be trustworthy:
    - ☐ Tell the truth
    - ☐ Do what you say you will do
    - ☐ Do not gossip
    - ☐ Do not share others' secrets
    - ☐ Use safe words (see below)
    - ☐ Maintain a safe body
    - ☐ Learn from your mistakes and try not to make the same mistake twice
- ☐ Be fair:
    - ☐ Take turns

- ☐ Share
- ☐ Play by the rules
- ☐ Do not take advantage of others
- ☐ Do not compare others
- ☐ Do not show favoritism
- ☐ Apologize when you make a mistake

Excellence

Put your best effort into everything in which you participate, including:

- ☐ Relationships
- ☐ School
- ☐ Therapy
- ☐ Sports
- ☐ Extra-curricular activities

How to achieve excellence:

- ☐ Be respectful of yourself and everyone with whom you come in contact:
  - ☐ Consider how other people would feel before acting
  - ☐ Do not insult or say something that could offend others
  - ☐ Treat everyone as if they are special and important
- ☐ Acknowledge your own and others' strengths:
  - ☐ Understand that everyone has unique gifts and talents
  - ☐ Look for them in yourself and others
- ☐ Appreciate and enjoy the differences between yourself and others:
  - ☐ Recognize that differences make the world interesting
  - ☐ Honor different cultures
- ☐ Contribute positively and generously to others' lives:
  - ☐ Compliment others when you appreciate their strengths
  - ☐ Offer information that is helpful to them
  - ☐ Help them with tasks
  - ☐ Make a gift for them
  - ☐ Listen and be with others when they feel sad
  - ☐ Be fun when you get together
- ☐ Be patient and tolerant:
  - ☐ Do not judge others

- ☐ Try to forgive others when they make mistakes. Holding grudges only hurts you

☐ Pay attention to other people and listen carefully to what people say:

- ☐ Look at people's eyes or forehead when they speak to you
- ☐ Wait for them to complete everything they want to say before speaking
- ☐ Respond thoughtfully and politely
- ☐ Stay on topic

☐ Have a positive and joyful attitude:

- ☐ Know that people enjoy being around people that make them feel good
- ☐ Be aware that your attitude makes a tremendous difference to the outcome of your encounters
- ☐ Realize that when you have a good attitude, things always go better

☐ Practice good sportsmanship:

- ☐ Be humble when you win—do not brag
- ☐ Be gracious when you lose—do not throw a fit or make excuses
- ☐ Help your team-mates
- ☐ Do not argue
- ☐ Play fair
- ☐ Learn from your mistakes
- ☐ Encourage others when they make mistakes
- ☐ Accept sports calls and decisions gracefully

☐ Even when the day goes badly, focus on everything for which you are grateful:

- ☐ Understand that when you focus on the things in life that go well, you feel happier
- ☐ Challenge yourself to see the good things that come out of life's challenges

Examples: Specific contexts at home

Hosting a play date

☐ When friend arrives say, "Hi ________. I am so glad you came over"

☐ Stay with your play date

☐ Conversation:

- ☐ Take turns initiating conversation
- ☐ Respond when others talk to you (Prutting and Kirchner 1987)
- ☐ Use whole-body listening when others are talking with you (Winner 2005)

☐ Eat at the same table as your play date

☐ Take turns choosing activities

☐ Share your toys

- ☐ Use words that communicate that you are happy to have him/her at our house
- ☐ Use the social fake (see p.139) if you are not happy to have him/her at our house
- ☐ At the end of the play date, walk your friend to the door
- ☐ When your friend is walking out of the door to leave say, "Goodbye. Thank you for coming"

Interacting when eating with family or guests

- ☐ Conversation:
  - ☐ Whole-body listening (Winner 2005)
  - ☐ Stay on topic
  - ☐ Take turns talking
  - ☐ Initiate comments
  - ☐ Listen when others talk
  - ☐ Ask questions and listen to the response
  - ☐ Respond when someone talks to you (Prutting and Kirchner 1987)
  - ☐ Use a Level 2 voice

Interacting with your brother or sister

- ☐ Respect your brother/sister's thoughts, feelings, and needs. That means:
  - ☐ Listen to what (s)he has to say
  - ☐ Respond only with safe words and actions
  - ☐ You do not need to agree
- ☐ Safe words (Levels 1–3)—words that are either neutral or make the other person feel good
- ☐ Safe body
- ☐ Level 2–3 voice
- ☐ No provoking

When your brother/sister is upset

- ☐ Have caring behavior:
  - ☐ Ask how you can help him or her
  - ☐ Try to do what (s)he needs
- ☐ Use a Level 1 voice
- ☐ If you cannot use a Level 1 voice or if you are feeling overwhelmed:
  - ☐ Leave the room
  - ☐ Find an adult

General table manners

- ☐ Put napkin in your lap
- ☐ Use the napkin, not your hand or shirt, to wipe your mouth
- ☐ Cut food into bite-size pieces
- ☐ Chew with your mouth closed
- ☐ Stay seated until everyone is finished
- ☐ Sit up straight
- ☐ Elbows off the table

Table manners: Specific situations

- ☐ Eating rolls:
  - ☐ Break off a piece of the roll before buttering
  - ☐ Use a knife to put butter on the plate
  - ☐ Then, use the knife to put butter on the roll
- ☐ If you have food in your teeth:
  - ☐ Excuse yourself to the bathroom to get the food out
  - ☐ Do not pick teeth at the table
- ☐ If you do not like the food:
  - ☐ Do not comment on how bad the food tastes
  - ☐ Do the "social fake" with the host or hostess
  - ☐ Leave the food on the plate
- ☐ If you spill a drink or food:
  - ☐ Use a fork or spoon to put spilled food on the side of the plate
  - ☐ Use paper towels to clean food or drink that could stain, not nice napkins
  - ☐ Say "Excuse me"

Everyday manners

- ☐ Wait patiently for your turn
- ☐ Listen attentively when others speak
- ☐ Clean up after yourself
- ☐ Help people in need
- ☐ Respect people different from you
- ☐ Be kind to people that help you regularly, such as:
  - ☐ Teachers
  - ☐ Babysitters
  - ☐ Grocery store clerks
- ☐ Say "Thank you" when someone does something nice for you

Everyday manners: Specific situations

- ☐ When meeting people:
  - ☐ Look them in the eye (or at the forehead)
  - ☐ Say "Hello"
  - ☐ Smile
- ☐ When you receive a gift:
  - ☐ Say "Thank you"
  - ☐ Do the "social fake" if you do not like it
  - ☐ Write and send a thank-you note within one week
- ☐ Say "Excuse me" when you:
  - ☐ Burp
  - ☐ Bump into someone
  - ☐ Fart

Everyday manners with elderly people

- ☐ Allow them to walk through the door first
- ☐ Offer your seat if they do not have one
- ☐ Assist them if you can see they need help or if they ask for support
- ☐ Let them sit in the front seat of a car

Behavioral expectations: School

Your child will be most successful when you explicitly teach him the behavioral expectations of the school. Your child needs to know the school rules, as well as the teacher's behavioral expectations for his or her classroom. There may be special expectations that apply to the library, the gym, or the school shop. You and teachers will lay the foundation for success at school when you define these expectations for your child.

School handbook

Look in your child's school handbook or on the school's website for the school rules:

- Choose the abridged rules that are intended for the younger children because they are usually written in simpler, more concrete terms.
- Copy the rules into your guide.
- Preview them with your child and review whenever necessary or helpful.

School day

Teachers may discuss some of their expectations for behavior during the school day, and may assume that students are already aware of others. Regardless of whether teachers talk about expectations, you should cover them in an explicit, visual format in order to ensure that your child with AS understands.

- Talk to teachers about classroom behavioral expectations.
- Note special behavioral expectations for the library, gym, shop, school bus pick-up, recess, field trips, and so on.
- Use the list and examples provided in this section as a springboard to think about behavioral expectations that would support your child at school.
- Once you create school expectations unique to your child's needs and situation, preview them with your child and have a copy available for review in each situation and environment until she integrates the expectation and demonstrates mastery.
- When you create your expectations toolbox, put one expectation per page with succinct, simple, accessible instructions. Less writing per page helps the child with AS avoid visual overload.

Expectations pertaining to general contexts at school may include:

- ☐ Being a student
- ☐ Being a student and looking like a student by working at my table spot
- ☐ Learning about directions
- ☐ Sharing my ideas
- ☐ How to persevere or keep doing work in which I am not interested
- ☐ Sensory tool rules

Expectations for specific contexts at school may include:

- ☐ Expected versus unexpected events and why (this is an abridged list—the full list can be found in the digital checklists):
  - ☐ Independent reading
  - ☐ Rug time
  - ☐ Cursive
  - ☐ Recess
  - ☐ Assembly
  - ☐ Closing circle
  - ☐ Class name: ________
- ☐ The recess plan

- ☐ Computer lab rules
- ☐ Birthday celebrations in ________ classroom
- ☐ Class visitors—Another class
- ☐ Group conversations
- ☐ Book club and rug time
- ☐ What to do if I am upset or someone else is upset
- ☐ When it is cold outside
- ☐ Class field trip

(LIST DEVELOPED WITH DYMENT, J.H.)

Examples: General school contexts

The lists and explanations below serve as examples of school behavioral expectations, which you can consider a springboard to making your own lists. Work with your child's special educator and/or teachers to define behavioral expectations for every context of your child's school day. Feel free to:

- use the space provided in the template checklists you have downloaded to add points to the expectations
- or create entirely new behavioral expectations that would support your child
- include both explicit behavioral expectations and those that are unstated.

Being a student

- ☐ Follow directions
- ☐ Ask questions
- ☐ Ask for help, when you need it
- ☐ Complete work
- ☐ Work nicely with others:
  - ☐ Safe words
  - ☐ Safe body
  - ☐ Level 2 voice
- ☐ Listen to others
- ☐ Do your best work

(BLUMENFELD, E., PERSONAL COMMUNICATION, 2011)

The following series of tools uses Social Stories™ to teach behavioral expectations at school. This format works well with children with AS because it shares information in a patient and reassuring way that makes it easier to understand. Alexander's special educator wrote these Social Stories™.

Being a student and looking like a student by working at my table spot

I am very good at "being a student" in school. Most of the time I complete my work, I participate and I try hard. My teachers and parents are proud of me for this.

My teachers also think it is important that I "look like a student."

There are many ways to look like a student. One way is to complete my work at my table spot or the quiet work spot inside ________classroom.

It is important and helpful to work at my table spot because:

1 When I look like a student, people will think these positive thoughts about me:

- ___________ (name) is a student, just like me.
- I have something in common with _________ (name). We are both students.
- ___________ (name) is smart and he tries hard.
- I need help. Maybe __________ (name) can help me.

2 If I'm not sure what to do, I can look around the room and see what my classmates are doing.

3 If I need help, there are at least ___ (number) teachers in the room to help me.

My teachers understand that I prefer to work alone, so they will not require me to work at my table spot all of the time. Instead, I can work at the quiet work spot sometimes.

My teachers will be very proud of me when I try to "look like a student" by completing my work at my table spot. I will feel proud of myself, too.

(DYMENT, J.H., USED WITH PERMISSION)

Directions are important

Hi! My name is ________ and I am a student at ________ School. I am learning about directions at school.

During the school day, there are times when teachers and other adults working at the school will tell students what they need to do. This is called giving directions.

Directions are important because they let students know what they are supposed to do, and they help students understand what is expected. Directions can be given anywhere in school, such as in class, at specials, in the hallways, in the cafeteria, and outside at recess.

Sometimes following directions can feel difficult or confusing. I might not want to follow some directions that are given to me. It is my teacher's job is to give directions, and my job as a student is to follow them. If I need help following or understanding a direction, I can ask a teacher or another student for help.

When I follow directions, I am doing my job as a student.

(BLUMENFELD, E., ADAPTED FROM GRAY 2010, USED WITH PERMISSION)

Sharing my ideas

Hi! My name is ________ and I'm a student in ________ grade.

Recently I made some recommendations to my teachers about good books to share with the class. My teachers are happy when I share my ideas with them in a positive way.

Recommending books also shows that I'm thinking of others. This is something that I'm working on, and my teachers are proud of me.

Several other students in my class have also made book recommendations to my teachers. Teachers are open to student ideas and also have ideas of their own.

To be fair to everyone, all ideas are heard and considered. My teachers have heard my idea about reading ________ and have considered it. They think it is a good idea and are willing to read it to the class at the next read-aloud.

I understand that this will be my turn for choosing the read-aloud book. The next few read-aloud books will be chosen by teachers and other students, so that everyone gets a chance.

(BLUMENFELD, E., USED WITH PERMISSION)

How to persevere or keep doing work in which I am not interested

My name is __________. I am a smart _______ grader who attends _______ School. I am learning "how to persevere" or keep doing schoolwork when I might not be interested in it.

My schedule shows certain times at school when I have to do certain things. For example, there is a time for:

- ☐ Reading
- ☐ Social studies
- ☐ Science
- ☐ Art
- ☐ Math
- ☐ Breaks

Some of these things are "academic" activities and some of them are "non-academic" and/or free-time activities.

The amount of time for academic activities is determined by what our curriculum for the day is and what my work is. The time is set each day. "Non-academic" activities and free-time activities are always flexible. My free-time activities at school change based on how much time I have available after I do my work.

When I have an assignment or have to learn about a topic that does not seem interesting to me at first, I will "just do it."

"Just doing it" will be helpful because, once I do it, it will be done. "Just doing it" will also be helpful because I might decide that I actually am interested in learning something about the topic. "Just doing it" means I will get my work done and then I can have some free time.

Since I like my free time, I will try to focus on getting my work done—and "just do it"!

Of course, if I have questions about how to do the assignment or if I am confused about something, then I will remember that my teachers think it is smart when I ask for help!

(BLUMENFELD, E., USED WITH PERMISSION)

Sensory tool rules

Hi! My name is ______ and I am a student in ______ grade at _______ School.

In _______ grade, we have sensory tools that we can use independently. They are located ________________.

If using a tool would help me concentrate or help make my body feel "just right," then I can get a tool and use it at almost any time during the day.

When I use a sensory tool, there are rules I have to follow in order to be safe.

- ☐ When I use balls or stretchy strips, I need to keep them in my hands where my teacher can see them at all times.
- ☐ If a teacher asks me to put a sensory tool away, even if I don't feel like I am finished with it, it is my job to follow directions and put it away.
- ☐ If I want to use the body sock, I need to keep my bottom on the floor.
- ☐ If I try to use the sensory tool rules, I will earn my safe body and following directions stars. I will feel proud of myself, and my teachers will feel proud of me too.

(BLUMENFELD, E., USED WITH PERMISSION)

Examples: Specific school contexts

The examples given here in the book are just for reference and fun lists as well as blank templates can be found in the digital checklists.

Expected versus unexpected events and why

Morning meeting

Expected	Unexpected...Why?
☐ Students sit on their rug spots ☐ Students show that their brain and body are in the group ☐ Students raise their hand if they want to participate	☐ Calling out (This would be distracting to others who are trying to learn) ☐ Sitting somewhere other than my rug spot (This would be distracting to others who are trying to learn. I also might be in someone's way or might not be able to see or hear the meeting if I am not on my rug spot)

(DYMENT, J.H., USED WITH PERMISSION)

Math

Expected	Unexpected...Why?
☐ Students sit on their rug spot for the lesson ☐ Students raise their hand when they want to participate or when they are called on ☐ Students show that their brain and body are in the group ☐ Students think about the math that is being taught	☐ Calling out (This would be distracting to others who are trying to learn) ☐ Sitting somewhere other than my rug spot (This would be distracting to others who are trying to learn. I also might be in someone's way or might not be able to see or hear the meeting if I am not on my rug spot) ☐ Daydreaming or thinking about something other than math (If I am thinking about something other than math, I might not learn new math ideas)

(DYMENT, J.H., USED WITH PERMISSION)

Writer's workshop

Expected	Unexpected...Why?
☐ Students sit at their table spots, most of the time ☐ Students raise their hand if they have a question for the teacher (Students often have questions for the teacher during writer's workshop!)	☐ Calling out or talking to your neighbor is unexpected because many students need a quiet environment to write ☐ Reading a book during Writer's Workshop is unexpected because the purpose of this time is to practice writing

(DYMENT, J.H., USED WITH PERMISSION)

Independent reading

Expected	Unexpected...Why?
☐ Each student is silently reading their own book	☐ Reading with a partner is unexpected because this particular time is for reading independently ☐ Talking to a friend during IR is unexpected because the purpose of this time is to practice and enjoy reading

(DYMENT, J.H., USED WITH PERMISSION)

Lunch

Expected	Unexpected...Why?
☐ Students sit in their assigned seat in the cafeteria ☐ Students eat their lunch ☐ Students make "small talk" and "have conversations" with each other ☐ Students clean up their own garbage ☐ Students sometimes help others clean up their garbage ☐ Students take turns wiping down the table ☐ Students line up with their classmates when lunch is over	☐ Leaving garbage at the table is unexpected because one of our jobs is to clean up after ourselves ☐ Sitting silently at lunch *all the time* is unexpected because people usually use lunch as a 'social time.' Sitting silently at lunch sometimes is ok. Sometimes people need some silent time too

(DYMENT, J.H., USED WITH PERMISSION)

Lunch in classroom

Expected	Unexpected...Why?
☐ Eat your lunch ☐ It is OK to share things with your teachers during lunch ☐ It is not OK to ask teachers to do something besides listen	☐ Ask teachers to do something for me during lunch (It is important for teachers to have time to eat and enjoy their lunch. They need a break too)

(DYMENT, J.H., CREATED STRUCTURE; BLUMENFELD, E., PERSONAL COMMUNICATION, 2011, PROVIDED CONTENT, USED WITH PERMISSION)

Lunch group

Expected	Unexpected...Why?
☐ Go to lunch group from _____ (time) until _____ (time) on ________ (day) ☐ Sit at the table ☐ Eat my lunch ☐ Participate with the group ☐ Follow the directions of _____ (speech and language pathologist) and ______ (aide)	☐ Using unsafe or unkind language at lunch group is unexpected because it makes people feel hurt and sad. The purpose of lunch group is to build friendships and learn from each other

(DYMENT, J.H., CREATED STRUCTURE; BLUMENFELD, E., PERSONAL COMMUNICATION, 2011, PROVIDED CONTENT, USED WITH PERMISSION)

Adaptive physical education (APE)

Expected	Unexpected...Why?
☐ Walk with _____ (aide) to APE ☐ Either go outside or to the auditorium ☐ Complete my exercises ☐ Follow directions of ______ (APE teacher) and ______ (aide)	☐ Doing my own thing during A.P.E. is unexpected because this is a time for me to practice specific skills with ____________ (teacher). If I need some time to do my own thing, I can ask ______________ and they can help me put it into my schedule

(DYMENT, J.H., CREATED STRUCTURE; BLUMENFELD, E., PERSONAL COMMUNICATION, 2011, PROVIDED CONTENT, USED WITH PERMISSION)

Art

Expected	Unexpected...Why?
☐ Walk by myself to class ☐ Stay for 45 minutes (unless I have permission from _____ (art teacher) to go to the bathroom or to the nurse) ☐ Follow the directions of _____ (art teacher)	☐ Using art tools in ways other than how my art teacher shows me is unexpected because it is our job to make sure the tools are taken care of so everyone can use them during art class

(DYMENT, J.H., CREATED STRUCTURE; BLUMENFELD, E., PERSONAL COMMUNICATION, 2011, PROVIDED CONTENT, USED WITH PERMISSION)

Music

Expected	Unexpected...Why?
☐ Walk to music on my own ☐ Stay at least 10 minutes ☐ Follow the directions of ____ (aide) and _____ (music teacher) ☐ Ask questions if I have them	☐ It is unexpected for students to sit in music class confused. It is hard to participate in music when I am confused. If I am confused, teachers expect me to ask a question

(DYMENT, J.H., CREATED STRUCTURE; BLUMENFELD, E., PERSONAL COMMUNICATION, 2011, PROVIDED CONTENT, USED WITH PERMISSION)

Rug time

Expected	Unexpected...Why?
☐ Stay at least until timer goes off ☐ Follow the rug rules	☐ It is unexpected to leave the rug before the timer goes off because my teacher gives us important information while we are at the rug. If I leave before the timer goes off, I will miss important information, which will make it difficult for me to complete my work

(DYMENT, J.H., CREATED STRUCTURE; BLUMENFELD, E., PERSONAL COMMUNICATION, 2011, PROVIDED CONTENT, USED WITH PERMISSION)

Book club

Expected	Unexpected...Why?
☐ Come to book club ☐ Stay for at least 15 minutes ☐ Listen to the ideas of others ☐ Share my ideas and opinions with others	☐ It is unexpected for me to 'steal the show' during book club because other people like to share their ideas as much as I do. When I listen to the ideas of others, they will want to listen to my ideas too

(DYMENT, J.H., CREATED STRUCTURE; BLUMENFELD, E., PERSONAL COMMUNICATION, 2011, PROVIDED CONTENT, USED WITH PERMISSION)

Writing

Expected	Unexpected...Why?
☐ Follow the directions of the teachers ☐ Write on your own for at least five sentences	☐ It is unexpected to draw during writing because the purpose of writing is to practice our writing skills

(DYMENT, J.H., CREATED STRUCTURE; BLUMENFELD, E., PERSONAL COMMUNICATION, 2011, PROVIDED CONTENT, USED WITH PERMISSION)

Recess

Expected	Unexpected...Why?
☐ At recess, it is a good idea to look for someone who might need someone to play with ☐ Ask the student if he or she would like to play a game or join you in an activity ☐ You can look for a game that you like and ask if you can join	☐ It is unexpected to play alone *all of the time* during recess because recess is mean to be a 'social time.' It is ok to play alone *some of the time*. Sometimes people enjoy a little alone time

(DYMENT, J.H., CREATED STRUCTURE; BLUMENFELD, E., PERSONAL COMMUNICATION, 2011, PROVIDED CONTENT, USED WITH PERMISSION)

Computer break

Expected	Unexpected...Why?
☐ Only look at appropriate things ☐ Use headphones if others are around ☐ Sign off when teachers say it is time ☐ Follow the directions of the teachers	☐ It is unexpected to look at inappropriate things during computer break because it can make others feel unsafe or confused

(DYMENT, J.H., CREATED STRUCTURE; BLUMENFELD, E., PERSONAL COMMUNICATION, 2011, PROVIDED CONTENT, USED WITH PERMISSION)

Computer lab

Expected	Unexpected...Why?
☐ Leave mouse pads in place ☐ Be careful and calm with the equipment ☐ Follow the directions of the teachers	☐ It is unexpected to be careless with the equipment because the equipment is there for everyone at school to use and share. The equipment is very expensive and therefor it is difficult to replace if it is used carelessly or if students don't use a calm body in the lab

(DYMENT, J.H., CREATED STRUCTURE; BLUMENFELD, E., PERSONAL COMMUNICATION, 2011, PROVIDED CONTENT, USED WITH PERMISSION)

Hall

Expected	Unexpected...Why?

☐ Stay to the right, especially on the stairs
☐ Say "hi" to adults and students when they say "hi" to you
☐ Have a safe body
☐ Walk
  ☐ Hands and feet to yourself
  ☐ Things on the wall stay on the wall
  ☐ Leave other people's property undisturbed
☐ If someone touches you or if there is too much noise:
  ☐ Try your best to keep your cool
☐ If someone is in your way when walking down the hall:
  ☐ Politely say "Excuse me"
  ☐ Allow the person time to move out of your way before you go on
☐ Try to remember that the hall is a place where unexpected things can happen:
  ☐ People can accidently touch you
  ☐ Noise can be too loud
  ☐ People walk in different directions
  ☐ It can feel chaotic and confusing
	☐ It is unexpected to walk down the staircase on the left side because I may bump into people walking up the stairs. Usually, people stay to the right, which allows space for everyone to go up and down the stairs in a safe way
	☐ It is unexpected to ignore people I know in the hallways because it makes people feel good when I say hello. They may think I don't want to see them if I ignore them in the hallway
	☐ It is unexpected to run in the hallway because you might trip or run into someone else. The hallway is a place where a lot of people travel, and it is our job to help everyone stay safe when we can

(DYMENT, J.H., CREATED STRUCTURE; BLUMENFELD, E., PERSONAL COMMUNICATION, 2011, PROVIDED CONTENT, USED WITH PERMISSION)

Assembly

Expected	Unexpected...Why?
☐ School assemblies ☐ Sit with the class for 10 minutes ☐ Keep a calm body ☐ If you cannot stay for 10 minutes, tell your teacher that you need a break ☐ Follow the directions of the teachers ☐ Performances ☐ If you are uncomfortable, tell the teacher you need a break ☐ Return, if possible, when you feel calm ☐ Follow the directions of the teachers	☐ It is unexpected to run out of an assembly because people might think I am hurt, sick or in danger ☐ It is unexpected to boo at an assembly because the performers probably worked hard and practiced their performance. It would hurt their feelings if I boo at the assembly

(DYMENT, J.H., CREATED STRUCTURE; BLUMENFELD, E., PERSONAL COMMUNICATION, 2011, PROVIDED CONTENT, USED WITH PERMISSION)

Closing circle

Expected	Unexpected...Why?
☐ Students sit on their rug spots ☐ Students show that their brain and body are in the group ☐ Students raise their hand if they want to participate	☐ Calling out (This would be distracting to others who are trying to learn) ☐ Sitting somewhere other than my rug spot (This would be distracting to others who are trying to learn. I also might be in someone's way or might not be able to see or hear the meeting if I am not on my rug spot)

(DYMENT, J.H., USED WITH PERMISSION)

The recess plan

My name is __________. I am a _____ grader at _________ School.

This year I have mostly been going to recess with my class. Some days I have played on the structure with others, some days I have tossed the ball around, and some days I walk or run around on my own.

It is my job as a student to go to recess when all ______ graders go. I have done a good job with this.

When it is cold outside, recess is not always something I want to do. My teachers understand this but they also want to help me do my job.

Because of this, they came up with a plan for recess that I can follow. The plan is:

- ☐ Go outside for at least ten minutes.
- ☐ Join a game, toss a ball, play on the structure, or walk around on my own.
- ☐ So that I know when the ten minutes is up, I will bring a timer to keep in my pocket. My teacher will set the timer for me, and my job is to keep it in my pocket until it beeps. When it beeps, ten minutes have passed.
- ☐ I will turn off the timer and walk inside to my classroom. It is my responsibility to return the timer to a teacher in my classroom in good condition.

My teachers will be proud of me when I try to follow the recess plan. I will also earn stars and work on my involvement and independence.

(BLUMENFELD, E., USED WITH PERMISSION)

Computer lab rules

Hi! My name is _______ and I am a student of the _______ School.

The _______ School has a policy about computer use. This policy is important for me to know since I use computers so often. I am usually very careful when I use the computers. The school policy is:

Anyone who does NOT handle computers, laptops, keyboards, mouse pads, or headphones gently will lose their privilege to use them.*

- The first time it happens, privileges are lost for 1 day.
- The second time it happens, privileges are lost for 1 week.
- The third time it happens, privileges are lost for the rest of the school year.

(*Banging on keyboards, throwing mouse pads or headphones, slamming laptops shut or on a surface, and hitting the screen are all actions that equal a strike.)

The reason for this policy is because students need to understand that not handling this equipment gently can lead to very expensive repairs.

Using computers is a privilege and I can try to do my best to follow the school policy so I can keep this privilege.

I can earn my stars for following directions, keeping a safe body, and being a student when I handle computer equipment gently.

(BLUMENFELD, E., USED WITH PERMISSION)

Birthday celebrations in ________________ (classroom)

Hi! My name is _________ and I am a student in _____ grade.

When someone in class has a birthday, there are special things we do together to celebrate.

In _____ classroom, we can share wishes for each other on our birthdays. When someone shares a birthday wish, they might say something like "I hope you have a great year," or "I hope you get a good gift for your birthday."

After someone shares a birthday wish, the person whose birthday it is says, "Thank you."

The birthday boy or girl can choose to have people share wishes out loud or in writing.

When it is my birthday, I can say "I'd like my wishes to be shared out loud," or "I'd like my wishes to be shared in writing."

If I do not want any wishes, it is okay to say, "I'd rather not have any wishes, thank you."

On my birthday, I can bring in a treat to share with the class. I can choose a classmate to help me pass out my treat, or I can pass it out by myself.

If people wish me a "Happy Birthday" during the school day, I can say, "Thank you."

I will feel proud of myself if I try to follow the _______ classroom birthday celebrations plan! My teachers will feel proud of me too.

(BLUMENFELD, E., USED WITH PERMISSION)

Class visitors: Another class

Who?

☐ Another class—buddies

What can I expect?

☐ We will do a project with them

☐ We might read with them

☐ We will work together

☐ They will want to have a conversation

What is my job?

☐ Be friendly

☐ Work with my buddy

☐ Try to talk with my buddy

☐ Follow the rules of the classroom

☐ Be a student

☐ Participate positively

☐ Try to spend at least five minutes with them

(DYMENT, J.H., USED WITH PERMISSION)

Group conversations

Where?

- ☐ Recess
- ☐ Group
- ☐ Lunch
- ☐ Lunch group
- ☐ Meals
- ☐ Working in groups

What should I do?

- ☐ Face the speaker
- ☐ Whole-body listening
- ☐ I might start a conversation with a question
- ☐ Include everyone
- ☐ Add comments that are on topic
- ☐ Wait for my turn to talk
- ☐ Don't raise my hand

How do I know if it is my turn to talk?

- ☐ A pause in the conversation
- ☐ People will look at me
- ☐ Someone might ask me a question

(DYMENT, J.H., USED WITH PERMISSION)

Book club and rug time

What should I do?

- ☐ Take turns—one person at a time
- ☐ Raise my hand to speak
- ☐ Whole-body listening
- ☐ Face the speaker
- ☐ Be respectful and polite
- ☐ Stay on topic

What should I think about?

- ☐ What should I say?
- ☐ Is this on topic (wait if the comment is off topic)?
- ☐ Does this help move the conversation along?
- ☐ Is this a comment or a question?
- ☐ Is this something the whole class needs to hear?
- ☐ Share the spotlight

(DYMENT, J.H., USED WITH PERMISSION)

What to do if I am upset or someone else is upset

Things to do if someone else is upset (unless they ask for help):

- ☐ Let them be alone
- ☐ Keep doing what I am doing

The reason to let them be alone:

- ☐ They may feel uncomfortable if someone stares or tries to talk with them
- ☐ They may not want to be the center of attention if they are upset
- ☐ They won't know what is going to be said to them and that is stressful

Things I can say to someone else if I am upset and want to be alone:

- ☐ "I'd like to be alone right now"
- ☐ "Can you give me a moment?"

Thing to do if I am upset and need some space:

- ☐ Ask an adult I trust to help me let people know I need some time and space

(BLUMENFELD, E., USED WITH PERMISSION)

When it is cold outside

My name is ________. I am a student in ________ grade at ________ School.

When it is cold outside, I do not like to go to recess. When it is nice outside, I usually go to recess. This year when it was nice out, I did things at recess such as ________ (activity), ________ (activity), and ________ (activity).

At school, my job is to be a student. When it is recess time, being a student means participating in recess. Sometimes, an announcement is made that students will have indoor recess. This means I can do my job inside. Otherwise, recess is always outside. This means I need to do my job outside.

Doing my job as a student outside at recess when it is cold out is not my first choice. My teachers want to help me do my best at being a student. They know I can be a student even when it might feel hard.

My teachers came up with a plan to help me and to show me that they know I am working hard. If I work hard at being a student, and I go to recess for at least ten minutes, then I can come inside and use a laptop during lunch. This means if I go out for at least ten minutes, then I can come in early *and* use a laptop!

When it is cold out, I can use these strategies to help myself get outside:

- ☐ Bundle up! (Wear a coat and warm clothes)
- ☐ Choose what I will do outside before I go

My teachers know that it is hard for me to go to recess in the cold. They will feel proud of me when I try to do my job as a student and go out to recess. I can earn extra laptop time if I go, too!

(BLUMENFELD, E., USED WITH PERMISSION)

Class field trip

Fifth Grade Field Trip to the Boston Nature Center

On Monday, the fifth grade will be visiting the Boston Nature Center.

We are going to the Center to learn about birds. More specifically, we will be learning about:

- ☐ The challenges that migrating birds face on their travels
- ☐ How to identify a bird based on sounds and markings
- ☐ Observing birds in different habitats

Here is what our day will look like:

I will come to school and

- ☐ Have a pretty regular morning with a full morning meeting
- ☐ We will work from 8:30–9:15

Because we will be leaving school at 9:30, we will start to get ready around 9:15, including:

- ☐ Having a snack
- ☐ Using the restroom

At 9:25 we will walk downstairs and get ready to board the bus. We will need to listen carefully to directions about:

- ☐ Where to sit
- ☐ How many students will sit in each row

We will sit in the same seats on the way there and the way back, unless teachers decide to make changes.

We should arrive at the Center around 10:00. We will all meet together for about 15 minutes while people from the Center welcome us and give us some information about the day.

During this time, it is expected that we:

- ☐ Sit with our group
- ☐ Listen to the experts from the Center

After the welcome, we will split into two big groups. One group will go to the "Migration Challenge." At this location, students will discover challenges faced by migrating birds. This will be for about 40 minutes. During this time, it is expected that we stay with our group, keep a safe body, and participate positively.

The other group will go on a Bird Walk. This group will split into two smaller groups and each group will have a leader from the Center. For the bird walk, students will have a chance to use binoculars to search for birds in different habitats. We will also use field guides and sounds to identify as many birds as we can.

During this time, it is also expected that we:

- ☐ Stay with our group
- ☐ Participate positively
- ☐ Keep a safe body

After our group goes to one of these places, the groups switch and go to the other. Students will spend 40 minutes or so at each activity.

After this, students will all gather back together for a game called "Migration Madness." Classroom rules apply all day, including during this game time.

We will have a final wrap-up together back in the Center, and then we will thank our guides and get back on the bus around 12:30. We should be back to school around 1:00.

(BLUMENFELD, E., USED WITH PERMISSION)

Behavioral expectations: Community

Your child will be most successful when you explicitly teach her the behavioral expectations of various contexts in the community. Be sure to note the rules in your guide.

Professionals with whom your child interacts may discuss some of their expectations for behavior. Some places you visit may have rules posted that all guests need to follow. In some situations, neither of these things will happen. You should be sure to go over expectations in an explicit, visual format in order to ensure that your child with AS understands.

- You can define some community behavioral expectations on your own.
- Others, such as rules for camp, you will want to develop in conjunction with individuals who support your child in the community.
- Use the list and examples provided in this section as a springboard to think about behavioral expectations that would support your child in every context in which she participates in the community.
- Once you create community expectations unique to your child's needs and situation, preview them with your child and have a copy available for review in each situation and environment until she integrates the expectation and demonstrates mastery.
- When you create your expectations toolbox, put one expectation per page with succinct, simple, accessible instructions. Less writing per page helps the child with AS avoid visual overload.

General behavioral expectations in the community may include:

- ☐ Riding:
  - ☐ On a bus
  - ☐ In a car
  - ☐ On a plane
  - ☐ On a train
- ☐ When at:
  - ☐ A restaurant
  - ☐ An ice skating rink
  - ☐ A toy store
  - ☐ A drug store
  - ☐ A department store
  - ☐ A library
  - ☐ A birthday party
  - ☐ A park
  - ☐ A beach
  - ☐ A movie
- ☐ Running errands
- ☐ Vacations (define rules for various environments and activities)
- ☐ Religious or spiritual venues
- ☐ When eating as someone's guest

(LIST DEVELOPED WITH DYMENT, J.H.)

Behavioral expectations for contexts involving professionals in the community may include:

- ☐ Extra-curricular activities:
  - ☐ Sports
  - ☐ Drama class
  - ☐ Music class
- ☐ Working with AS professionals (at their office):
  - ☐ Psychologist
  - ☐ Psychiatrist
  - ☐ Neuropsychologist
  - ☐ Social worker
  - ☐ Coach

- [ ] Social pragmatics specialist
    - [ ] Occupational therapist
    - [ ] Executive functioning specialist
    - [ ] ABA specialist
- [ ] Camp (explain rules for various environments and activities)
- [ ] Field trips

(LIST DEVELOPED WITH DYMENT, J.H.)

The lists and explanations below serve as examples of community behavioral expectations, which you can consider a springboard to make your own lists. Feel free to:

- use the space provided in the template checklists you have downloaded to add points to the expectations
- or create entirely new behavioral expectations that would support your child
- include both explicit behavioral expectations and those that are unstated (the "hidden curriculum").

Examples: Behavioral expectations in the community

Car expectations

- [ ] Try to keep your hands on your lap or on your toys and have a quiet body when sitting in the back seat:
    - [ ] Touching other kids, unbuckling seatbelts, and touching doors or windows are unexpected behaviors and can make others angry with you or not want to be in the car with you
- [ ] Try to keep your legs down and still:
    - [ ] Kicking the seat in front of you is an unexpected behavior and can make others angry with you or not want to be in the car with you.
- [ ] Use a Level 3 voice:
    - [ ] Yelling in the car is unexpected and can make others angry with you or not want to be in the car with you

Behavioral expectations in different environments

Environment/ place	Expected behavior	Positive consequences
Ice skating rink	☐ Keep your body safe (try to avoid bumping into people) ☐ You must have skates on when you are on the ice ☐ Skate in the same direction as everyone else ☐ Steer clear of the boards ☐ Get off of the ice to eat snacks	☐ Keeps everyone safe and happy

Bus (city bus or school bus)	☐ Do not scream or yell
	☐ Do a quiet activity:
	  ☐ Read a book
	  ☐ Listen to music with headphones
	  ☐ Just sit quietly
	☐ Do not disturb others
		☐ Calm bus ride

Toy store	☐ Do not grab something and yell loudly that you want it ☐ Pay for what you take ☐ Don't try to buy a bunch of toys	☐ Others feel happy ☐ You feel good ☐ Calm toy store trip
Park	☐ Run around and play ☐ Do not feed the wild animals ☐ Respect the play equipment ☐ Use equipment the way it is supposed to be used ☐ Respect the grounds and plantings	☐ Makes you happy ☐ You have fun ☐ Equipment will be there next time ☐ You can go again ☐ Others will feel happy
Recess	☐ Keep a calm voice ☐ Stay in the playground area ☐ Talk ☐ Play a game ☐ Run around ☐ Hang out on a bench ☐ Include others ☐ Use words if a situation gets upsetting	☐ Keeps you safe ☐ Get exercise and fresh air ☐ Everyone gets a chance to do what he/she wants

Beach	☐ Wear sunscreen	☐ Keeps skin healthy
	☐ Keep sand on the beach	☐ Shows respect for others
	☐ Shake off your towel away from others and close to the ground	☐ Keeps you safe
	☐ In the water, stay close to shallow parts	
	☐ Respect the lifeguards and their rules	
	☐ Stay close enough to family/ friends so you can still see them	

(BLUMENFELD, E., FROM CLASS DISCUSSION, USED WITH PERMISSION)

Eating as someone's guest

Use all general table manners and:

- ☐ Stand behind your seat until the hostess sits, then sit
- ☐ Make only positive comments about the food
- ☐ Say "Thank you" when served
- ☐ Wait until everyone is served and the hostess raises her fork before eating
- ☐ Ask for an item to be passed—do not reach over people
- ☐ Say "Thank you" to the hostess after the meal
- ☐ Talk with everyone at the table, particularly the two people seated next to you
- ☐ Offer to help clear items off the table

Behavioral expectations with psychologist

Check-in

- ☐ Identify physical or emotional stress:
    - ☐ Tired
    - ☐ Sick
    - ☐ Angry
    - ☐ Annoyed
- ☐ High points and low points:
    - ☐ High points help see that life is not so black and white
    - ☐ Low points—can address in session
- ☐ Homework—address any lows in the session

Suggest or collaborate on a plan to address physical or emotional stress before proceeding

- ☐ Mindfulness
- ☐ Snack
- ☐ Chat about high points of past week
- ☐ Talk about distress of the day
- ☐ Short nap

When I do not want to discuss a topic or event

- ☐ Tell why
- ☐ Collaborate on a solution
- ☐ When do I think I can talk about the topic?

Review agenda

- ☐ Choose "choice time" activity
- ☐ Discuss focus of session
- ☐ Check agenda item when complete

During the session

- ☐ Tell the psychologist directly if I notice I am becoming overwhelmed, angry, or agitated
- ☐ When I can, tell the psychologist I need a mindfulness break. When I don't independently, the psychologist will ask me to take a break and I will
- ☐ I will let the psychologist know if I understand what she is saying and if I agree
- ☐ If something is distracting me, I will tell the psychologist and we will make a plan to address it so I can refocus on the session. The distraction plan could include:
    - ☐ Adding a reminder onto the agenda
    - ☐ Deciding what we will do, when, and for how long

End of session

- ☐ Homework assignment
- ☐ Special interest time—end with fun

(PSYCHOLOGIST, USED WITH PERMISSION)

Behavioral expectations at camp

Rules for morning drop-off

- ☐ We find our group
- ☐ We look at the schedule
- ☐ We do not climb the trees
- ☐ We do not bend the branches
- ☐ We stay with the group
- ☐ We use safe bodies
- ☐ We use safe words
- ☐ We listen to our counselors
- ☐ We ask a counselor if we need help

(PARTRIDGE, M., USED WITH PERMISSION)

Bus rules

- ☐ We sit where our counselors tell us
- ☐ We stay in our seats
- ☐ We keep our bottom on seat
- ☐ We use safe bodies
- ☐ We use safe words
- ☐ We listen to our counselors
- ☐ We ask a counselor if we need help

(PARTRIDGE, M., USED WITH PERMISSION)

Walking rules

- ☐ We line up single file
- ☐ We stay behind the line leader
- ☐ We watch for the red light/ green light signs
- ☐ We always stay with the group
- ☐ We use safe bodies
- ☐ We use safe words
- ☐ We listen to our counselors
- ☐ We ask a counselor if we need help

(PARTRIDGE, M., USED WITH PERMISSION)

Swim rules

- ☐ We follow the swim checklist
- ☐ When a counselor says we are ready, we begin to swim
- ☐ We always stay with the group
- ☐ We use safe bodies like watching where we jump
- ☐ We use safe words
- ☐ We listen to our counselors, especially when they give us the countdown to end of swim
- ☐ We ask a counselor if we need help

(PARTRIDGE, M., USED WITH PERMISSION)

Group activity rules

- ☐ We always stay with our group
- ☐ We listen to the directions of the activity leader
- ☐ We try our best to do the activity
- ☐ We participate in the activity
- ☐ If we need a break, we ask our counselor
- ☐ We use safe bodies
- ☐ We use safe words
- ☐ We ask a counselor if we need help

(PARTRIDGE, M., USED WITH PERMISSION)

Rules for afternoon pick-up

- ☐ We walk safely to pick-up
- ☐ We stay with the group
- ☐ We do not climb the trees
- ☐ We do not bend the branches
- ☐ We use safe bodies
- ☐ We use safe words
- ☐ We listen to our counselors
- ☐ We ask a counselor if we need help

(PARTRIDGE, M., USED WITH PERMISSION)

How to use the toolbox

Now that you have created your behavioral expectations toolbox, you will be able to:

- decrease stress and confusion for your child by clarifying and helping him or her align behavior to expectations in every environment in which he or she interacts

- implement structure for home education and have guidelines for a unified approach to parenting
- create more productive and pleasant relationships between your child and their teachers and service providers now that expectations in their environments are explicit
- help your child generalize skills by using the same strategies in multiple environments.

Chapter 7

Important Adults

As Alexander's mother, I am one of the most important adults in his life. With a tremendous investment of love and energy over time, Alexander and I have developed a very solid relationship. I now understand the keys to interacting positively with him after years of learning from my successes and my mistakes. I have developed a sense of when to listen, use humor, remain firm, express compassion, take a stand, educate honestly, counsel, be quiet, and walk away. I know the nuances of his moods, expressions, and demeanor. Our interactions are rather like dancing. I naturally have the rhythm and have learned the steps, but we still sometimes trip or step on each other's toes.

My understanding, flexible, and accommodating nature has many upsides for Alexander, but a downside is that he gets confused and anxious when other adults interact with him with a slightly different style. For example, I sometimes negotiate with Alexander. Usually he starts homework at 3:30 in the afternoon. Occasionally, when it is 3:30, Alexander tells me that he just needs to finish watching a video clip. I recognize that transitions from a preferred to a non-preferred activity are difficult, and I might tell him that I will give him five minutes to complete the clip but he must begin homework at 3:35. I set a timer for five minutes, and at 3:35 he starts without complaint. I have found this accommodation effective in many situations. I have the luxury of time and structure to offer it, which I realize other environments don't always have.

When other adults aren't able to negotiate with Alexander, problems sometimes occur. If another adult takes a firm stand and enforces that Alexander must do as he's been told after the first request in the general course of the day, Alexander often perceives the adult as mean. He is expecting the dance that happens with me to happen with other people, and when they don't or can't comply he gets thrown off. Because I interact differently with him at home, he receives the other adult's way of interacting as an unexpected affront. He gets furious and expresses his anger. The adult often, in turn, perceives him as disrespectful or rude.

The problems are that Alexander does not understand the other adult's perspective, the adult does not grasp Alexander's perspective, and Alexander does not yet know how to navigate different relationship styles. This dynamic is a common issue for us. I have found that we resolve it most efficiently when I serve as the translator. I explain the adult's perspective to Alexander and vice versa, assess and address the components of the struggle, remain calm, and access my best collaborating skills (see Chapter 4).

This story provides just one example of how adults' lack of knowledge about Alexander can lead to negative social or emotional outcomes. The purpose of this chapter is to help you think about how to share the right information with both your child and important adults in his life to achieve positive outcomes.

Parents' role with important adults

As a case manager, your role as it relates to important adults is the following:

- Develop a solid, trusting relationship with your child and help foster your child's relationships with important adults at home.
- Make sure that your child's teacher or special educator (your point person at school) understands your child and that your child and his point person have every tool necessary to build a healthy, productive relationship. You can support this process through collaboration and communication (see Chapter 4).
- Advocate for important adults in the community to forge a supportive relationship with your child. Educate your child about the adult in the community and vice versa.

This chapter and your guide will facilitate this process.

Important adults in every environment

Preview important information about your child with adults

Share your guide

Share pertinent parts of your guide with adults new to your child at home, at school, and in the community. Your guide will give these adults the tools and information they need to begin their relationship with your child in a positive way.

Anticipate potential issues

Anticipate where miscommunications may occur based on your child's unique profile. Communicate with important adults in your child's life to increase understanding so they do not over-react to your child.

Remember that preventative work is less burdensome than repair work. Identify the issues that have the potential for most harm for the relationship and proactively address these points. For example, if your child is over-reactive to touch, you might highlight that adults will severely damage the relationship if they touch your child. Or, if your child is like Alexander, you could explain that your child has a common misperception that teachers that set strict limits are mean, and he will respond in kind. Your guide will help you present these important points.

Preview information about new adults with your child

Use tools to orient your child to adults at home

You will find tools in this chapter's Parents Take Charge section that will help you orient your child to adults at home. These tools will tell your child about which adult is coming into the house, what the adult's role is, what the child should know about the adult, and what the child's role is when interacting with the adult.

Use tools to orient your child to new teachers at school

You will find tools in this chapter's Parents Take Charge section that will help you introduce your child to new important adults at school. These tools tell the child about what the teacher's classroom looks like, what his or her teaching style is, how the teacher helps to keep students organized, how it sounds in his or her classroom, and what the child's role is in the classroom.

Use tools to orient your child to important adults in the community

You will find tools in the Parents Take Charge section that introduce your child to important adults in the community. These tools tell your child what the professional's job is, why he sees the professional, and what his role is.

Educate your child about different styles of relationships

The goal is to teach your child how to interact successfully with many different types of people. Relationships with different adults can look and feel different.

For example, parents in the same household often have different styles that children need to learn. In our home, I embrace schedules and consistency, but I also like to be wacky and fun. I enjoy meditation, yoga, cultural events, art, learning, and talking about feelings and deep topics. I strive to be emotionally calm. I am devoted to helping my children through struggles. Interpersonal relationships are my priority. Family is very important, and I am very social, too. My husband, Michael, is more spontaneous. Sports and being athletic are important to him. Fun is a priority. He relates to our boys more through doing activities with them than talking. He likes people, but does not need to socialize or interact as much as I do. He is understanding, yet firm. He has a sense of humor and loves to laugh, but he is not wacky. He can be edgy—if someone crosses the line, he reacts. He prefers blunt honesty to social niceties. These differences don't make some relationship styles right and some wrong.

You can help your child be more understanding if an adult doesn't treat him in a manner that he considers "just right." This skill will support him in every environment. He will ultimately integrate this skill through the support of the tools in this chapter and ongoing communication and education in multiple environments.

Repair relationships

If a relationship between your child and an important adult is damaged, start by dissecting the components of the relationship struggle. In the example I gave at the beginning of the chapter concerning negotiation, the components of the struggle are that Alexander and the adult do not understand each other's perspectives and the adult and I have different styles. The teacher's intent is to get work done. She is communicating directly and efficiently as she might with any other student. Alexander perceives her intent as mean and reacts on his perception by making rude comments. The teacher may understandably want to give Alexander a consequence for his rudeness. However, these consequences exacerbate the situation and make Alexander angrier.

Communication from a parent can be helpful at this stage. With parental intervention, the teacher can recognize that the child's rudeness is a manifestation of his misperception. Rather than potentially escalating the situation by reacting with a consequence, the teacher could respond in a manner that would educate the child and build understanding and trust. For example, she might acknowledge that she is doing work differently than the child is used to, explain why, and emphasize that she is on his side and wants to help him work like a student.

We want to give both the child and the teacher the opportunity to understand each other so that they can both operate at their best. When the child recognizes that the teacher's style is different, understands why, and feels supported, his anxiety will decrease and he will be able to change his behavior. When the teacher understands that the rudeness isn't personal, she can react differently. Your role is to help each of them understand the other's perspective.

Highlight the value of human connection

When a typically developing child has a positive interaction with his aunt or his teacher, he smiles and walks away feeling positive. He can make the connection that because he forged close relationships with these adults, he will likely build a close relationship with other adults such as his babysitter or his camp counselor.

Your child with AS is unlikely to make this connection on her own, so there is value in teaching this concept in an overt way. First, she builds close relationships with her family members, and she might notice a warm, fuzzy feeling. She can take that template and use it as a model to build similar relationships with other people.

For example, I can teach Alexander that when he talks with his aide about movies, there is more value than simply engaging in his special interest. By sharing his special interest with another person, he also gets to experience a warm sense of connection. I can help him see that once he learns how to develop this type of relationship with one adult outside of his family, he can develop a similar relationship with other adults in different environments.

Positively reinforce your child regarding important adults

You can positively reinforce your child's behavior when he interacts in an expected way with important adults. For example, at home, I would use the tools in the home section of the Parents Take Charge portion of this chapter to educate Alexander about interacting with house visitors. I might reward Alexander with five minutes of extra computer time if he sits down and interacts with my friend and me for fifteen minutes using the guidance I provided. At school, your child's special educator might reward your child for interacting well with the principal after providing a similar education. You can help your child learn how to relate with important adults when you positively reinforce what he does well. You can provide direct, honest, non-judgmental feedback about the behaviors that do not work when interacting with important adults.

Important adults at home

Relationships within the home are very important for children with AS. Parents, relatives, and babysitters can both provide acceptance for the child's unique AS expression and teach him how to interact with his world. The work that parents put into helping their child understand and build relationships will directly shape his future interpersonal success and happiness.

Parent–child relationship

Children with AS need a safe, nurturing, and predictable person in their life for many of the same reasons neurotypical children do. The difference is that children with AS are more dependent on their parents for a longer period of time, and the parenting role is more involved and complicated. Parents have an intuitive and highly nuanced understanding of their child's communication style and needs. They can help the child interpret her world and educate anyone with whom she interacts about her unique profile. Parents should be an anchor for their child through early childhood, school, and into adulthood.

The role of other important adults

In addition to parents, other adults such as aunts, uncles, and grandparents can play a significant role in supporting children with AS with social growth. These adults do not necessarily have to be involved in setting limits and disciplining the child, so their relationships are often free from some of the conflict that can naturally occur between parents and their children. Family members can engage the child with AS through his particular special interests. For example, when Alexander's special interest was whales, my in-laws took him on whale watches, read him whale books, bought him whale toys and stuffed animals, brought him to a new aquarium that housed beluga whales, and supported his whale stationery sale. This dynamic opens opportunities for connection, learning, and positive interactions.

You can also point out to your child that we have different types of relationships with different people. For example, your child may have a favorite aunt and find another aunt grouchy. He will need explicit instruction that he still must be polite to the grouchy aunt even if he doesn't feel the same way about her.

Important adults at school

Relationships with teachers and other staff members

Individuals with AS often miss the social expectations of students when interacting with teachers and staff members. They can get themselves in trouble by making social mistakes and inadvertently offending people. A goal is to educate the child with AS about the hidden rules, such as that we all have different roles and that we must behave in accordance with these roles. A child may not identify himself as a "student" or the adult as his "teacher," and may not have an understanding of what those roles mean. In addition, a single person may perform different roles at different times, which can be confusing. For example, a teacher may yell orders to get the group to behave in a way that allows them to get things done. Most kids forgive the teacher for yelling because they understand that. A child with AS may perceive the teacher as being mean because he doesn't recognize that her role is to keep the group on task.

A problem could then arise when that teacher gives him a directive. He may feel confused about why he needs to listen to this adult and angry that she is trying to lead him. He may believe that his parents can tell him what to do, but no one else can. He may not understand that the role of the teacher is to instruct, guide, and support and the role of the student is to learn, follow guidance, and be respectful. In this case, proactive, clear, and simple social education about the expectations of student/teacher interaction expectations helps the child avoid an unnecessary and unpleasant misunderstanding with his teacher.

Similarly, many students with AS don't know that there is a hierarchy among the staff at school and that they should be more deferential to their principal than to their teacher. When the staff bring the principal into a more serious situation, a student with AS may perceive it simply as two adults telling him to do exactly the same thing. The child with AS may not recognize that the principal is more likely to talk to his parents, make a decision about whether he can attend certain events, or determine if he can go on to the next grade. Students with AS have the ability to respond in a more expected way and experience greater harmony and success when they are explicitly taught the hidden curriculum.

Classroom visitors

Children with AS often experience visitors to their classroom as yet another stressful transition to cope with. Visitors might include the speech and language pathologist, occupational therapist, substitute teacher, principal, educational consultant, outside psychologist, or buddies from another grade. Children with AS benefit from understanding who will visit, when, and the purpose of the visit. They interact with visitors most successfully when someone previews this information and they understand the behavioral expectations. For example, Alexander's special educator in fourth and fifth grades sat down with the class to preview how to interact with substitute teachers. The class discussed that the teacher may not enforce the same rules as the regular teachers. The behavioral expectations that they agreed upon were the following:

- Follow the substitute teacher's rules.
- Do not interrupt, even if the teacher follows different rules (he or she may have permission from the regular teacher).
- When the substitute does something that is different from how it is usually done, either:
  - » tell the person nicely that this is not what we usually do
  - » go along with it.
- Treat the substitute with respect.
- Use the class contract (rules regarding how to treat others) to help make the guest teacher feel welcome.

Whenever it was possible, the special educator let the class know in advance when they would have a substitute teacher. This type of preview helped prepare the class to interact successfully with their substitute teacher. Once they developed the tool, they had the tool available to preview every time the class had a substitute teacher.

Important adults in the community

A number of factors can influence your child's interactions with important adults in the community. You can play a major role in supporting these relationships by:

- selecting the best professionals and activities to address your child's profile-related struggles and needs
- communicating and collaborating with the important adults
- evaluating therapies and activities and understanding resistance

- scheduling with balance and peace in mind
- explicitly educating your child about his activities and important adults
- priming your child for successful interactions with adults later in life.

Select professionals and activities

Throughout the course of your child's life, you will likely engage with a variety of outside professionals to support your child's specific needs. As a case manager, you can determine which professionals best serve your child's struggles and collaborate with the professional to support maximum therapeutic results. The following list and descriptions of professional service providers can assist you with your decisions. You can utilize the professional's guidance to support your home environment and to share information with the school.

You can collaborate more effectively with professional service providers by sharing the guide you create. Professionals think broadly and specifically about their AS client and benefit from a comprehensive picture of the child's unique profile, successful interventions, and AS-specific social teaching. The guide decreases the time the professionals need to invest in getting to know the child and provides the keys to successful interaction. Professionals will more quickly know how best to target their approach for greatest therapeutic impact.

Educational consultant

School districts may hire outside experts to consult with the school if a student with AS is not making effective progress and the staff and teachers think greater support or knowledge would be useful. Educational consultants seem to be most successful when the school district pays for the consultant's services. The staff and teachers understand that the expert is working for them and is not overly influenced by the parents' perspective. Staff and teachers trust that the relationship is honest and direct. Under this arrangement, they also have input into the consultant's communication with parents. Parents and consultants can make better progress when they communicate well and earn each other's trust (see Chapter 4). The team's shared confidence in the consultant's expertise can relieve stress for everyone and strengthen working relationships. When both the school and parents believe that the consultant is working for the best interest of everyone involved and is achieving results, the consultant is often given the flexibility to focus on the areas that need the most support.

Families can opt to pay for a consultant if the school either doesn't have the resources available or doesn't feel the service is necessary. Initially, this dynamic makes the consultant's work more challenging because access to the school will be more limited and communication with the teachers will likely be less open and trusting. While not the ideal set-up, this option is a good second choice because the service can still significantly help a student who is not thriving at school.

Neuropsychologist or occupational therapist (assessment)

After an initial evaluation to determine eligibility, the school district is responsible for assessing the student with AS every third year as long as the child continues to meet the criteria for service delivery. Parents may want to engage an outside professional, such as a neuropsychologist or an occupational therapist, to further test their child if they are not satisfied with the scope or results of the school-delivered assessments. Data gathered from testing is very important because it helps inform best intervention strategies and academic approaches for the child with AS.

Assessment reports vary greatly in terms of quality and thoroughness. Often the reports list a number of recommendations for the child with AS, but they do not prioritize their importance. Parents should take advantage of report feedback sessions, during which the professional will present his or her report and walk parents through the findings, to gain maximum benefit from the assessment process. Parents can ask the professional to prioritize recommendations for their child with AS so they understand what issues they need to address immediately versus those that can wait. They can use the feedback session as an opportunity to ensure that the evaluator answers their questions. Parents can take the most important points and input them into a template (see "Report feedback tool" in the Important adults: Community section of Parents Take Charge) for easy sharing and access.

Psychologist or social worker

Parents might consider hiring a psychologist or social worker who specializes in AS, because children with AS are often emotionally vulnerable and family, school, and community dynamics can be complex and intense. The quality of life for individuals and families can improve when a professional guides and educates the family about AS and addresses their individual needs. Sharing your guide will provide a longitudinal perspective that will maximize the benefits of working with such a professional.

Therapists working directly with children with AS should have experience with or specific interest in working with individuals on the autism spectrum.

Therapists trained in cognitive behavioral therapy are often good choices because of their experience treating anxiety. The thoughts of children with AS often get in the way of their success, and a professional who understands how to reverse counterproductive thinking can be very helpful.

Children with AS may not need to see a therapist on a regular basis. At times therapy is not very useful, depending on the issues at hand. For example, some children with AS can talk well, appear to have great insight, and be self-referential, but they are unable to put their insights into practice. A therapist would likely be helpful to children like this. On the other hand, some children with AS cannot use therapists to help with their social issues until they are much older. These individuals learn later in life how to reflect, and to think about and try new strategies.

Therapy might be helpful when a child is beginning to understand his diagnosis and experiencing grief about not being typical. They may also need help with specific anxiety issues. Both children with AS and parents can weigh in on therapy goals with the therapist at any time in the course of treatment.

Home-based Applied Behavior Analysis (ABA) specialist

ABA providers emphasize that their approach is validated by scientific research. They examine the antecedents and consequences that tend to encourage or reduce specific behaviors and develop treatment plans by measuring and analyzing the child's responses to relevant changes in their environments. Prior to school age, parents often receive these services as part of an early intervention (EI) program. School-age children can get home-based ABA services through the school district if the team recommends it through the Individualized Education Program (IEP) process.

Therapeutic services, specialized groups, and summer camps

Various interventions available in the community provide a different kind of support for children with AS than most schools offer. Therapeutic horseback riding and summer camps for children with AS are some examples. These programs allow children to participate in activities that might be overwhelming without AS-specific support.

Social Thinking® or social skills groups

Most children with AS benefit from participating in social pragmatic or Social Thinking® groups that target their particular social impairments. Social skills assessments and observations by parents and clinicians can begin to uncover the child's specific needs. Parents can also share part of their guide with the child's group leader in an introductory meeting to help the leader quickly grasp the most salient aspects of the child's AS profile. When discerning the best match for their child, parents should ensure that the program's philosophy is aligned with their family perspective. If the child's major deficit involves specific social skills such as turn-taking or asking for help, then a social skills group would be most useful. Alternatively, if the child struggles most with his or her approach and thinking about social interactions such as perspective-taking and putting social interaction into context, then a group utilizing Michelle Garcia Winner's Social Thinking® approach may best address his or her needs.

Grouping compatible children together can make a major difference in the effectiveness of the sessions. Program coordinators should consider the whole child and put in the same groups children with similar perspective-taking skills, cognitive levels, and interests. It is also helpful to achieve a balance between extroverts and introverts. Groups created with intention will function better than those created by simply matching the next six 12-year-olds that sign up with the organization.

After a child with AS participates in his weekly social skills or Social Thinking® group, his leader commonly will e-mail parents a summary of the meeting. Parents can integrate the tools and concepts into their home life to help generalize the information. They can also forward the e-mails to the child's special education teacher for potential use at school. As we've learned in previous chapters, best results occur when all settings coordinate social learning utilizing the same tools and language.

Occupational therapy (service delivery)

Occupational therapy is important for children with AS whose sensory systems have a profound impact on their ability to stay calm and go about their daily lives. As we will discuss further in Chapter 8, an occupational therapist can evaluate a child's sensory profile and construct an individualized sensory diet. Once the sensory diet is developed, parents can share it with the child's support team to ensure that his sensory needs are monitored and supported throughout the day.

Occupational therapists work with children with a variety of diagnoses and challenges. Not all clinicians have experience working with children on the autism spectrum. The best therapist–child matches occur when the occupational therapist has experience with and interest in AS. When meeting with the intake coordinator, parents can explain what type of individual their child works with most effectively. For example, they might say that their child works best with someone who takes a slow approach, provides structure, uses visual supports, and talks quietly, rather than with someone who has high energy and can be impulsive. When parents meet the occupational therapist assigned to their child, they can use the presentation they created from the workbook to succinctly explain their child's unique profile.

Psychiatrist

There are no medications for the core deficits of autism. However, psychiatrists can support children with AS by treating comorbid symptoms such as anxiety, irritability, impulsivity, depression, and attention issues. This intervention can make a significant difference in an child's ability to access the academic and social curriculum at school.

Extra-curricular activities

Parents should not expect that extra-curricular activity leaders have the training to work with the AS population. Collaborators within the child's school can often make suggestions about which extra-curricular activity providers work well with children with AS and which ones to avoid. Once parents decide which activity will be the best fit for their child, they can give the leader a short list of what helps their child.

Schedule therapies and activities for balance and peace

Children with AS cannot access professionals' support when they, their parents, and their family are too stressed by the schedule. In my zeal to do as much as I could to support Alexander, I developed a schedule that overwhelmed all of us. When Alexander was in kindergarten and first grade, I scheduled tennis, a psychologist appointment, occupational therapy, play dates, and social pragmatics for every week. I scheduled play dates and appointments for Will, and I had my own full life. Though I had great intentions of doing all that I could for everyone, I did not realize that I overdid it. Alexander's experience in each environment started to suffer. He was asked to discontinue OT and we had to cut back on his therapy appointments. He could not access all of the great therapies and activities because he had too much on his plate.

Parents should monitor and tweak their child's balance of therapies and extra-curricular activities on an ongoing basis. We all run the risk of over-scheduling our children with AS. We can expect some resistance from them about going to all activities. The key is to differentiate whether the resistance is about the child being truly overloaded or suffering from anxiety about a particular activity. If the child is consistently overwhelmed by a therapy or extra-curricular activity, that may be a sign that it is time to discontinue it. If the child is anxious, you may be able to help him work through the anxiety and ultimately be successful.

You may not always know which activities call for perseverance. You can gauge your child's reactions not only prior to the activity, but during and after as well to evaluate how it is working. Remember that children with AS tend to give more weight to what happened at the end of an event. For example, your child's camp day may have gone well overall, but if he struggled at the end of the day he could leave the camp thinking that it was horrific and that he never wants to return. You will want to go over the day with your child to understand the issues he did have and try to head off future problems, but you probably don't want to discontinue an activity if most of it goes well.

Parents can develop their child's schedule in such a way that balances his needs with those of the parents and siblings. Parents should not give up their own personal interests and involvements in order to take their child to every therapy available. They can choose therapies and activities based on the degree of positive impact they have on the child with AS. A risk is that parents can fall into the habit of going to a specific therapy every week regardless of results. If the benefits seem to be diminishing, parents should discuss with the clinician and decide whether it is time to discontinue.

Helping your child access support from service providers

Children with AS may experience meetings with important adults in the community such as service providers as yet another stressful transition with which they must cope. Your child will be better able to access support from service providers when he understands who the professional is, why he sees the professional, and his responsibilities when meeting. The Parents Take Charge section will help you easily communicate this information to your child in a visual format.

This process also primes children with AS for later interactions with these adults. Children with AS are often compliant about going to service providers and interacting with other adults in the community when they are younger. However, they often become resistant and don't want to go when they become teenagers. If parents don't think about helping the child at an early age make the connection about *why* they participate in various therapies and explaining the adult's and child's roles when interacting, a problem often arises later. If you haven't primed your child with this information, he might reject the help he needs in later years because he doesn't see the need to go and doesn't understand why he goes. He may start feeling bad about himself, and the common knee-jerk reaction is to reject the support.

AANE "Wallet Card"

Your child may come into contact with important adults in the community in emergency situations. He may feel scared or unsafe based on the nature of the situation. His interactions with first responders such as police officers, fire fighters, and medical technicians could go poorly as a result of his fear. The Asperger/Autism Network provides a tool called a "wallet card" on their website (www.aane.org under Articles and Resources). This card will help your child share information about his disability and how to interact with him. You can write the names and numbers of two people whom the first responders can call to help. The AANE website gives explicit instructions about this tool and how to coach your child in these situations. This tool can proactively prevent potentially traumatic interactions with first responders and support everyone in emergency situations.

Other Important Adults in the Community

This section of the chapter has focused mostly on your child's interactions with various professionals and service providers, but we also wanted to provide some guidance about adults with whom he or she will come into contact in daily life. With important adults in the community, your child will likely encounter less role clarity than at home, at school, or at therapy appointments. For example, the clerk at the coffee shop may help you politely, but not talk with you when you see him on the street after his shift. The baseball coach may also be a family friend. You can help your child navigate these relational changes by providing explicit education about how his role and adults' roles can change as contexts change in every environment.

Celebrate successful relationships at home, at school, and in the community

One of the most beautiful gifts that Alexander has brought me is the people that have both come into our lives and risen to the occasion as a result of his AS. Exceptional people related to home, school, and the community have impacted our lives profoundly. This group includes family, close friends, babysitters, special educators, general educators, coaches, speech and language pathologists, social workers, aides, occupational therapists, psychologists, educational consultants, neuropsychologists, psychiatrists, and graduate school professors. These people have formed the village that has helped us raise Alexander. They have worked through Alexander's crises and celebrated his successes with us. They have both educated and guided us about how to support Alexander and provided the support themselves. They have joined us in this journey through honest communication and collaboration. Each person has offered his or her unique gifts generously, and they have helped Alexander and me grow. I express my gratitude to them often. I wonder how I can properly convey the depth of my appreciation for such precious and valued gifts, but I still try.

Throughout your child's youth, you will undoubtedly also encounter remarkable adults who understand your child and interact with him in a manner that supports him and helps him grow. They will go the extra mile to help him. I encourage you to celebrate and acknowledge these individuals, too. They can impact your child's life in extraordinary ways.

Generalization

As you have seen throughout this chapter, the process for helping your child interact effectively with important adults is the same for every environment in which he interacts:

- Preview important information about your child to adults.
- Preview information about new adults with your child.
- Educate your child about different styles of relationships.
- Repair relationships.
- Highlight the value of human connection.
- Positively reinforce your child regarding important adults.

When your child uses the tools for interacting with different adults across all environments, he will develop the skills to interact effectively with different adults, operating with different styles for different reasons.

Parents Take Charge

Creating Your Child's Important Adults Toolbox

These workbook exercises help you educate your child about the important adults in his life at home, at school, and in the community. The tools work as a simple guide for your child and a teaching template and collaboration toolbox for you and the professionals that support him.

Important adults: Every environment

Strategies for developing successful relationships with important adults in every environment

- ☐ Preview important information about your child with adults.
- ☐ Preview important information about adults with your child.
- ☐ Educate your child about different relationship styles.
- ☐ Dissect issues and share each perspective if the relationship gets damaged.
- ☐ Teach your child the value of human connection.
- ☐ Positively reinforce your child regarding important adults.

Important adults: Home

These exercises will help you to understand and articulate the important skills for interacting with adults that will lead your child to independence with navigating relationships with adults at home. Note these tools in your guide.

- Use the list and examples provided in this section as a springboard to think about interaction skills that would support your child in knowing how to relate with important adults at home. If you do not see an important adult interaction skill that is important for your child, simply create one using these examples as models.

- Once you create important adult interaction tools unique to your child's situation, preview them with your child and have a copy available for review in each situation and environment until he integrates the tool and demonstrates mastery.
- Once you create important adult interaction tools unique to your child's needs and situation, parents, babysitters, and anyone else in a home care role can use these tools to teach your child how to master each skill.
- Important adult interaction tools should be introduced one at a time as part of home education.
- Once the child becomes competent with one important adult interaction tool for home, continue practicing it and start teaching another one.
- When you create your important adults toolbox, put one important adult interaction tool per page with succinct, simple, accessible instructions. Less writing on each page helps the child with AS avoid visual overload.
- Parents can further support the process by using video modeling (video someone executing the steps listed here) to both show and describe how to perform the important adult interaction skills.

Important adult interaction tools at home may include:

- ☐ Important adult template
- ☐ Interacting with your mother and father
- ☐ Interacting with a caregiver
- ☐ Interacting with house visitors

Examples: Interacting with important adults at home

The lists below serve as examples of interacting with important adults at home, which you can consider a springboard to making your own lists. Feel free to:

- use the space provided in the template checklists you have downloaded to add points to the lists
- or create entirely new tools that would support your child.

Important adult template

- ☐ Which adult is coming into the house
- ☐ What the adult's role is
- ☐ What the child should know about the adult
- ☐ What the child's role is when interacting with the adult

Interacting with your mother and father

- ☐ Feel free to share what you think and feel, such as:
  - ☐ Opinions
  - ☐ What is upsetting you
  - ☐ What makes you happy
- ☐ Communicate your needs
- ☐ Safe words (Levels 1–3)
- ☐ Safe body
- ☐ Level 2–3 voice

Interacting with a caregiver

- ☐ Safe words (Levels 1–3)
- ☐ Safe body
- ☐ Level 2–3 voice
- ☐ Communicate your needs

Interacting with house visitors

- ☐ Use welcoming words. Communicate you are happy to have them at our house:
  - ☐ Use the social fake if you are not happy to have them at our house
- ☐ Be thoughtful with your actions. For example:
  - ☐ If they spend the night, be quiet in the morning if you wake up first
  - ☐ Create cards to welcome them
  - ☐ Offer them food or drink and get it for them
- ☐ Conversation:
  - ☐ Initiate conversation
  - ☐ Use whole-body listening
  - ☐ Respond when addressed
- ☐ Safe words (Levels 1–3)
- ☐ Safe body
- ☐ Level 2–3 voice

Important adults: School

You and teachers will lay the foundation for success at school when you educate your child about the important adults in his school life. Teachers may discuss some information about important adults at school, and may assume that students are already aware of other information. Regardless of whether teachers talk about important adults, you should cover this topic in an explicit, visual format in order to ensure that your child with AS understands.

- Use the list and examples provided in this section as a springboard to think about important adult tools that would support your child at school.
- Once you create important adult tools unique to your child's needs and situation, preview them with your child and have a copy available for review in each situation until she integrates the expectation and demonstrates mastery.
- When you create your important adults toolbox, put one tool per page with succinct, simple, accessible information or instructions. Less writing per page helps the child with AS avoid visual overload.

Educating your child about important adults at school may include:

- ☐ Educating your child about teachers and staff
- ☐ Previewing new teachers
- ☐ Supporting your child's interaction with teachers and staff
- ☐ Supporting your child's interaction with teachers who usually come into the classroom
- ☐ Education about class visitors
- ☐ Supporting your child's interaction with substitute teachers
- ☐ Discussing with your child: do adults know everything?

Examples: Interacting with important adults at school

The lists and explanations below serve as examples of important adults at school tools, which you can consider a springboard to making your own lists. Work with your child's special educator and/or teachers to define behavioral expectations for every context of your child's school day. Feel free to:

- use the space provided in the template checklists you have downloaded to add points to the tools
- or create entirely new important adults at school tools that would support your child.

Suggestions for educating your child about teachers and staff at school may include:

- Look in your child's school directory or on the school's website for a list of the teachers and staff members at his school and what roles they have to help orient your child to the school community.
- Copy the list of teachers and staff members and their roles into your guide.
- Preview them with your child and review whenever necessary or helpful.
- If you have access to pictures of teachers and staff members, add these to make this tool more effective.

The following are a few examples of teacher and staff member roles that could make up your guide. The full lists can be found in the templates you have downloaded.

Teachers and staff at ________________ School

____________ **School staff**	
Names	**Positions**
	Principal
	Vice Principal
	Secretary
	Pre-K
	K
	1st
	ELL

Teachers and staff at ______________ School

______________ School staff	
Names	**Positions**
	Guidance
	Office Instructional Aide
	Librarian
	Nurse
	Physical Education
	Psychologist
	Special Education
	Technology

Information about ______________ (name of Science, English Language Arts, Social Studies, Science, Math, Health, Music, Art, Foreign Language Teacher)

You can use this tool for every new teacher that your child encounters for every subject to support maximum clarity. This is an excellent tool to use when students transition from year to year (see Chapter 9, Navigating Transitions and Changes.)

About his room

- ☐ His classroom is located ______________
  - ☐ On the __________ floor of the building
  - ☐ Across from the _________ room
  - ☐ In ____________ building
- ☐ His classroom is called ______________ (use name of room)
  - ☐ Science lab
  - ☐ Social studies room
  - ☐ Art studio
  - ☐ Math room
- ☐ Students sit on ____________
  - ☐ Chairs
  - ☐ Stools
  - ☐ The floor
- ☐ Students use ____________
  - ☐ Tables
  - ☐ Desks

- [ ] Each table has __________ (number) of chairs so students can work in a group
  - [ ] The room has a ______________ (special feature)
    - [ ] Reading corner
    - [ ] Safe Spot
    - [ ] Sensory tool area
  - [ ] The ________________ (special feature of the room such as reading corner, Safe Spot, or sensory tool area) contains ______________ (list contents)
    - [ ] Rocking chairs
    - [ ] Wooden chairs
    - [ ] Cushions
    - [ ] Sensory tools
    - [ ] Books
  - [ ] The room has _____________ (special contents)
    - [ ] Plants to make the environment inviting and cozy
    - [ ] Lamps with soft lighting
    - [ ] Homework bins for finished homework
    - [ ] Containers for:
      - [ ] Markers
      - [ ] Crayons
      - [ ] Paper
      - [ ] Scissors
  - [ ] The classroom has ____________ (displays)
    - [ ] Science materials
    - [ ] Posters

About his teaching style

- [ ] His facial expression, body language, and tone of voice are____________
  - [ ] Friendly
  - [ ] Soft
  - [ ] Caring
  - [ ] Enthusiastic
  - [ ] Animated
- [ ] He is passionate about ___________ (subject)
  - [ ] Science
  - [ ] Math
  - [ ] Social Studies

- ☐ English Language Arts
  - ☐ Foreign Language (list specific one)
  - ☐ Health
  - ☐ Physical Education
  - ☐ Music
  - ☐ Art
- ☐ He __________ (describe how he presents himself to students) when teaching
  - ☐ Smiles
  - ☐ Moves his hands
  - ☐ Stands still
- ☐ He knows a lot about ______________ (subject)!
  - ☐ Science
  - ☐ Math
  - ☐ Social Studies
  - ☐ English Language Arts
  - ☐ Foreign Language (list specific one)
  - ☐ Health
  - ☐ Physical Education
  - ☐ Music
  - ☐ Art
- ☐ He speaks ______________ (describe how he speaks)
  - ☐ Loudly
  - ☐ Softly
  - ☐ In a neutral tone
- ☐ When he teaches he ____________________ (describe what he does)
  - ☐ Stands in front of his classroom
  - ☐ Walks around the room
- ☐ He uses ____________ (teaching tool)
  - ☐ Projector
  - ☐ SmartBoard
  - ☐ Chalkboard
- ☐ When kids are working, he ______________ (describe what teacher does)
  - ☐ Walks around to talk to them in groups
  - ☐ Walks around to talk to them individually
  - ☐ Sits quietly at his desk

- [ ] He loves ____________ (words to describe what he loves to do) to ______________ grade students
    - [ ] Reading
    - [ ] Writing
    - [ ] Speaking
- [ ] He wants students to ____________ (describe expectation for class)
    - [ ] Freely make guesses and predictions
    - [ ] Raise hands to answer questions
    - [ ] Call out answers
    - [ ] Sit in seats quietly
- [ ] When he reads books aloud, he uses different tones of voice for different characters
- [ ] He ____________ (describe his demeanor)
    - [ ] Is serious
    - [ ] Is funny
    - [ ] Has a great sense of humor
- [ ] He sometimes ________________ (list special activity) in class
    - [ ] Plays music
    - [ ] Reads books aloud using different tones of voice for different characters
    - [ ] Shows videos
- [ ] He often ______________ (describe how teacher reinforces his students and what is important to him)
    - [ ] Compliments students when they participate in class
    - [ ] Gives students stars when they listen well

How does he help kids stay organized?

Examples might be:

- [ ] Students in his class have ________________ (list school supplies that keep child organized)
    - [ ] Binder
    - [ ] Notebook
    - [ ] Folder
- [ ] He writes things down on the _____________ (chalkboard, projector, whiteboard, etc.) such as:
    - [ ] The agenda for the day
    - [ ] A schedule
    - [ ] Important findings from class
    - [ ] Important information for me to copy
    - [ ] Steps to follow during class

- ☐ Homework assignments
- ☐ Class assignments
- ☐ Directions

☐ He always passes out a class agenda in the form of a checklist so students know what to expect

☐ He encourages students to plan or draw out the story and thoughts on a graphic organizer

☐ He asks students to think about "big ideas" or "themes"

☐ He uses a SmartBoard to:

- ☐ Explain class assignments
- ☐ Show movie clips
- ☐ Discuss assignments

How does it sound in his classroom?

☐ His classroom is usually ________ (describe noise level such as "quiet") because ___________ (explain why the noise level is that way such as "he wants students to think and work calmly")

☐ When the classroom becomes loud, he ______________ (describe teacher's strategy for controlling noise such as "raises his hand to reduce the noise level or to get students' attention. When he raises his hand, my job is to raise my hand too. Then he will know he has my attention")

My job in his classroom

☐ Attend class

☐ Learn ____________ (subject) with

- ☐ _________ (teacher's name)
- ☐ _________ (special educator's name)
- ☐ _________ (aide's name)
- ☐ My classmates

Other things to include

If possible, include pictures of important features of the classroom such as:

☐ Teacher:

- ☐ Teaching class
- ☐ Giving feedback to students

☐ Classroom:

- ☐ Desks
- ☐ Tables

- ☐ Floor seating
- ☐ Chairs
- ☐ Materials displayed in the classroom

☐ Special features in the room:

- ☐ Reading corner
- ☐ Safe Spot
- ☐ Sensory tool area

(CREATED BY HAQ, M., AND MODIFIED BY DYMENT, J.H., USED WITH PERMISSION)

Support your child's interactions with teachers and staff

Where can I expect to see teachers and staff?

- ☐ Out at recess
- ☐ In the hallways
- ☐ In the office
- ☐ At specials
- ☐ In other classrooms
- ☐ During all school events
- ☐ In the computer lab
- ☐ In the cafeteria

My job when I see these teachers:

- ☐ Listen
- ☐ Follow directions
- ☐ Remember class rules
- ☐ Be polite
- ☐ Be flexible
- ☐ Ask questions
- ☐ Say "hi" when they say "hi"

(DYMENT, J.H., USED WITH PERMISSION)

Teachers who usually come into class

Where?

- ☐ Classroom

Who?

- ☐ Speech and language pathologist, ______ (name)
- ☐ Occupational therapist, ________ (name)
- ☐ Language teacher, _________ (name)
- ☐ APE teacher, ___________ (name)
- ☐ Guidance counselor, __________ (name)
- ☐ Principal, __________ (name)

My job when they are in the room:

- ☐ Listen
- ☐ Follow directions
- ☐ Follow class rules
- ☐ Ask questions
- ☐ Be polite
- ☐ Be flexible

(DYMENT, J.H., USED WITH PERMISSION)

Education about class visitors

Who?

- ☐ Teachers from other schools, educational consultants, psychologists, and so on
- ☐ They will probably wear a School Visitor sign around their neck

What can I expect?

- ☐ They will want to watch my teachers
- ☐ They will want to learn how things go in my classroom
- ☐ They probably will not have a conversation with me
- ☐ My teachers will keep our schedule the way it usually is
- ☐ Our routines will be the same (unless noted as a Plan B)

(DYMENT, J.H., USED WITH PERMISSION)

What is my job?

- ☐ Be friendly if someone speaks to me
- ☐ Continue to do my work
- ☐ Follow classroom rules

Interacting with substitute teachers

- ☐ He/she may not enforce the same rules as your regular teacher
- ☐ While he/she is acting as your teacher, you need to follow his/her rules
- ☐ Do not interrupt, even if he/she is following different rules. He/she may have permission from the regular teacher
- ☐ When he/she does something that is different than how it is usually done, you can tell her really nicely that this is not what we usually do, or you can go along with it
- ☐ Treat him/her with respect
- ☐ Use the class contract to help make the guest teacher feel welcome

(BLUMENFELD, E., FROM CLASS DISCUSSION, USED WITH PERMISSION)

Do adults know everything?

Hi! My name is __________ and I'm a student in ________ grade at __________ school.

A lot of times, when I need help with something or if I am wondering about something, I'll ask an adult in my classroom. I would like that person to know the answer to my question and tell it to me. Sometimes that is exactly what happens. Sometimes this doesn't happen and it can be very frustrating.

Most adults do know a lot of things, like how to take care of themselves, how to do their jobs, and how to find help when they need it. The truth is that adults don't know everything. They can get confused and make mistakes. This happens to all people, and it is okay.

All people, children and adults, have things that they don't know about. This is okay. If I ask an adult about something and they do not know the answer, I might feel frustrated but I can try to be patient and remember that adults usually do the best they can, but they don't know everything.

(BLUMENFELD, E., ADAPTED FROM GRAY 2010, USED WITH PERMISSION)

Important adults: Community

Your child will be most successful when you explicitly teach her about the important adults with whom she interacts in various contexts in the community. Be sure to note the rules in your guide.

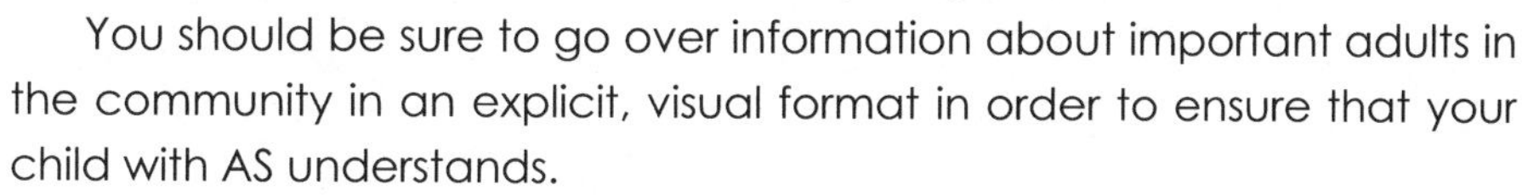

You should be sure to go over information about important adults in the community in an explicit, visual format in order to ensure that your child with AS understands.

- You can define some information about adults in the community on your own.
- Others you may want to develop in conjunction with individuals who support your child in the community.
- Use the list and examples provided in this section as a springboard to think about information about important adults in the community that would support your child in every context in which she participates in the community.
- Once you create community tools unique to your child's needs and situation, preview them with your child and have a copy available for review in each situation until she integrates the content and demonstrates mastery.

When you create your important adults toolbox, put one tool per page with succinct, simple, accessible information and instructions. Less writing per page helps the child with AS avoid visual overload.

Important adults in the community may include:

- psychologist
- coach
- education consultant
- occupational therapist
- psychiatrist
- cognitive behavioral therapist

- speech and language pathologist
- neuropsychologist
- applied behavior analysis therapist
- camp counselor.

Examples: Interacting with important adults in the community

The lists and explanations below serve as examples of important adults in the community tools, which you can consider a springboard to make your own lists. Feel free to:

- use the space provided in the template checklists you have downloaded to add points to the tools
- or create entirely new important adults in the community tools that would support your child.

List of private service providers that currently help your child

This list includes all of the professionals that comprise your child's treatment team. It will organize you and orient your child.

Name	Title	Address	Phone number	E-mail
	Clinical psychologist			
	ASD coach			
	Educational consultant			
	Occupational therapist			
	Psychiatrist			
	Cognitive behavioral therapist			
	Speech and language pathologist			
	Neuropsychologist			
	ABA therapist			

For each professional, create a separate page explicitly explaining:

- ☐ What is the professional's job?
- ☐ Why does the child meet the professional?
- ☐ What is the child's job when meeting?

Clinical psychologist

A psychologist can help you:

- ☐ Sort out your feelings
- ☐ Determine the steps you need to take to feel better

Why do you talk to him?

- ☐ He is someone who accepts you unconditionally
- ☐ He is safe
- ☐ He can help you understand about Asperger's Syndrome
- ☐ He can help you work to solve struggles at school or home or with any relationship
- ☐ You can feel free to share anything with him
- ☐ He wants to help you feel happy and teach you how to feel successful

What is your job?

- ☐ Tell him how you are doing and feeling
- ☐ Discuss anything that is bothering you
- ☐ Discuss anything with which you would like help
- ☐ Answer his questions

ASD coach

A coach listens to what you want in life and advises you how to achieve your goal (Korin 2011).

Why do you talk with her?

- ☐ She can help you do something you have asked for help with: "learning how to not embarrass myself"
- ☐ She can help you understand how your body works and teach you strategies for calming down when you feel upset
- ☐ She can help you learn about friendships

What is your job?

- ☐ Let them support you in reaching your goals
- ☐ Discuss anything with which you would like help
- ☐ Answer their questions

Educational consultant

An educational consultant helps teachers understand you and enhance your social and academic experiences.

Why does he come to your school?

- ☐ He understands what helps people with Asperger's Syndrome do well in school
- ☐ He wants to support you in having a good experience at school
- ☐ He brings great ideas to your teachers to help you

What is your job?

- ☐ Tell him what would help you at school
- ☐ Be polite to him

Occupational therapist

Her job is to support you with sensory integration. This means she will teach you how to get your body feeling just right so you can feel calm.

Why do you go to an occupational therapist?

- ☐ To support your body in feeling just right
- ☐ To help you feel less bothered by unexpected touch and loud noises
- ☐ To help you feel more comfortable and calm
- ☐ To build muscles and help balance—this will help with comfort in writing and sitting
- ☐ To help with motor planning—think out and physically do tasks

What is your job?

- ☐ Follow their directions
- ☐ Participate in the activities
- ☐ Have a positive attitude
- ☐ Be polite

Psychiatrist

A psychiatrist is a therapist and also a doctor. He can prescribe medications (Zaks 2006).

Why do you talk with him?

- ☐ Many people with Asperger's Syndrome and anxiety take medication
- ☐ He is an expert in giving medication to individuals with Asperger's Syndrome and anxiety
- ☐ He is working to support you to feel calm, comfortable, and happy

What is your job?

- ☐ Tell him how you are doing and feeling
- ☐ Discuss anything that is bothering you
- ☐ Answer his questions
- ☐ Remember to take your medications

Cognitive behavioral therapist

He specializes in cognitive behavioral therapy used to reduce symptoms of OCD. Cognitive behavioral therapists ask you to do concrete exercises to:

- ☐ Lessen your worries in certain situations
- ☐ Face your fears
- ☐ Handle your behavior differently (Zaks 2006)

Why do you talk with him?

- ☐ He is an expert in OCD
- ☐ He can help you learn how to feel less worried
- ☐ He will provide strategies to support you
- ☐ You can feel free to talk with him about anything that worries you
- ☐ He wants to help you feel calm and happy

What is your job?

- ☐ Complete the homework assigned to you
- ☐ Have a positive attitude
- ☐ Answer his questions

Speech and language pathologist

A speech and language pathologist teaches you how to make and keep friendships and communicate socially.

Why do you talk with him?

- ☐ To learn how to interact effectively in social situations
- ☐ To understand expected verbal and non-verbal communication in various environments

What is your job?

- ☐ Participate with the group
- ☐ Have a positive attitude
- ☐ Maintain safe words and body
- ☐ Practice the skills that you learn

Neuropsychologist

The job of a neuropsychologist is to provide a series of assessments to understand your strengths and to identify effective ways to improve your academic life.

Why do you talk with him?

- ☐ The neuropsychologist will use the information gleaned from the assessments to teach parents and teachers how to best support you

What is your job?

- ☐ Complete the assessments
- ☐ Have a positive attitude
- ☐ Answer his questions
- ☐ Do your best work

ABA therapist

The ABA therapist leads a social group and ABA therapy.

Why do you talk with her?

- ☐ She teaches you how to have expected behavior in school and in social situations (how to play well with friends)
- ☐ She teaches you how to stay calm, maintain a safe body, and be flexible

What is your job?

- ☐ Listen to her
- ☐ Apply what she is telling you to do at home, school and in the community
- ☐ Follow her directions

Report feedback tool

You can bring this "Report feedback tool" to the feedback session of a neuropsychological assessment for your child. Remember to ask the professional to prioritize recommendations for your child so you understand what issues you need to address immediately versus those that can wait. You can input the most important points into this template. This template will help you organize your efforts and communicate effectively about the report with professionals in the school and community.

Child's name:

Evaluator:

Date:

Most important recommendations:

1

2

3

4

5

6

How to use the toolbox

Now that you have created your important adults toolbox, you will be able to:

- decrease stress and confusion for your child by clarifying and helping him understand who the adult is, why he sees the adult, and what his role is in every environment in which he interacts
- implement structure for home education and have guidelines for a unified approach to parenting
- create more productive and pleasant relationships between your child and his teachers and service providers now that roles and expectations in their environments are explicit
- help your child generalize skills by using the same strategies in multiple environments.

Chapter 8

Managing Crises and Emotions

When Alexander was in fourth grade, his stress levels and behavior escalated quickly and almost daily, whether at school, at home, or with service providers. Once, in a social pragmatics group, another group member threatened to chop Alexander with an axe. Alexander became extremely upset and hurled a board game box top at the boy. Other members of the group reacted by screaming. Amidst the yelling and chaos, the group leader tried desperately to regain control. The assembled mothers in the waiting room overheard the eruption, and the enraged mother of the boy who threatened Alexander stormed into the group's meeting room. She grabbed her son and berated me in the waiting room for several minutes on their way out. My memory of the conversation is that she accused my son of being a troublemaker and wanted him removed from the group.

I was shocked that a mother of a child with special needs was so judgmental of another child with special needs. Surely she understood that I wanted Alexander to be capable of controlling his emotions so that he could participate in and benefit from the group. When this woman yelled at me, I began sobbing. I didn't think I should be crying in front of children or in a professional setting, which made me feel more humiliated. I couldn't flee the building quickly enough.

I had built a positive relationship with the founder of this social pragmatics group's organization over the several years that Alexander had attended classes there. He called me at home that night, and though he was gracious about my crying, he told me he thought it was unsafe for Alexander to return to the group. I understood, but the fact remained that Alexander was expelled from that group.

During this time Alexander was transitioning to fourth grade, which represented a change in teachers, classroom, and students for the first time since second grade. Despite our preparation, the transition challenged everyone involved when Alexander regressed into crisis. Two significant incidents happened within weeks of each other, and both were handled ineffectively because Alexander's teachers didn't yet know about his AS profile-based struggles.

In addition to the school and extra-curricular struggles, life at home was peppered with daily explosions. My travel every third weekend to attend a one-year graduate program in a nearby state further disrupted Alexander and led to outbursts. These weekends away at school were difficult for all of my family members. I received multiple calls from my younger son, who was distraught that I was away and felt completely ungrounded without me. He either screeched into the phone or sobbed hysterically. He and Alexander fought most of the weekend, and my husband was overwrought. I felt overwhelmed and at a loss about how to help Alexander.

Managing crises and emotions across environments

Encouraging self-regulation

As these examples make clear, our family struggled with crises and meltdowns in all kinds of situations. Children with AS can get upset for any number of reasons, including sensory issues, transition struggles, and interpersonal conflicts. Life can begin to feel like everyone is walking in a minefield, never certain when an explosion will occur. Parents can lessen the impact on the child and the people with whom he interacts by using self-regulation, or emotion management, tools.

For instance, parents can use visual tools to support the child when dealing with an upset. You can share Figure 8.1 in this chapter with caregivers and professionals so that they understand the meltdown cycle and respond to the child's escalation cues before it is too late. (We will discuss the meltdown cycle in more detail later in the chapter.) The advantage of using visual tools is that they do not require talking, which will often stress a child with AS further. The ultimate goal is that the child with AS will learn to recognize his escalation warning signs himself and utilize methods to avoid a meltdown.

The level of self-awareness of the child with AS influences the choice of self-regulation strategies and the level of adult support he or she will need. Adults should establish their approach well ahead of time. As an example, a successful strategy for a child who is anxious with low self-awareness might involve an adult watching carefully for behavioral signs of arousal and intervening with step-by-step visual supports, few words, and an even demeanor to remind the child of what his calming techniques are. If a child is more self-aware, then an agreed-upon cue might be sufficient to help the child initiate putting a self-regulation strategy into place himself. The goal is to calm the child, not to process the incident in the moment, because that would likely lead to further upset.

Using strategies such as "How Does Your Engine Run?" (Williams and Shellenberger 1996) can increase the self-awareness of a child with AS by teaching him about his level of physiological arousal. The program educates children to figure out if their engine is running too slow, too fast, or just right. The engine analogy works well because young children can relate to it. In addition, older children can be taught the fight or flight animal model of stress and coping to help them understand their own body and stress responses and make appropriate accommodations.

Phil Schwarz, co-author of *Ask and Tell: Self-Advocacy and Disclosure for People on the Autism Spectrum* (Hane *et al.* 2004), champions the concept that autism is not an excuse for bad behavior. Like everyone else, an individual with AS is expected ultimately to learn how to manage his emotions and function within the community. Achieving these results may require more of an investment on the part of parent case managers, the child, and his team than for typically developing children, but this effort is necessary.

Direct instruction: sharing emotions with children with AS

Parents, teachers, and professionals can teach emotion management skills to the child with AS by routinely sharing their own emotions and discussing how they manage them. Children with AS benefit from explicit instruction, and adults can seize a teaching opportunity by providing a narrative of how they address their own emotional wellbeing. If adults process their emotions internally without sharing how they deal with them, they are missing the chance to be good models of how to cope with emotions. If children with AS never see or hear about their adults being upset, angry, or sad, they may fear that there is something wrong with their own emotions.

That said, parents, teachers, and professionals should make sure they are modeling positive behaviors and refrain from dramatic reactions such as throwing tantrums. The same applies to disagreements between parents. Out-of-control verbal or physical conflicts should not happen in front of any child. However, parents can use an argument as a teaching tool to illustrate how to resolve differences in an appropriate way. If parents get angry and say something they shouldn't with the child present, then they can apologize in front of the child. This process actively models how children with AS can deal with their own interpersonal conflicts.

Create a star chart

In addition, star charts can be implemented at home and school, as well as in the community, to support self-regulation. This strategy acknowledges and positively reinforces behaviors that are most important for success. Parents and teachers can choose the three behaviors that they most want to encourage in their child. For example, the child might earn stars for following directions, being a student, and using a safe body. Expectations are explicitly explained with visual support. Behavior requirements and rewards should be based on the child's profile. Some children might only need rewards once or twice per day, while others might require them three or more times per day to remain engaged and perform successfully. The child must earn a certain number of stars during a specified time period to receive a preferred reward such as working on the computer for five minutes. This structure motivates the child to regulate himself. Parents and teachers can adjust the program over time as the child integrates the desired behaviors. The Parents Take Charge section will help you create star charts for use both at home and at school.

Sensory diet accommodations

Your child's sensory profile can be as important as his cognitive profile when it comes to understanding how to support his needs. As we discussed in Chapter 3, sensory disorders can come in a variety of presentations and combinations. The system of individuals with AS can be over-reactive, under-reactive, or input seeking; others may have a difficult time discerning sensation differences. Some struggle with posture, balance, or motor planning due to sensory-based motor issues (Kranowitz 2010, p.28). These struggles can negatively impact the child's behavior.

Occupational therapists evaluate the child to develop an understanding of his sensory profile. They can then recommend an activity plan, or sensory diet, to support the child's unique sensory struggles, teach him how to make his body calm, and help him cope with his day. For example, if a child is highly sensitive to loud noises, he may be allowed to wear earplugs or earphones at certain times of the day, and teachers may preview fire alarms and construction noises. If a child is over-reactive to touch, teachers may avoid physical contact and be prepared to help a child return to baseline if he is inadvertently touched. It is essential for you to understand and share your child's sensory profile and diet with the school to help prevent emotional outbursts and crises at school and best position him for success. The tools for sensory struggles in the Parents Take Charge section of Chapter 4 also provide excellent strategies.

Handling meltdowns effectively

The meltdown cycle

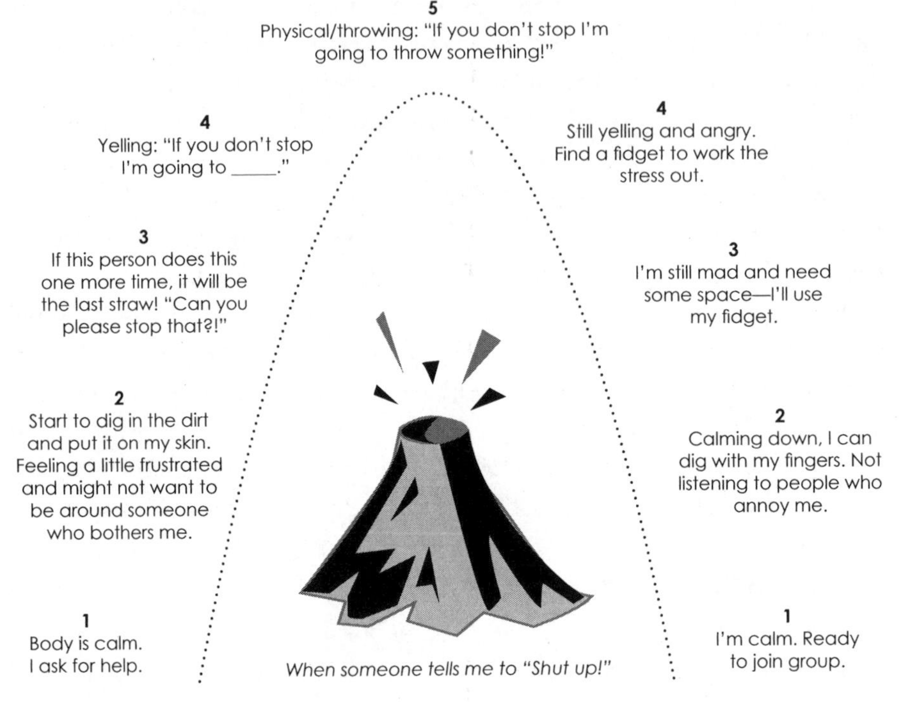

Figure 8.1 The meltdown cycle

The meltdown cycle for a child with AS follows a predictable trajectory. Understanding the meltdown cycle, knowing how to manage it, and making thoughtful interventions are major components of stopping the escalation process and helping to prevent crises. Figure 8.1 is included in the template checklists you have downloaded and can be used to help teachers and your child to understand what happens as the child's arousal level escalates, reaches a climax, and calms down. The goal is to help the child stop the escalation process as soon as possible by identifying his escalation cues and putting a plan into action according to his level of upset.

In the first phase of the meltdown, which Brenda Smith Myles refers to as the "rumbling" phase, the child with AS will display a variety of behavioral changes. Some are more apparent, while others may seem minor and unrelated. The more obvious behaviors might include verbal or physical aggression or emotional or physical withdrawal. Behaviors that are less easy to connect with escalation might be tensing muscles, grimacing, or tapping feet (Myles and Southwick 2005). In the meltdown visual here, after someone tells the child to "shut up" he begins in the rumbling phase by digging in the dirt and putting the dirt on his skin.

Adult intervention is very important during the rumbling phase. Specific calming techniques will vary from child to child, depending on their unique profile and preferences. For example, the adult can distract the child, remove him from the situation, and have him read in a quiet space or engage in physical activity. They can provide a written or visual cue to tell the child to use a calming strategy, or ask the other child to move. The adult must remain calm and use few words. Too many words can further escalate a rumbling situation (Myles and Southwick 2005).

Myles refers to the second phase as "rage" (Myles and Southwick 2005). If adults are unable to diffuse the situation during the rumbling phase, the child will likely progress into rage. Once the child reaches this phase, the meltdown usually must run its course. Meltdowns are challenging in every environment because the child often appears angry and aggressive. Outbursts can include yelling, flipping of desks, or other behaviors that classmates, group participants, and family members will understandably find dangerous and scary. It helps when the staff recognize that the child's thinking brain turns off when he reaches a heightened level of escalation, and the resulting behaviors are impulsive and out of his control. In the meltdown visual, the child became physical and started throwing things during the rage phase.

The most important considerations for adults during the rage phase are helping the child recover and preserving his dignity. Having a pre-determined Safe Spot where the child is away from others and feels comfortable usually helps. The team should agree upon the strategy for this phase and preview it with the child before a crisis. A child will likely become further aroused if adults implement surprising strategies during the heat of rage (Myles and Southwick 2005).

The final phase of the meltdown is "recovery" (Myles and Southwick 2005). In the meltdown visual, the child moved from still yelling and being angry to being mad, needing space, and using a fidget, to calming, digging with his fingers, and not listening to people who annoy him. After he finally calmed, he was ready to join the group.

During this phase, an adult that the child trusts and knows can help him calm by quietly getting him involved in a special interest activity. Adults should be certain that the child is completely calm before asking him to work or join the group. The entire cycle could resume if the child has not fully recovered.

Make a crisis response plan

You can create crisis response plans to let adults at home, at school, and in the community know how to best handle a meltdown. These written plans can explicitly list the things the child should try when he gets upset, and adults can prompt him with the list as his behavior escalates. The plan should be previewed with the child with AS when he is calm, which helps him to know what to expect and to follow instructions from the person in charge when the strategy is needed.

Working with your child's team to develop a crisis response plan in advance will help to manage crises most effectively. The team must know who will serve as the leader and provide direction. The team also needs to make decisions ahead of time about whether and where to move your child or the class, group, or family members when his behavior escalates beyond a certain point. You should communicate to the team what typically happens when your child has a meltdown and what supports him. For some children with AS, a hands-on approach settles the child more quickly. For others, the same approach results in intensified arousal to the point that people are more likely to get hurt.

The team should also devise a plan for respectful communication and resolution after the incident. Everyone should establish up front how the child's parents will be informed and if, when, and how the parents of the other classmates or group participants are told. The Parents Take Charge section of this chapter will guide you through creating a crisis response plan.

Remaining calm during meltdowns

It is not always easy, but caregivers and professionals can best manage tantrums by remaining calm. When the adult maintains a steady and unruffled demeanor, the child can recover more quickly.

We realize that managing meltdowns can be very difficult, emotionally and logistically. Adults can be triggered by the volume and verbal content of the child's tantrum. They might have other children with competing needs to think about during the escalation. To handle the outburst effectively, they must immediately regulate themselves to avoid making the situation worse.

The Parents Take Charge section of this chapter addresses this struggle and helps parents prepare themselves for meltdowns. You can use the same visuals at home, at school, and in the community to provide consistency and structure for your child. You can manage your child's daily schedule to minimize the chances of escalation. We will help you identify your child's triggers and signals of upset, so that you have a better chance of quickly reversing the meltdown cycle.

Making amends after an outburst

If a child has a meltdown that negatively affects someone else, an adult should initiate a repair plan after the child regains composure. The adult can help the child with AS think about the incident, understand what happened, and make the situation and relationships right to the greatest extent possible. The repair plan should teach the child that his actions had an impact on others and that he needs to take responsibility for them.

It is important that you (or the adult in charge) do not treat the repair plan as a punishment for doing something wrong. The only exception is when it is absolutely clear that the child had access to her "thinking brain" and deliberately engaged in unacceptable behavior. In those cases, the child should face consequences. It is also important to wait until the meltdown is over before trying to process what happened with your child and discuss making amends. Trying to talk about it during the outburst will not be effective and will likely lead to further escalation of her behavior.

The unique challenges of managing crises and emotions in the community

Most of the strategies for self-regulation and dealing with meltdowns that we have discussed have focused on the home and school environments. It is harder to manage crises and emotions in the community because there are more unexpected aspects of community life and fewer opportunities to coach professionals and adults. Community environments such as social pragmatics groups or private occupational therapy can use the tools from the Parents Take Charge section as they are or customize them to support emotion management during their sessions.

In the larger community, be thoughtful about the situations you put your child in based on his sensory profile. For example, if he has an over-reactive sensory system and cannot tolerate unexpected touch, a trip to the library will likely be more successful than a trip to an amusement park. The risks are higher in the community because a public meltdown leads to greater ramifications than a private meltdown at home. Help your child learn by providing tools and education, exposing the child to the world in a manner that stretches him, and limiting the opportunities for situations that he can't handle.

As Alexander has gotten older, been educated about self-regulation, and used tools to help him manage his emotions, he is better able to navigate certain community outings. Recently, he was invited to watch his best friend's improvisation performance. While his sensory issues still impact him tremendously, he was able to cope with the loud cheering and clapping and the unexpected nature of improvisation. He covered his ears and groaned when the noise level escalated, but he sat through the entire performance and even stayed later to congratulate his friend. While it pained me to see him struggle, the fact that he made it through the entire performance and nurtured his friendship by being there was huge progress.

As a mother, I want to introduce Alexander to the beauty that life has to offer. I want him to experience his community, nation, and world. Given his profile, this has not been possible in the way I originally envisioned. Instead, we embark on this process at a slower pace and in a different manner, taking small steps together. My overall goal is to maximize successful community outings.

Common emotional struggles for children with AS

Emotional struggles significantly impact self-regulation and can contribute to increased meltdowns. This section covers common emotional struggles for children with AS, including anxiety and depression, stress from one environment bleeding into other environments, social withdrawal, and strain caused by sleep issues. Once you understand the common emotional struggles, you can help your child by taking steps to provide support to address the issues. Once the issues are addressed, your child will be capable of greater self-regulation and there will be fewer meltdowns.

Anxiety and depression

Although mood disorders such as anxiety and depression are not part of the make-up of every child with AS, they often go hand in hand. Psychiatrists view these disorders as comorbid, or co-occurring, with AS.

Many behaviors of children with AS can be understood by answering the question: "What could be producing anxiety in my child right now that could be influencing this behavior?" In an extreme, but real, example, a child with AS in school raged at his teacher in a filthy, misogynistic rant. A counselor interrupted him by saying, "You must be anxious about something." He replied "No shit, Sherlock!" and explained that he was anxious about an upcoming school play in which he had a minor role. He calmed quickly with this insight. Despite the fact that he behaved this way because of anxiety, the child was required to repair the relationship with the teacher at whom he raged.

Your child's mood struggles may make home and school atmospheres explosive, emotionally intense, and draining. You can address this issue by training the support team at home, at school, and in the community about your child's moods and how to recognize the behaviors associated with them. This education can rally the team to work together to help stabilize his mood, which decreases the emotional toll on everyone. For example, if one of your child's idiosyncratic signs of being anxious is pacing, you can instruct siblings to identify that sign and give their brother space because he is probably getting nervous. This will allow the child with AS time to calm down and could prevent an outburst.

Caregivers and professionals can implement a number of techniques to decrease the stress of the child with AS. They can help the child put their struggles into perspective by using Michelle Garcia Winner's "The Size of My Problem" visual scale (see "The Size of My Problem" Box). Adults can soothe the child's concerns by clearly explaining why and how everything will be fine and work out, if that is true. At home, parents can teach their child how to breathe deeply, talk her through a meditation, offer a massage, use a sound machine to cancel noise, or have the child sleep with a weighted blanket at night. Cardiovascular exercise for at least twenty minutes each day releases stress hormones and decreases anxiety.

Depression can have its own causes. The child's perception of his lack of success can lead to feelings of hopelessness, self-doubt, and sadness. Some children meet the criteria for major depression or bipolar disorder. Others experience a chronic and relatively mild depression called dysthymia. Symptoms of depression can include pervasive sadness, pessimism, or irritability, decreased pleasure, appetite disturbance, fatigue, and impaired concentration.

Treatment for these disorders may include medication. Cognitive behavioral therapy can also provide benefits to the child with AS. This type of therapy often works well because children with AS find it logical that thoughts affect feelings, feelings affect behaviors, and so on. For the child with AS who wholeheartedly believes that one error on a math assignment will cause his eventual destruction as an adult, the calm and rational CBT therapist will chain thoughts together to show why this is an illogical conclusion.

The Size of My Problem

Michelle Garcia Winner is known for breaking down complex social concepts and explaining them in a way that people can easily understand. She has developed a vocabulary to help adults and children communicate with a common language. "The Size of My Problem" is one example. As she explains on her website www.socialthinking.com:

Understanding the size of the problem helps students appreciate that when our reaction does not match the situation at hand (either too big or too small), this can result in people having uncomfortable thoughts about us. One of the responsibilities we all share when interacting with others is doing our part to keep the group on an even keel.

Introducing medication

Based on Alexander's intensifying behavior in multiple environments during fourth grade, his psychologist broached the topic of medications with us. I was terrified to make a decision that could put him at risk of serious side-effects that could impact his health simply to make life easier. How could I live with myself if something happened? However, after much debate and many talks with both his psychologist and psychiatrist, we recognized that he needed more support, and we introduced medications.

As the year progressed, Alexander's stress continued to mount, and he developed obsessive-compulsive disorder. We added another medication to his cocktail to give him some relief from his new anxiety disorder, which caused an adverse reaction.

In all of my experiences with Alexander, living through his adverse reaction was the most agonizing. He became so depressed that he regularly voiced suicidal thoughts. His art became very dark, and the content changed from whales to guns. He often wore hoods because he wanted to be invisible. He had no interest in a social life, and he had limited tolerance for anything that I would consider minimally irritating. During that period, it felt like he was either yelling or crying all the time. At times, we were afraid to leave him by himself. He was suffering so much. My heart ached.

Outside of the adverse reaction, I have a very difficult time teasing out the impact of each medication on Alexander. His sleep has improved dramatically. He is able to regulate himself much better. I imagine that the improved self-regulation has to do with a combination of education and medications.

Our situation does not apply to everyone. You can initiate a conversation about medication with your child's pediatrician, therapist, or psychiatrist if you ever wonder if this type of therapy might help your child.

Bringing school-related stress home

As I mentioned at the beginning of the chapter, Alexander's emotional struggles at school spilled over into our life at home. A child's school-related stress can have a tremendous impact on the family's home life. Children with AS work extremely hard to manage their days and be successful at school. Their inner resources have often been exhausted by the time they come home. Worn out from exerting themselves all day at school, they may have less tolerance for sensory input that aggravates their systems. They may feel assaulted and their behavior escalates immediately and dramatically, even when the input isn't intended to upset them. For example, they might explode at someone who inadvertently makes an unexpected loud noise such as slamming a door or dropping a pan.

A child with AS who is stressed at school often experiences low self-esteem. When he feels bad about himself, he may suffer from negative self-talk or project his judgments about himself onto other people. For example, a child with AS may berate his siblings when they exhibit negative behaviors he recognizes in himself.

After-school schedules often need to be different for a child with AS than for a typically developing child. A child with AS may need more time to decompress when he gets home from school. Parents of a typically developing child often insist that he complete his homework as soon as he returns from school before he can go outside to play. A child with AS may need an hour or so to himself to pace, play on a therapy ball, or simply rest before he is able to do another challenging or stressful task.

Social withdrawal

When Alexander was struggling at school and at home, he announced to me that he wanted to stop having play dates. I knew play dates stressed him, but his request still concerned me. With great sadness, I agreed to suspend them, recognizing that he didn't have the energy or the interest to participate. I worried about the consequences of Alexander isolating himself socially, but I also understood that forced socialization wouldn't work and could potentially backfire. We didn't need any more burned social bridges.

Some children with AS socially withdraw as they get older. Identifying the possible causes can be complicated. They may articulate that they don't want to be with peers and that they feel forced to socialize. Sometimes this is a way to declare independence from their parents. They may express that their need for social interaction is not the same as their parents' need, and they want to delineate what they can and cannot tolerate.

If your child with AS withdraws socially or has any change in overt behavior, you can become a detective and try to generate a hypothesis about the reason for the change, which will inform your next steps. Is your child suffering from a medical issue? Is she experiencing increased anxiety about school? Is she having increased sensory issues? After identifying the cause, you can help your child address the underlying problem.

Sleep issues

Alexander has always struggled with sleep. He had a hard time getting to sleep and would often wake up for several hours during the night. When he had his adverse reaction to medication and suffered resulting suicidal thoughts, he woke every night for several hours. Because he was in such a fragile state, I got up with him every night. The sleep deprivation that resulted for both of us made an already emotional and difficult situation worse.

Sleep issues are common among children with AS and lead to emotional dysregulation, or turmoil. You can support your child with AS by teaching good sleep habits from a very early age and reinforcing them as your child grows. For example, you can encourage your child to treat the bed only as a place to sleep, as opposed to a place to play, watch television, or work on the computer. This strategy keeps expectations clear and trains your child that when he or she gets in bed, it is time to go to sleep. Keeping sleep times fairly consistent is also helpful. *The Harvard Medical School Guide to a Good Night's Sleep* (Epstein and Mardon 2007) is a good resource for sleep hygiene. Your early investment in developing a sleep strategy helps children with AS significantly in the long run.

Generalization

Adults in every environment can help a child generalize skills to manage crises and emotions by using a similar approach and common language.

- Encourage self-regulation:
  - » Teach the child self-awareness.
  - » Share about your own emotion regulation process.
  - » Create star charts.
  - » Implement sensory supports, if necessary.

- Handle meltdowns:
  - » Understand the meltdown cycle.
  - » Develop crises response plans.
  - » Remain calm.
  - » Teach the child how to make amends.
- Provide support for common emotional struggles.

Help him in every environment to identify his:

- triggers
- emotions attached to the triggers
- behaviors attached to the triggers
- strategies to put in place when he is triggered.

When professionals and adults point out the triggers and attached emotions and behaviors in each environment, he starts to realize when he gets upset and he independently makes the connection to put the strategy in place. For example, when Alexander gets angry at home, he often says that he is getting mad and that he is going to go upstairs to his room. At school, he will often initiate a break to a quiet space. When we visit a relative's home, he will often retreat into his room when he feels overwhelmed. The goal is for the child to either manage on his own or to accept help.

Parents Take Charge

Creating Your Child's Managing Crises and Emotions Toolbox

These workbook exercises help you build a plan to help manage crises and emotions at home, at school, and in the community. Each tool approaches this topic from a different angle, and works as a simple guide for your child and a teaching template and collaboration toolbox for you and the professionals that support him.

Managing crises and emotions: Every environment

As we've discussed previously, children with AS often have struggles that impact all the environments in which they interact. Taking a unified approach to managing your child's crises and emotions, across environments, can lead to greater success in every context.

- Using the list below and examples in this section as a starting point, work with your child's special educator and/or teacher(s) and people who support him in the community to determine the tools that he needs to master first. If you don't see a tool that is important for your child, simply create one using the examples as models.
- Introduce managing crises and emotions topics one at a time in a coordinated effort across contexts.
- Use the same language in every setting when introducing the tool.
- Preview the tool with your child before use in each environment.
- Have a copy available for review in each situation and environment until your child integrates the concept and demonstrates mastery of it.
- Once the child becomes competent with one managing crises and emotions topic, continue practicing it and simultaneously start teaching another one in every environment.

- When you create your managing crises and emotions toolbox, put one tool per page with succinct, simple, accessible instructions. Less writing per page helps the child with AS avoid visual overload.

Strategies for managing crises and emotions in every environment

- ☐ Encourage self-regulation:
  - ☐ Teach the child self-awareness
  - ☐ Share about your own emotion regulation process
  - ☐ Create star charts
  - ☐ Implement sensory supports, if necessary
- ☐ Handle meltdowns:
  - ☐ Understand the meltdown cycle
  - ☐ Develop crisis response plans
  - ☐ Remain calm
  - ☐ Teach the child how to make amends
- ☐ Provide support for common emotional struggles
- ☐ Help the child in every environment to identify his:
  - ☐ Triggers
  - ☐ Emotions attached to the triggers
  - ☐ Behaviors attached to the triggers
  - ☐ Strategies to put in place when he is triggered

Examples: Managing crises and emotions in every environment

The lists below serve as examples of tools that can be used in multiple environments to help manage crises and emotions, which you can consider a springboard to making your own lists. Feel free to:

- use the space provided in the template checklists you have downloaded to add points to the tools
- or create entirely new managing crises and emotions tools that would support your child using these tools as models.

Tools for managing crises and emotions may include:

- ☐ Crisis response plan
- ☐ Meltdown cycle visual
- ☐ Sensory diet accommodations
- ☐ Things the child can do to calm down
- ☐ Strategies that support the child to relax
- ☐ Create separate star charts for home and school
- ☐ Develop a Social Story™ to introduce your child's star chart

Example crisis response plan

Who is in charge?

- ☐ Parents
- ☐ Babysitters
- ☐ Grandparents
- ☐ Special educator
- ☐ Instructional aide
- ☐ Service provider (list specifically)

Who gets involved (if backup is needed)?

- ☐ Familiar people with whom he has formed a relationship: former aide, former special educator, and speech and language pathologist
- ☐ Not administration
- ☐ Preview with _____ (child's name) who gets involved and when

What typically causes escalation?

- ☐ Unexpected touch—everyone should be prepped to avoid touching him
- ☐ Loud and unexpected noises
- ☐ Visual chaos:
  - ☐ Clutter
  - ☐ Balls or other items flying through the air
- ☐ Unexpectedly not getting his way
- ☐ Changes and transitions—particularly when not previewed
- ☐ Not understanding the schedule or plan
- ☐ Perceived slights
- ☐ Impulsive or unexpected behavior
- ☐ Disorder
- ☐ When his behavior is already escalated, the following can push him over the meltdown edge:
  - ☐ Being in his visual line
  - ☐ Talking with him
  - ☐ Attempting to reason with him
- ☐ Emotional environment—he does best when the environment is calm and quiet

What are the signs of escalation?

- ☐ Growling
- ☐ Grimacing
- ☐ Flexing with stiff and straight arms and hands fisted
- ☐ Shouting
- ☐ Pushing, hitting, or kicking
- ☐ Tearing things

Calming strategies

- ☐ Get him to move to his quiet area
- ☐ An adult reads to him
- ☐ Exercise
  - ☐ Throw ball
  - ☐ Ride stationary bike
  - ☐ Walk
- ☐ Approach calmly and slowly
- ☐ Maintain a non-judgmental and helpful attitude
- ☐ Talk very little—notes often work better
- ☐ A clear message that the adult is trying to help him

Visual support

This should be created before the school or community relationship begins and be readily available:

- ☐ Five-point scale (see Chapter 4)
- ☐ Writing notes
- ☐ Using wipe board to draw visuals
- ☐ Preview managing crises and emotions tools with him before any crisis

Move the child or class, group, peers, or siblings

- ☐ If possible, Plan A is for ______ (child's name) to move. Provide him with the choice that he can go to the Break Spot or the class, group, or sibling will need to leave the room
- ☐ If not possible, then Plan B is for the class, group, or sibling to move
- ☐ Important to preview with him at the beginning of the year or relationship

What is the plan for communicating with parents?

- ☐ The special educator or service provider will communicate with mother or father about incidents

What should happen in terms of sharing incident with other classroom parents?

- ☐ The school team or service provider will decide whether or not the families of other students should be notified about an incident
- ☐ Before notifying other families, the child's parents should be contacted and a plan should be worked out collaboratively

Resolution after the incident—repair plan

The purpose here is to educate, not punish:

- ☐ Determine a plan for re-entry to classroom, and preview what he will be working on when he gets back to class
- ☐ Have the child write an apology note or note of explanation, if necessary
- ☐ Draw cartoons to explain what happened and what could be done differently
- ☐ Be consistent in response—no surprising consequences
- ☐ No trips to the principal's office

Use the meltdown cycle visual to educate your child and others

Parents can use the visual below to help the child and everyone involved with him to understand what happens as the child escalates, reaches a climax, and calms down.

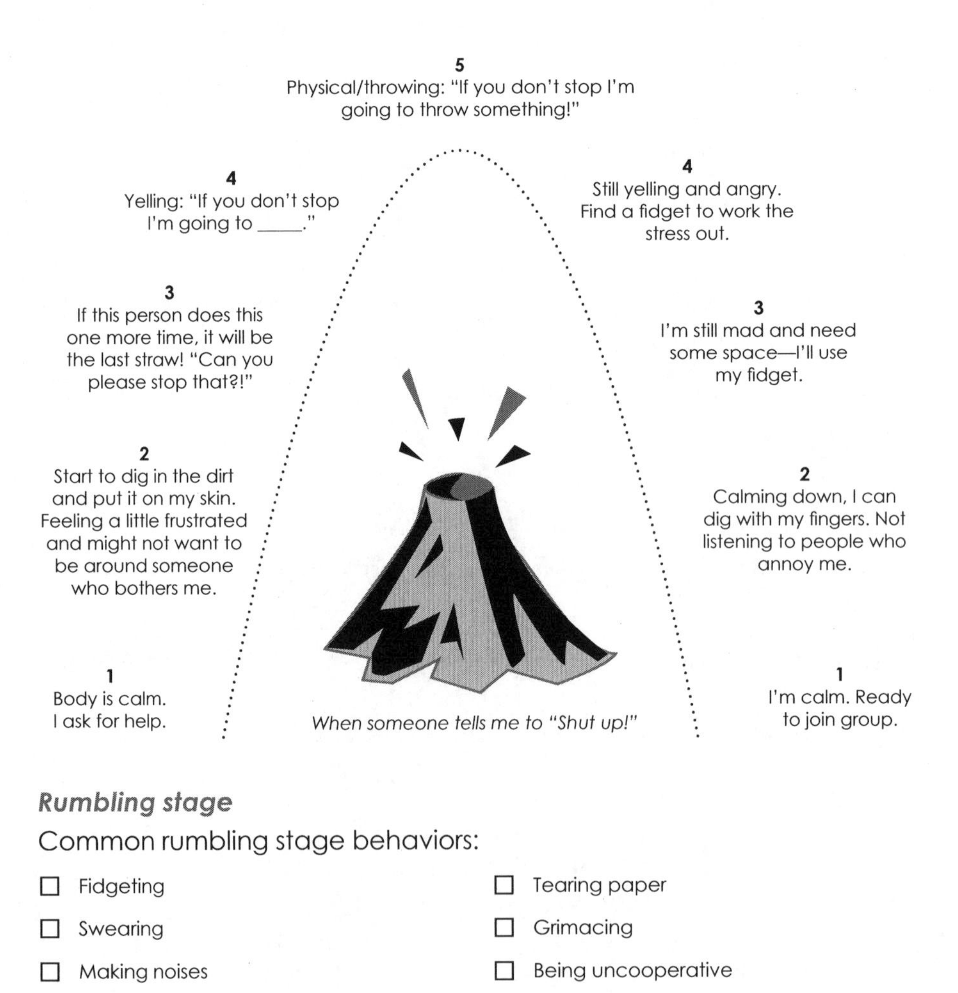

Rumbling stage

Common rumbling stage behaviors:

- ☐ Fidgeting
- ☐ Swearing
- ☐ Making noises
- ☐ Tearing paper
- ☐ Grimacing
- ☐ Being uncooperative

- ☐ Crying
- ☐ Clenching muscles
- ☐ Name calling
- ☐ Raising or lowering voice
- ☐ Making threats

(MYLES AND SOUTHWICK 2005, P.27)

Suggested rumbling stage interventions:

- ☐ Calmly removing the person from the situation
- ☐ Using your body to modify behavior. Standing closer may offer support, or giving space may be more effective
- ☐ Using non-verbal signals to communicate
- ☐ Using humor
- ☐ Trying to get the child back on track using his or her schedule
- ☐ Bringing up and showing interest in the child's special interest
- ☐ Redirecting
- ☐ Using a neutral place where the student can go to regroup
- ☐ Walking and talking with no conversation
- ☐ Acknowledging the child's difficulties: reinforce the rule the child should follow. Let the child know you can help

(MYLES AND SOUTHWICK 2005, PP.27–31)

Effective adult behaviors during the rumbling stage:

- ☐ Stay calm
- ☐ Speak calmly and quietly
- ☐ Take deep breaths
- ☐ Don't engage in a power struggle
- ☐ Rethink student goals
- ☐ Be flexible

(MYLES AND SOUTHWICK 2005, P.32)

Adult behaviors that can escalate a crisis:

- ☐ Raising voice or shouting
- ☐ Making assumptions
- ☐ Preaching to the child
- ☐ Backing the child into a corner
- ☐ Telling the child "I'm in charge here"
- ☐ Pleading
- ☐ Bribing
- ☐ Insisting on having the last word
- ☐ Bringing up unrelated events
- ☐ Using confrontational body language
- ☐ Making remarks like "You kids are all the same"
- ☐ Being sarcastic
- ☐ Attacking the child's character
- ☐ Being accusatory
- ☐ Nagging
- ☐ Holding a grudge
- ☐ Acting superior
- ☐ Throwing a tantrum
- ☐ Using unnecessary physical force
- ☐ Mimicking the child
- ☐ Drawing other people into the conflict
- ☐ Comparing the child with siblings, other students, and so on
- ☐ Insisting the adult is right
- ☐ Having a double standard: "Do as I say, not as I do"
- ☐ Commanding, demanding, dominating
- ☐ Rewarding the student for unacceptable behavior
- ☐ Using putdowns

(MYLES AND SOUTHWICK 2005, P.33)

Rage stage

Typical rage stage behaviors:

- ☐ Impulsivity
- ☐ Being highly emotional
- ☐ Being explosive
- ☐ Damaging or destroying property
- ☐ Hurting himself
- ☐ Externalizing behavior such as yelling, hitting, kicking, and biting
- ☐ Negative behaviors directed towards the self

(MYLES AND SOUTHWICK 2005, P.33)

Rage stage interventions:

- ☐ Protect the child
- ☐ Protect the environment
- ☐ Protect others
- ☐ Don't discipline the child
- ☐ Remove the audience
- ☐ Don't be confrontational
- ☐ Plan a "graceful" exit strategy
- ☐ Follow a plan
- ☐ Obtain assistance
- ☐ Encourage the child to go to a neutral place to cool off, as appropriate
- ☐ Don't speak much
- ☐ Prevent a power struggle
- ☐ Rethink the child's goals
- ☐ Be flexible
- ☐ Set a timer to suggest to the child that there is a beginning and end to the event

(MYLES AND SOUTHWICK 2005, P.34)

Effective adult behaviors during the rage stage:

- ☐ Control your own "flight or fight" tendency
- ☐ Remember that less is more
- ☐ Remain calm and quiet
- ☐ Don't take behaviors personally
- ☐ Disengage emotionally
- ☐ Be aware of your non-verbal cues
- ☐ Breathe deeply

(MYLES AND SOUTHWICK 2005, P.35)

Recovery stage

Typical recovery behaviors:

- ☐ Sleeping
- ☐ Denial of behaviors displayed during meltdown
- ☐ Withdrawal into fantasy
- ☐ Saying sorry

(MYLES AND SOUTHWICK 2005, P.36)

Recovery stage interventions:

- ☐ Allow the child to sleep
- ☐ Support use of relaxation techniques
- ☐ Don't refer to the rage behaviors
- ☐ Support with structure

- ☐ Consider the child "fragile"
- ☐ Plan to teach the child alternatives to tantrums, rage, meltdowns, and shut-downs
- ☐ Determine appropriate option for the child:
    - ☐ Redirect to successful activity or special interest
    - ☐ Give space
    - ☐ Be sure the interventions are presented at or below the child's functioning level
- ☐ Check to see if the child is ready to learn
- ☐ Don't make excessive demands

(MYLES AND SOUTHWICK 2005, P.37)

Effective adult behaviors during the recovery stage:

- ☐ Remain calm and quiet
- ☐ Take time for yourself to regroup

(MYLES AND SOUTHWICK 2005, P.37)

Sensory diet accommodations

If possible, ask your occupational therapist to write a report detailing your child's sensory struggles and sensory diet recommendations to use at home, at school, and in the community. Provide a copy of it to your child's special educator, service providers, and, if applicable, his school occupational therapist. See also Chapter 4 for additional sensory support strategies.

Example of a report

Name:

Date:

Therapist:

________ (child's name) has been seen for sensory integration treatment from ______ (occupational therapist) from ______ (date) to the present. He is seen one time a week for 45 minutes of direct therapy. Intervention has focused on self-regulation, improving tolerance to movement, improving postural and functional strength, improving tolerance for multisensory activities, and bilateral coordination. Activities that involve unexpected touch, certain movement activities (spinning, swinging), and activities that require motor planning (especially games that involve collaboration among a peer or peers) can be overwhelming and over-stimulating for ________ (child's name). ________ (child's name) has been successful with participating in multisensory activities within the clinic and within the school environment by using a variety of strategies. He is able to participate in games with multiple peers within the clinic and has been able to participate in his general education gym class with support from his adaptive physical education teacher. Below are the strategies that have been most helpful in supporting ________ (child's name).

Strategies for self-regulation/group participation

- ☐ Proprioceptive input before a stimulating activity (gym class, lunch room, etc.). Some examples are: weightlifting, using a medicine ball, and wall pushups.
- ☐ Use a hand signal (thumbs up/down) or a code word to communicate to an adult when ________ (child's name) is becoming overwhelmed.
- ☐ Sometimes ________ (child's name) needs a break during group activities, but does not need to leave the group or room. Using a water bottle with a straw, doing wall pushups, or eating a crunchy or chewy snack have been helpful during breaks.
- ☐ Collaborate with ________ (child's name) on an "exit" plan if he needs to leave the group (where can he go safely to regroup).
- ☐ Allow ________ (child's name) to leave the group at any time. When he is in a safe, quiet place, then he is able to discuss why he needed to leave the activity, what triggered this, and what can be done for him to return to the group. Most times he returns to the activity.

Accommodations for the classroom

- ☐ Discuss with ________ (child's name) what he can do if he becomes overwhelmed with an activity and provide him with quiet spaces to help him regroup and become organized. (for example, quiet corner in a classroom, going for a short walk in a quiet hallway).
- ☐ Allow ________ (child's name) to stand at the end of the line or allow him to leave the class a few minutes early to change classes to minimize the risk of unexpected or unwanted touch.
- ☐ Warn ________ (child's name) of loud noises such as before a fire alarm or school bell.
- ☐ ________ (child's name) may need assistance with prioritizing tasks and assignments. He may need assistance to identify the sequence of the task and help to collect the appropriate materials needed to complete the task.
- ☐ ________ (child's name) may need adult assistance to facilitate collaboration with peers during group projects.
- ☐ ________ (child's name) may need a checklist or adult assistance to recognize errors in his work and may need assistance to develop strategies to improve work.
- ☐ Use a visual timer or a programmed watch or provide a verbal warning before changing tasks. This will help ________ (child's name) with classroom transitions.
- ☐ Have a laminated schedule attached to his book bag to help organize the day for smoother transitions.
- ☐ Use consistent places to store ________ (child's name)'s assignments and classroom materials to assist in developing organizational skills such as color-coded folders, binders, or pencil cases.

(CAPONE, K., USED WITH PERMISSION)

Things the child can do to calm down

Using very few words, show your child this list as his upset mounts. He can choose his strategy by pointing. Parents, childcare providers, and professionals at school and in the community can take the strategy lead from the child. If the child cannot choose, the adult can choose for him. Preview this process with the child before you implement it.

- ☐ Go to your room and take a break
- ☐ Ask an adult to read to you
- ☐ Run around the house—outside
- ☐ Go to the sensory gym and work out
- ☐ Go fast on the elliptical machine
- ☐ Talk with someone whom you trust about what is bothering you
- ☐ Write in a journal
- ☐ Engage in a preferred activity
- ☐ Tell a story
- ☐ Type a story
- ☐ Use the ball
- ☐ Write
- ☐ Draw
- ☐ Chew gum
- ☐ Read a book
- ☐ Take deep breaths
- ☐ Talk to someone who can help
- ☐ Make an explicit, visual plan, after not being so upset
- ☐ Ask for space
- ☐ Take a pre-determined break
- ☐ Jump rope
- ☐ Use a pull-up bar
- ☐ Swing
- ☐ Ride stationary bike
- ☐ Take a walk

(BLUMENFELD, E., PERSONAL COMMUNICATION, 2011; DYMENT, J.H., PERSONAL COMMUNICATION, 2013)

Strategies that support the child to relax

Parents, childcare providers, and professionals at school and in the community can help the child build these strategies into his schedule.

- ☐ Read
- ☐ Deep breathing
- ☐ Yoga.
- ☐ Use the weighted blanket
- ☐ Exercise
- ☐ Mindfulness
- ☐ Listen to music
- ☐ Listen to a story
- ☐ Preferred stuffed animal
- ☐ Preferred activity
- ☐ Drawing
- ☐ Write lists
- ☐ Create a visual plan
- ☐ Screen time
- ☐ Movie

Create separate star charts for home and school

- Choose the three most important positive behaviors you would like to reinforce.
- Fill in the star chart grid with those behaviors.
- Insert time frames into the star chart grid.

Reward:

- Award a star for each time segment that the child achieves positive behavior goals.
- Reward the child with a preferred activity if he earns the designated number of stars per time frame.
- The reward could be five minutes of screen time or another approved activity.

Example of a star chart grid for home

	Safe body	**Level 2 voice**	**Follow directions**
6:00–6:30			
6:30–7:00			
7:00–7:30			
	If I earned 10 out of 12 stars I earn my reward		
2:30–3:00			
3:00–3:30			
3:30–4:00			
4:00–4:30			
4:30–5:00			
	If I earned 16 out of 20 stars I earn my reward		
5:00–5:30			
5:30–6:00			
6:00–6:30			
6:30–7:00			
	If I earned 13 out of 16 stars I earn my reward		

For my reward:

- ☐ I can choose computer time or TV time or another approved choice activity
- ☐ I will get five minutes on it

Example of a star chart grid for school

	Following directions: **Listening and following any direction given**	**Being a student:** **Participating in adult-directed activities during scheduled times throughout the day**	**Using a safe body:** ☐ **Keeping hands and feet to myself** ☐ **Not breaking or throwing objects**	**Bonus stars**
8:00–8:30				
8:30–9:00				
9:00–9:30				
9:30–10:00				
	If I earned 10 out of 12 stars I earn my reward			
10:00–10:30				
10:30–11:00				
11:00–11:30				
11:30–12:00				
	If I earned 10 out of 12 stars I earn my reward			
12:00–12:30				
12:30–1:00				
1:00–1:30				
1:30–2:00				
	If I earned 10 out of 12 stars I earn my reward			

- ☐ I can take a friend with me to the computer lab if that is what I choose as my reward
- ☐ If I choose the computer, I will get five minutes on it
- ☐ I can earn bonus stars for being a good friend and an exceptional student

(BLUMENFELD, E., USED WITH PERMISSION)

Develop a Social Story™ to introduce your child's star chart

Example of a star chart Social Story™

Hi! My name is ______.

During the day, I use a star chart. With my star chart, I can earn stars for:

- ☐ Following directions
- ☐ Being a student
- ☐ Using a safe body
- ☐ Using a Level 2 voice

With the star chart, I can also earn extra stars for:

- ☐ Being a good friend
- ☐ Being an exceptional student

If I earn 10 out of 12 stars, I can earn a five-minute computer break!

With the star chart, I can earn up to three breaks a day. I can earn a break at 10am, 12pm, and 2pm.

Every 30 minutes, my __________ (parents, teachers, or service providers) will check in with me to talk about how many stars I'm earning. My __________ (parents, teachers, or service providers) want me to earn all my stars so that I can earn all three breaks during the day.

If I try to follow the star chart, I will feel proud of myself, my ________ (parents, teachers, or service providers) will feel proud of me, and I will earn more computer breaks.

(BLUMENFELD, E., USED WITH PERMISSION)

Example of a repair plan Social Story™

Using this repair plan example as a model, devise your own repair plan for home, school, and various contexts in the community to determine how your child will repair mistakes made with others during upsets.

Hi! My name is _________.

Like other people, when I am mad, I might do something that hurts people's feelings.

When I hurt people's feelings, they may not want to spend time with me or be my friend.

If I follow the repair plan, the other person will probably feel better. They will probably still want to spend time with me or be my friend.

When I hurt people's feelings, it is my job to try to make it better by using a repair plan.

This is the plan:

- ☐ First, calm down before trying to make it better
- ☐ Choose one of these apologies:
  - ☐ I can say "I'm sorry" in a Level 2 voice, looking at the person
  - ☐ I can write the person a letter

My teachers, service providers, friends, and parents will be proud of me when I try to follow the repair plan.

(DYMENT, J.H., USED WITH PERMISSION)

Managing crises and emotions: School

Your child will be most successful when you explicitly teach him how to manage crises and emotions at school. You and teachers will lay the foundation for success at school when you explicitly teach your child what to do when he is upset.

Teachers may discuss some of their expectations for managing crises and emotions during the school day, and may assume that students are already aware of others. Regardless of whether teachers talk about what to do when your child is upset, you should cover these points in an explicit, visual format in order to ensure that your child with AS understands.

- Talk to teachers about helping to manage crises and emotions.
- Use the list and examples provided in this section as a springboard to think about managing crises and emotions tools that would support your child at school.
- Once you create school tools to manage crises and emotions unique to your child's needs and situation, preview them with your child and have a copy available for review in each situation and environment until she integrates the concepts and demonstrates mastery.
- When you create your managing crises and emotions toolbox, put one expectation per page with succinct, simple, accessible instructions. Less writing per page helps the child with AS avoid visual overload.

Tools for managing crises and emotions at school may include:

- ☐ Break Spot plan
- ☐ My 5-point scale for school
- ☐ My 5-point scale, if I am at a 5!

Examples: Managing crises and emotions at school

The Social Stories™ below serve as examples of how to support emotional regulation at school, which you can consider a springboard to making your own tools. Work with your child's special educator and/or teachers to develop tools to help your child manage crises and emotions. Feel free to:

- use the space provided in the template checklists you have downloaded to add points
- or create entirely new tools that would support your child.

Break Spot plan Social Story™

Hi! My name is _______ and I am a _____ grader at ________ School.

At ________ School, there is a room called the Break Spot. It is a place where students can go to have some quiet time to themselves. Students in all grades can use the Break Spot.

Sometimes when I am upset, I like to take quiet time to myself to cool down. My teachers understand this about me.

If I need to take quiet time to myself, I can tell my teachers, "I need to go to the Break Spot." They will understand and one of them will walk down with me.

Sometimes, my teachers might see that I am having a hard time and tell me, "It's a good time for the Break Spot."

When my teachers say this to me, they are trying to help me get to a quiet space, where I can cool down.

When I get to the Break Spot, there are a few things I can do:

- ☐ Use sensory tools on my own or with a teacher
- ☐ Lay down
- ☐ Have a teacher read to me
- ☐ Read by myself

My teachers feel proud of me when I try to use the Break Spot plan. I will feel proud of myself too.

(BLUMENFELD, E., USED WITH PERMISSION)

My 5-point scale for school Social Story™

Hi! My name is ________ and I am a student in _______ grade at ______ School.

During the school day, I can earn stars for following directions, being a student, and keeping a safe body. I can also earn stars for being a good friend, doing a good deed, or working extra hard.

My teachers check in with me every 30 minutes during the day to check on my stars. At this time, I also update them on how I am feeling.

5	I need to leave!	I need to take a break in the Break Spot*
4	I need some space	I need to take a movement break outside of my classroom OR I would like to go to the Break Spot
3	Please do not talk	I need some time alone in the Safe Spot or I need a movement break
2	I am a little nervous	I can work in my classroom at my table spot or in the Safe Spot
1	I can handle this	I can work at my table spot

** The Break Spot is a separate room designated as a place for Alexander to go when he is really stressed. The Safe Spot is a designated place within the classroom or learning center for him to retreat if he is feeling overwhelmed. If appropriate for your child, you may consider establishing similar spots with your child's teachers.*

When I point to a number on the 5-point scale, my teachers and I will know what I need, and where I need to go. My teachers want to help me feel calm and safe at school.

If I try to use my 5-point scale, it might help me feel safe and comfortable in school. I will feel proud of myself, and my teachers and parents will feel proud of me too.

(BLUMENFELD, E., INSPIRED BY BURON AND CURTIS 2003, USED WITH PERMISSION)

If I am at a 5 Social Story™

If I am at a 5, I can go to the Break Spot to take some time to calm down.

When my teachers or I see that I am at a 5 and I need to go to the Break Spot to calm down, I have three minutes to leave my classroom and go to the Break Spot.

If my three minutes are up and I have not left my classroom, my teachers will have students in my classroom leave the class together to give me some time and room to myself.

My teachers want to help me feel calm. To help me feel calm, they will follow the 5-point plan.

(BLUMENFELD, E., USED WITH PERMISSION)

Managing crises and emotions: Community

Your child will be most successful when you explicitly teach her how to manage crises and emotions in various contexts in the community. Be sure to note the rules in your guide.

Professionals with whom your child interacts may discuss some of their expectations for emotional regulation. Some places you visit may have rules posted that all guests need to follow. In some situations, neither of these things will happen. You should be sure to go over expectations for managing crises and emotions in an explicit, visual format in order to ensure that your child with AS understands.

- You will want to develop a plan for managing crises and emotions in conjunction with individuals who support your child in the community.
- Use the list and examples provided in this section as a springboard to think about emotional regulation expectations that would support your child in every context in which she participates in the community.
- Once you create a plan for managing crises and emotions in the community unique to your child's needs and situation, preview the tools with your child and have a copy available for review in each situation and environment until she integrates the concepts and demonstrates mastery.
- When you create your managing crises and emotions toolbox, put one expectation per page with succinct, simple, accessible instructions. Less writing per page helps the child with AS avoid visual overload.

Examples of tools for managing crises and emotions in the community may include:

- ☐ The Green, Yellow, and Red Zones
- ☐ How to earn back lost special activity time

The lists and explanations below serve as examples of tools for managing crises and emotions in the community, which you can consider a springboard to make your own lists. Feel free to:

- use the space provided in the template checklists you have downloaded to add points to the tools
- or create entirely new managing crises and emotions tools that would support your child.

Examples: Managing crises and emotions in the community

The Green, Yellow, and Red Zones

I am in the Green Zone when I am:

- ☐ Having a safe body
- ☐ Following directions
- ☐ Using safe words

If I am in the Green Zone at the end of the time block, then I can earn a star.

When I have 18 stars, I can earn a special choice.

I am in the Yellow Zone when I am:

- ☐ Not having a safe body
- ☐ Not following directions
- ☐ Not using safe words

When I am in the Yellow Zone, I need to take a break with my counselor. During my break I can read a special book with my counselor. When I am ready to return to the group and have a safe body, use safe words, and follow directions, I can return to the Green Zone.

I am in the Red Zone when I am:

- ☐ Not having a safe body
- ☐ Not following directions
- ☐ Not using safe words
- ☐ Not listening to my counselor's directions to take a break

(PARTRIDGE, M., MODIFIED FROM KUYPERS 2011, USED WITH PERMISSION)

How to earn back lost special activity time

- ☐ Safe body
- ☐ Following directions
- ☐ Safe words
- ☐ Participating
- ☐ Listening

(PARTRIDGE, M., USED WITH PERMISSION)

How to use the toolbox

Now that you have created your managing crises and emotions toolbox, you will be able to:

- decrease stress and confusion for your child by creating a plan for managing crises and emotions in every environment in which he or she interacts
- implement structure for emotional regulation and safety education and have guidelines for a unified approach to parenting
- create more productive and pleasant relationships between your child and their teachers and service providers now that a plan for supporting emotional regulation and managing crises and emotions in their environments is explicit
- help your child generalize skills by using the same strategies in multiple environments.

Chapter 9

Navigating Transitions and Changes

A major transition that we navigated as a family was moving back to the U.S. after living in London for three and a half years. As I shared with you in Chapter 5, the transition to London was very difficult for Alexander. With guidance from an AS consultant, our move back to the U.S. went much more smoothly.

This move home was tricky because we moved out of our London flat in mid-June and could not move into our new home until August 1. We stayed with relatives in three different cities over the course of the six weeks. In addition to staying in unfamiliar homes, we wanted to reconnect with friends because we had been away so long. In one city, we hosted a party with twenty-eight adults and children. In another, we hosted a steady stream of overnight guests. In the third city, we saw family members around the clock. Alexander was five years old, and this very easily could have been a recipe for disaster.

Our AS consultant helped us devise a strategy. She recommended that we buy an 8"×11" calendar book with one page devoted to every day of the year. We chose red because that was Alexander's favorite color. The pages were lined and divided into one-hour segments. Before leaving London, we filled in every schedule-related segment that we knew. As we learned more along the way, we added to the book. We made the calendar easier to access by gluing in pictures of everyone that we would see in each location by day, at the party, and for the overnight visits. We also glued in images of the activities that we planned. For example, at the party we rode on a boat, so we included an image of a boat. We put a picture of a plane on our travel days. If dogs lived at a home we were visiting, we inserted a picture of the dogs. We also needed to let Alexander know what was expected of him. In the margins beside each activity, we wrote explicit behavioral expectations for the event. If we knew a particular activity would be difficult for Alexander, we offered a Plan B option.

Our hand-made picture calendar let Alexander know where we would be when, for how long, with whom, and what was expected of him. We previewed the six-week span with him several times before leaving London. While on the trip, we previewed each new day the night before. We also explained his needs to the family and friends that we visited. With this training, the move back to the U.S. was much more successful than our move to London.

Parents' role with transition management

As a case manager, your role is to teach your child how to navigate transitions and changes at home, and to coordinate this process at school and in the community. This will call for knowledge, tools, and communication.

In this chapter you will learn about:

- why transitions and changes are so difficult for children with AS
- types of transitions and changes
- strategies to support transitions in every environment.

Navigating transitions and changes across environments

Why are transitions and changes so difficult for children with AS?

Struggles with transitions and changes are hallmark challenges for children with AS. Difficulties with cognitive flexibility and executive functioning, particularly in terms of planning and time estimation, make transitions and changes problematic. For example, if a child does not understand what 30 minutes feels like, he might react strongly to leaving a preferred activity for a 30-minute dinner if he incorrectly perceives that it will take "forever."

Many children with AS take comfort in repetition and sameness. By definition, transitions and changes decrease comfort and increase anxiety. Change is difficult, even when it is positive. For example, leaders in an Aspire program used a software tool designed to help individuals with AS assess their mood, energy, sleep, and food intake to teach the connection between these factors and happiness. One individual answered nearly every question in the exact same way over the course of the seven-week program. When asked about it, he responded that changing his answer from a Level 3 to a Level 4 on a scale of 1–5 happiness scale was so anxiety-producing that he willed himself to stay at a 3 because he could not tolerate the stress of the change. Similarly, children may struggle with a change from math class to gym, even if they find gym more exciting.

Types of transitions and changes

Children with AS encounter multiple transitions and changes every day. They occur all of the time and from moment to moment. Transitions and changes can be as big as moving to a new house, new school, or new country (which are often stressful for typically developing individuals, too), or as mundane as changing from working on the computer to exercising at home, going from class to class at school, or moving from one appointment to another in the community. Even transitions that are seemingly subtle, such as looking from the keyboard to the computer screen, can be problematic because they can cause children with AS to lose their focus. Transitions also include changes in the peers and adults in the child's life, such as new siblings, babysitters, childcare workers, or visitors at home; new teachers or peers at school; and new staff members or peers at community activities. Changes in schedules, plans, locations, and space design may also impact children with AS. Given the breadth of this challenging category, children with AS get little relief during the day from transition and change-induced stress.

Strategies to support every environment

Teach the concept of transition to your child

Transition and change are important words to explain and require direct instruction in every environment. You can talk about changes with a younger child. You might indicate that you understand that changes can be hard for your child. Assure him that there are things that you can do to support him and to help make them go easier.

Transitions are more all-encompassing. They are not just about the change that is more readily apparent to the child, but also about change at a higher level of abstraction such as the switch from being a student at school to a child at home. Not only is there a physical change, but there is also a role change. You can talk about transitions with older children and let them know that you will teach them how to cope with these.

Educate your child about "glitches" or "curve balls" and Plan Bs

Unexpected changes such as schedule changes at home, at school, or in the community occur regularly. You can help your child cope by assigning a name like "glitch" or "curve ball" to unexpected changes and teaching your child that he needs to go to Plan B when a glitch or curve ball occurs. This strategy primes your child to move into solution mode rather than staying stuck in the problem. Your child will generalize this concept most efficiently when all environments in which he interacts use the same language.

Assess your child's transition support needs

You can spend some time informally or formally collecting data during transition times. See if you can identify patterns regarding transitions and changes. For example, does your child struggle more with transitions during a particular time of day? Are activity changes or people changes more difficult? What activities does your child have the toughest time leaving? Once you identify patterns, you can provide different types of support accordingly. For example, a visual timer may be very important to use to support your child's transition from a preferred activity such as screen time, but verbal prompts might suffice when transitioning from less preferred activities such as homework.

You can best help your child by finding the balance between making accommodations to support success with ensuring that the child's life is not too structured and predictable. Your child needs transition assistance, but as he gets older, he also needs to learn and practice coping skills for inevitable life changes with the ultimate goal of dealing with them independently.

Preview transitions and changes

Children with AS cope better with transitions and changes when adults preview them either verbally or visually rather than springing the surprise on them. Social Stories™, notes, visual schedules, tables, and pictures are examples of the types of tools that you can use to preview changes. Your child will likely accept transitions and changes better when you explain why they are occurring. For example, you can share that the reason that his aide is not able to come to school today is because he is sick.

Your child's anxiety will decrease when he understands what will be the same and what will be different after a transition or change. For example, when a child transitions from one grade to the next, he will benefit from knowing very specifically what will stay the same and what will be different in terms of his teachers, schedule, classrooms, classes, peers, and so on. Unexpected transitions and changes can often lead to upset and crises.

When changing environments and staff members, involve your child. When possible, arrange to visit the new environment or meet a new babysitter, teacher, or staff member before the change occurs. Images are very effective. Either let your child take pictures when he visits the new environment, ask an adult to send you pictures, or use them in a Social Story™ to introduce the new environment. You might want to make a visual book like the one we created for Alexander during our move back to the United States so your child can review the images many times before the transition.

Plan transition periods between activities

Planning transition periods is as important as planning activities. Aspire's summer camp builds transitions into their schedules and orchestrates the environment to teach transition skills in a natural setting. The campers must bring backpacks to the camp with supplies for the day. Between activities, the counselors help the campers plan ahead. For example, they ask the children questions such as "What do you do with your wet suit after swimming?" and "What do you need from your backpack for your next activity?" These prompts help the children think about planning. In addition to giving the children an opportunity to strengthen their executive functioning skills, the weight of the backpack provides input to their bodies that helps them feel grounded. They build a therapeutic activity into a natural environment.

At school, Scott taught the staff how to plan transition periods for Alexander. For example, the school gave Alexander the job of bringing a basket of his class's lunch boxes in from the playground back to the classroom for the next event on the schedule.

At home, transitions go smoother when I give Alexander a job. For example, I might ask him to collect a bag that we need and to bring it into the car or bring groceries or luggage into the house from the car. That way he focuses on the task rather than on the stressful change.

Support transitions in the moment

Several techniques support children with AS during transitions. Counting down, giving reminders, using a timer, and providing a visual schedule are useful tactics to help make the transitions more concrete for your child. As we mentioned in Chapter 5, you can promote more flexibility when you add "ish" to a timeframe when you are not certain of the precise start time. For example, you can tell the child you will eat around noon-ish if you are not exactly sure when you can pull the meal together, but you know that it will be some time between 11:50 and 12:10. Many children with AS feel violated when you tell them a precise time like 12:00pm, and then you cannot meet that time. Struggles often arise as soon as the clock shows 12:01.

You can make transitions more peaceful for your child by staggering timeframes. Often transitions such as going into school at the start of the day and changing classes in busy halls are very chaotic and loud. If your child has an over-reactive sensory system, he will likely manage transitions better when he arrives a bit early to school to get settled and possibly transitions to classes a bit early or late.

As we also mentioned in Chapter 5, you can help your child develop the executive functioning skills of time estimation and prediction by using schedules and teaching what time segments feel like. When your child can better estimate and predict, he will be surprised less often by what he might otherwise interpret as an unexpected transition being sprung on him. When your child is clearer about where he is in his day and what transition is happening next, he feels a greater sense of control and peace.

Show your child that thoughts and emotions are connected to transitions

Based on your experience with your child, you can predict the thoughts and feelings the child will have and support him through the transition process. For example, if your child tells you that "school sucks" every time you prompt him to go to school, then you can offer replacement thoughts such as "School is hard for me right now" and "I can manage it." The emotion is likely anxiety. If you can help him change his thoughts, his feelings will likely change, too. If your child thinks that he can handle school, he will feel less out of control and his anxiety will lessen. You can explicitly point out the connection between transitions and thoughts and emotions to the younger child. When your child develops more, then the conversation can be more of a collaborative discussion. He will begin to make the connection for himself.

Use tools from other chapters to support transitions

Many of the tools throughout the book work together to help your child thrive at home, at school, and in the community. You can help your child with transitions and changes by previewing schedules, routines, behavioral expectations, and important adults. As we explained in earlier chapters, this information will help orient him, clarify environments, and decrease stress. Should issues with transitions and changes lead to meltdowns, you can use the tools in Chapter 8, Managing Crises and Emotions, to help your child regroup.

Follow up on transitions with your child

You can ask your child to reflect on how a transition went for him by rating how intense it was on a scale of 1 to 5. Determine with feedback from your child what worked and what would help in the future. If a transition went well, you can remind your child about the success the next time he faces a similar transition.

At home, at school, and in the community, your child with AS will learn how to cope with transitions when he receives positive reinforcement for the things he does well. Adults can help your child grasp what didn't work and why by providing explicit, non-judgmental education about what he is doing ineffectively and how to put the correction in place. When people in all environments positively reinforce successes, they will help your child recognize that he is capable of handling transitions and changes. Given that children with AS often receive negative feedback for their mistakes, this approach helps build their confidence.

It is also important to show compassion to your child. Often children with AS feel bombarded, confused, misunderstood, and stressed in many environments in which they interact. Transitions and changes are very difficult for many children with AS and assault them throughout the day. When your child knows that you understand her struggles, she will feel seen and heard. This dynamic calms your child and emphasizes that you get her, are on her side, and have the ability to provide a safe haven while supporting her growth.

Navigating transitions at home

As we've established, transitions are often difficult for children with AS to navigate in any environment. At home, children with AS must cope with many transitions, such as screen time to homework, homework to exercise, exercise to dinner, and people coming in and out. As we mentioned earlier in the chapter, even subtle shifts in attention can be viewed as a transition, as when your child shifts from looking at a computer screen to looking at a dog entering the room. Bigger transitions such as moving to a different home or gaining a new sibling can be particularly troubling. As you will see in the following examples of both larger and more mundane home-related transitions, transitions that have a significant impact on your child with AS will impact everyone in the household. When you use your transition tools, you can help your child manage transitions and changes at home and support a more harmonious household.

Moving to a new home

Moving to a new home is extremely stressful for any family, and even more intense for children with AS. They often do not know what to expect, their schedules and routines are impacted, they likely have to interact with new adults such as movers and construction workers, and their sensory systems are assaulted. Big transitions such as moves trigger many AS-related struggles and often lead to crises and upsets.

While on summer vacation in the U.S. during the time we lived in London, our landlord called with alarming news. Pipes burst in our London flat causing severe damage. When we returned, we first had to stay in a hotel followed by a temporary home for the next three months. Much of our furniture was damaged. Our home life was totally disrupted. All of the changes were so stressful for Alexander that he developed a tic that only stopped when we moved back into our flat after it was repaired. This experience helped me start to understand how difficult changes and transitions are for him.

We put a few strategies in place during this transition. Fortunately, our temporary apartment was around the corner from our home. Given that it can be hard to set a definite timeframe for work completion on these types of home projects, we gave Alexander an estimate of three to five months for when we would move back home. We visited the construction site about once a week to see the progress and discussed what the workers had completed and what they had left to do. This visual helped him. Additionally, we kept the rest of his routines and schedules in place. Had we known more at the time, we could have used more of the tools from the Parents Take Charge section of this chapter to better support Alexander.

Two years later, our AS consultant helped us support Alexander's transition into our new home in the U.S. when we moved back from London. When we decided on our new home, we took a trip back to the States to introduce Alexander to his new home and to visit his new school. We gave him a camera that he used to take a picture of every element outside and inside of the home, such as the driveway, the front door, a big picture view of the structure of the building, the kitchen, and the bedroom. His preview of the move was both the walk-through and the pictures. We made the pictures into a book and looked at them together regularly. We spoke about what would be the same in the house, such as our existing furniture, and what would be different, such as his new desk. We showed him a picture of the new desk.

After my difficult experience moving into our London home, which I shared in Chapter 5, we decided that we would not subject Alexander to the chaos of the move. My in-laws kindly helped us stagger the timeframe of the transition by keeping him at their home and supporting him with daily schedules and behavioral expectations for each context, which I provided. We also had a big picture calendar, which helped us provide a visual countdown to the move. We set the house up to the greatest extent possible before he came to his new home. By the time he arrived, most of the boxes were broken down, the house was cleaned, and his room was in order. Because we previewed it with him and didn't subject him to its most stressful aspects, this move was much more successful!

The birth of a sibling

The addition of a new family member is another major transition, which triggers many of the most intense AS-related struggles. Children with AS have to cope with multiple, unexpected changes. Parents are different before and after they have a new baby. They are often more excited, tired, and distracted than usual. Routines and schedules likely change, and parents may not be able to spend as much time with their child with AS. The house expectations can change too. For example, the child with AS might have to be quiet during certain times, such as when the baby is asleep. The family will often have visitors during this time. Both the visitors and the baby will increase the noise level in the home. All of these stressors build up quickly for children with AS and often lead to crises and upsets. Parents might have less bandwidth for dealing with the struggles of the child with AS because they are exhausted or fragile. Without AS-specific tools to support this transition (see the Navigating transitions and changes: Home section in Parents Take Charge), this life change can be very challenging.

Will's birth, which occurred four months after Alexander started preschool, represented another tremendous change. While we intuitively knew to maintain the schedule to the greatest extent possible, even our greatest efforts did not thwart Alexander's deep dislike and intolerance for change. He was angry and his tantrums became more intense. Soon after Will came home from the hospital, I made a conscious effort to spend quality time with Alexander. He refused to be with me because he was frustrated with the change and jealous about the time I spent with his brother. A few days after I returned from the hospital, I urged him to go for a walk with me. He had a temper fit that lasted about fifteen minutes and ultimately yelled loudly, "I hate you! I don't want to be with you!" I was hormonal, fragile, and tired from giving birth, sad that Alexander was struggling, and hurt that he didn't want to spend time with me. I went for a walk by myself and cried for about an hour. I wondered at the time why this was so hard. He held this furious, punishing position for close to three weeks.

Everyday changes

There are many kinds of everyday changes. They occur all of the time and incrementally increase the stress of the child with AS. These changes can include an increase in noise such as someone mowing the lawn in the neighborhood, a dog barking, or a child bouncing a ball. Other changes impact schedules such as an appointment being added or cancelled or someone arriving home late. New people coming into the home such as siblings or parents' friends can often be unwanted changes. Family members' mood and demeanor changes impact children with AS. All of these everyday changes can mount quickly and lead to crises or upsets at home.

My husband, Michael, usually arrives home from work around 7:30pm. Based on many years of experience, both of my children expect him at this time and major upsets occur when he runs late. We use several techniques to support Alexander with this change. When we know well in advance that his father will be late, we post the change on our family's visual weekly calendar, verbally preview the change, and remind Alexander multiple times. When the change is more last-minute, Michael calls home to talk with Alexander about the "glitch," including why the change occurred, and what Plan B can be. For example, if he will not arrive before Alexander goes to bed, they may make a special plan to watch a movie together the following night or over the weekend.

Navigating transitions at school

Transition to a new school

Change at school can also be very difficult for children with AS. Children with AS typically need strategies to cope with the multiple transitions they face throughout their school day. Some transitions, such as a change to a new school, are more difficult for children with AS and require more collaborative planning by parents and teachers. Transitioning to a new school or school year can take months for children with AS to master. Parents and teachers can work together to develop strategies to decrease transition time and stress. The plan can include having the child with AS visit the classroom and meet the teachers before school begins, understand how to get from class to class and how to negotiate the classroom, and arrive to school early to avoid sensory overload and get settled. Changes to new environments run most smoothly when the child's teachers have a sense of the child prior to the transition. You can give the team your school guide and review it with them before they begin to work with your child.

As we prepared to move from London, our educational consultant also trained me to organize my accumulated information relating to Alexander's AS to present to his new school. She advised me to create two case files, one for our family and one for the school, with his:

- diagnostic report
- speech and language assessment and follow-up reports
- occupational therapy assessment and follow-up reports
- school reports
- medical records
- immunization history.

In addition, I included:

- letters from his teachers about their experience with Alexander and his preferences, presentation, struggles, and overall history
- a report from our educational consultant listing recommendations based on successful strategies.

The files offered all the information, in an accessible format, that the school needed to transition Alexander. The experience taught me the importance of creating an organizational system for all AS information regarding my son, which later influenced my decision to create my school guide.

Additionally, the consultant recommended that I give Alexander a camera when we visited the school and let him know that his job was to take pictures of his new surroundings. Snapping photos helped him feel less anxious as well as useful. We created a photo album after the visit, which he reviewed numerous times before the school year began. As it did with his transition to our new home, studying the images of his new school, classrooms, and various teachers increased his familiarity and reduced his stress leading up to the first day of school. The outcome of our educational consultant's recommendations taught me that transition management is an effective tool.

All of the preparation supported Alexander's successful integration into kindergarten in the States. His teacher and I kept the lines of communication open, but the year was a relatively smooth one. He made friends, had play dates, and kept up with his schoolwork. His principal later told me that she would have never known that Alexander had AS had we not shared his diagnosis. His new classroom model better supported his needs due to large, daily visual schedules posted, previewed, and referenced throughout the day, fewer students in the classroom, and more adults to assist each student. The room was quieter, the day was clearly structured, the schedule was predictable, and the kindergarteners released their energy in a separate playground from the rest of the school. All of the built-in supports helped him thrive.

Transition to a new teacher, class, and school year

While perhaps not as stressful as a transition to a brand new school, the transition to a new school year, with new teachers, classrooms, classmates, and schedules, is often problematic for children with AS. Special educators play an important role in the transition from one grade to another. They can explicitly break the process down into more manageable pieces through the use of Social Stories™ or other visual tools. They can help the child decrease his anxiety by reminding him that change can often turn out well. They can bring closure to the year by reminding the child with AS of her biggest accomplishments and use that as evidence that she can succeed the next year. They can further relieve end-of-year stress by explaining all of the things that will be similar and pointing out what is already familiar about the things that will be different. They can re-orient the child when she returns to school by reminding her of the similarities from the previous year and telling her what she needs to do as a student. If a child voices particular distress about a change, such as not knowing if her aide will return, the teacher can address her concern as thoroughly as possible.

Every school year, we endured a learning curve that often lasted months, during which teachers tried hard to understand what worked for Alexander. During this same period, Alexander struggled terribly with all of the changes and transitions that new school years bring. I didn't know how to help. Alexander's profile is complex and errors inevitably occurred. Whenever a new teacher entered the picture, this ritual repeated itself and resulted in avoidable crises.

One day at the beginning of a school year Alexander became so upset that his teachers thought he should leave the room. When he refused, two well-intentioned teachers each took an arm and forced him out. Because of his over-reactivity to touch, he went into a full-blown meltdown and didn't recover for hours. The school ultimately called me to pick him up. When I arrived, I found him laying on the floor completely distraught in a room the size of a large closet with someone guarding the outside of the door. I was horrified that he had been treated this way. His teachers were very rattled. The situation was extremely difficult and affected trust for everyone.

This crisis could have been avoided. These teachers are bright, sensitive, capable, and motivated to do a great job. They simply did not yet know Alexander. I recognize in retrospect that I should have been proactive in sharing information about him. The year could have started much more easily. I wish I had shared that touch will automatically set him off, particularly if he is already upset, and provided calming techniques. In most cases, Alexander has a difficult time recovering from rough beginnings. I could have positively influenced his entire year by sharing information about his AS and strategies that support him.

Transition back to school from the weekend, vacation, or summer break

The first days back to school after weekends are usually difficult, but they are even tougher after a vacation and worst of all after summer break. The transition from the rhythm and routine of life at home and in the community to the rhythm and routine of life at school is difficult for children with AS. Part of the problem could be that they know that school is challenging for them. But, as you have seen throughout this chapter, a major contributor to the struggle is the fact that any kind of change is hard for children with AS.

To help with transitions back to school after the weekend, one of Alexander's special educators developed a positive reinforcement tool that she used with him every week (this tool can be found in the Parents Take Charge section). She sent him a note every weekend that highlighted his successes from the previous week and previewed anything that was coming up the following week. I read it to him on Sunday late in the day. This tool helped him feel good about himself and school, strengthened his relationship with her, and supported his transition back to school.

Significant classroom and staff changes

Changes of classrooms and staff that children both know will happen and do not expect are a part of school life. For example, as children progress to the later grades of elementary school, many will transition from having a homeroom base where most teaching occurs to changing classrooms for some subjects. This change is part of the known school culture. More unexpected transitions include changes in room design or size or a teacher going on maternity or paternity leave. Your child will likely manage these types of transitions best with the support of notes or Social Stories™, pictures for changes in design, and an opportunity to physically preview the space and meet the staff for changes in teaching in a homeroom to switching classrooms. (You can find examples of tools to support these types of transitions in the Parents Take Charge section.)

Everyday transitions at school

In addition to bigger transitions such as moving to a new school or navigating a new school year, students with AS encounter many challenging transitions throughout their days, including transitioning to school every day, changing from class to class and activity to activity, navigating different teaching styles, and handling changes in plans including additions or changes to the schedule. You and your child's team at school can help your child manage these transitions and changes by using the information in this chapter and the tools in the Parents Take Charge sections of this book.

Transition meetings

As a case manager, you can help your child with all of these transitions at school. You can start by requesting a transition meeting in late spring to rally his or her team to design proactively an effective transition plan for the upcoming year.

Whenever the team assembles to talk about your child, the gathering is considered an IEP meeting. Therefore, transition meetings are part of the IEP process. The law does not require transition meetings, but we recommend that you schedule them every year. The purpose of the meeting should be to determine the interventions and accommodations that can and should be in place to ensure a smooth transition to the next grade and to educate new team members about your child.

Once you establish a meeting date, you can develop agenda items and distribute your e-mail to the school liaison, special educator, and educational consultant. Examples of topics include creating a crisis response plan for the following year, clarifying academic and executive functioning support, discussing the best most compatible educator–child match and student grouping, verifying the training level of teachers and aides about AS, establishing carefully structured introductory meetings between the new teachers and the child with AS, and setting parent meetings with new teachers to share information about the child's unique profile. You can use the example agenda-setting e-mail for transition meetings (see the Navigating transitions and changes: School section in Parents Take Charge) as a model from which to work.

One of the benefits of having a transition meeting is that the incoming and outgoing teams have an opportunity to meet and speak about your child. You can take the opportunity to present your guide to the team. The outgoing team can tell the incoming team what tools and strategies from the guide worked particularly well. New teachers will not receive sufficient information to work with your child by simply reading your child's IEP. You will greatly assist new teachers and team members in quickly getting up to speed on your child's profile and needs and effectively transitioning your child to a new grade when you use your guide as a collaboration tool.

Navigating transitions in the community

Children with AS face similar types of transitions and changes and resulting struggles in the community as they do at school and at home. These transitions and changes may include:

- taking on a new activity such as an art or drama class, a sport, occupational therapy, or a social pragmatics group
- transitioning in and out of the activity (arrival and departure)
- working with new staff members and peers
- changing from task to task within the course of the activity
- receiving unexpected news of changes in the schedule or plan
- returning after a break.

The strategies and tools in this chapter and in the Parents Take Charge section will help you collaborate with adults in the community to support your child with transitions and changes. In addition to the tools in the Community section, you can adapt the Social Stories™ and tools in the School section to support your child in the community. As we mentioned earlier in the chapter, you can also use the tools in the Parents Take Charge sections of other chapters (Routines and Schedules, Behavioral Expectations, Important Adults, and

Managing Crises and Emotions) to provide complete transition and change support. Share pertinent parts of your guide with the adults in the community so they understand your child's profile and transition-related needs.

Change from activity to activity

Changes from activity to activity in the community can be extremely challenging for children with AS, particularly when schedule and people changes and sensory assaults are involved. The community is less predictable and controllable than other environments. These stressors can quickly escalate to crises, particularly when adults don't have the tools or knowledge to support the child.

Once we traveled for a week with another family. On the return trip, we had to take a train and then catch a cab home. During the transition between train and cab, someone accidentally bumped Alexander while waiting in a long, crowded line outside of a noisy train station. The next thing I knew, he yelled at the top of his lungs in front of everyone in line. We tried talking to him to calm him down and that aroused him further. My husband decided to take him to a more private area. He picked him up, which caused kicking, hitting, and louder yelling. I felt powerless, out of control, and embarrassed. In retrospect, I recognize and have compassion for the fact that Alexander's sensory system was completely overwhelmed with visual, tactile, and aural input on top of the transition between train and cab. At the time, I tried earnestly to do the best that I knew how to do, but I secretly feared that his tantrums reflected poor parenting skills.

If I could go back, I would have previewed a visual schedule and had it available in the moment with prompts so Alexander would know exactly what to expect and when. I would have provided earplugs or headphones with music he likes to try to cancel the noise. Instead of subjecting him to the crowded line, I would have found a quieter, less busy place in the train station and waited there with him while my husband waited in line. I would have made sure that he had an activity to occupy him while we waited. We wouldn't have touched him or picked him up, and we would have used minimal words and written simple communications on a notebook when necessary. I would have previewed with our family friends that this would likely be a tricky time for Alexander and that I would need to give him my undivided attention and support.

Struggle with change in the community, even if it is exciting

Scott knows a family that took their child with AS to Disney World. This child was secure with certain community outings. In fact, his favorite community outing was going to Walmart. He knew what to expect in the store and felt very comfortable there.

Even though this child had success with Walmart outings, he had a major meltdown at the Disney entrance. He cried and screamed that he did not want to go to Disney. Instead, he wanted to go to Walmart. Though Disney would likely be great fun for this child, the transition to something unknown was still difficult.

The family did not go to Disney that day. However, with transition-related support including the preview of Disney's entrance, they went in the following day and the experience was successful. It is important to remember that anything new, even if it is something seemingly enjoyable, can be stressful for a child with AS. Use the same planning and previewing tools you would with transitions that are more obviously stressful or unpleasant.

Generalization

Life brings changes all of the time. Some we can predict, and many we cannot. You can teach your child from an early age and in every environment that he is resilient and can handle it. Though children with AS often do not outgrow their struggles with transitions and changes, they can develop coping skills. You can explicitly teach children with AS flexibility and anticipation skills.

As you have seen throughout this chapter, the process for helping your child develop skills to cope with transitions and changes is the same for every environment in which he interacts:

- Teach the concept of transition and change to your child.
- Educate the child about glitches/curve balls and Plan Bs.
- Assess your child's transition support needs in each environment.
- Preview transitions and changes.
- Plan transition periods between activities.
- Support transitions in the moment.
- Help your child develop transition-related executive functioning skills.

- Show your child that thoughts and emotions are connected to transitions.
- Use tools from other chapters to support transitions.
- Positively reinforce your child's successes.
- Show compassion to your child.
- Set important adults in each environment up for success by sharing pertinent parts of your guide.

You can support generalization by educating your child about the process and communicating with his support team to make sure that the language used is consistent in every environment.

In conclusion: Supporting changes and transitions

Your child will be able to cope with and navigate transitions and changes best when you start this education and practice early and continue it consistently in every environment. As you have seen, many of the tools in different chapters will work with the tools in this chapter to support every aspect of transitions and changes. Schedules and routines, behavioral expectations, and important adults tools are essential components of previewing transitions. Managing crises and emotions tools will support your child if transitions and changes cause his behavior to escalate. Your child will have more success with independence when he can deal with transitions and changes effectively. We will discuss more about independence in the next chapter.

Parents Take Charge

Creating Your Child's Navigating Transitions and Changes Toolbox

These workbook exercises help decrease stress and increase clarity about transitions that your child will encounter at home, at school, and in the community. This toolbox works as a simple guide for your child and a teaching template and collaboration toolbox for you and the professionals that support him.

Navigating transitions and changes: Every environment

As we've discussed previously, transitions and changes are difficult for children with AS in every environment. Generalizing strategies for transitions and changes can expedite this process and lead to greater success in every context. Coordinate with your child's support team to use the same strategies in every setting when helping your child develop independence skills. Set important adults in each environment up for success by sharing pertinent parts of your guide.

Strategies for navigating transitions and changes in every environment

- ☐ Teach the concept of transition and change to your child
- ☐ Educate your child about glitches/curve balls and Plan Bs
- ☐ Assess your child's transition support needs in each environment
- ☐ Preview transitions and changes:
    - ☐ Social Stories™
    - ☐ Notes
    - ☐ Pictures
    - ☐ Visits
    - ☐ Meeting important adults
    - ☐ What will be the same and what will be different

- ☐ Plan transition periods between activities
- ☐ Support transitions in the moment:
  - ☐ Count down
  - ☐ Provide reminders
  - ☐ Use a timer
  - ☐ Provide a visual schedule
  - ☐ Stagger timeframes—have the child transition earlier than the group
- ☐ Help your child develop transition-related executive functioning skills
- ☐ Show your child that thoughts and emotions are connected to transitions
- ☐ Use tools from other chapters to support transitions:
  - ☐ Preview schedules and routines
  - ☐ Preview behavioral expectations for each context
  - ☐ Preview and meet important adults
  - ☐ Use tools from managing crises and emotions if your child gets stressed from transitions and changes
- ☐ Reflect on how the transition went for the child
- ☐ Positively reinforce your child's successes
- ☐ Show compassion to your child

Navigating transitions and changes: Home

The goal is to create strategies that will support your child with transitions and changes at home. These tools may vary greatly from child to child, depending on his profile. These exercises will help you to understand and use the strategies that will help your child cope with transitions and changes.

- Use the list and examples provided in this section as a springboard to think about strategies for transitions and changes that would support your child at home. If you do not see a strategy that is pertinent for your child, simply create one using these examples as models.
- Once you create tools unique to your child's needs and situation, preview the transitions and changes with your child and have a copy available for review in each situation and environment as he navigates the transitions and changes.

- Once you create strategies for transitions and changes unique to your child's needs and situation, parents, babysitters, and anyone else in a home care role can use these tools to teach your child how to cope with transitions and changes.
- Transitions and changes should be introduced one at a time, and learning to cope with them can be part of home education.
- Once the child becomes competent with coping with a transition or change, continue practicing it, make the connection to other similar transitions or changes, and start teaching your child how to cope with another transition or change.
- When you create your navigating transitions and changes toolbox, put one tool per page with succinct, simple, accessible instructions. Less writing on each page helps the child with AS avoid visual overload.

Transitions and changes at home may include:

- ☐ Moving to a new home
- ☐ Welcoming a new sibling
- ☐ Getting a pet
- ☐ Having people come into your home

The lists below serve as examples of strategies for transitions and changes, which you can consider a springboard to making your own lists. Feel free to:

- use the space provided in the template checklists you have downloaded to add points to the daily living skills
- or create entirely new transitions and changes strategies that would support your child.

Examples: Navigating transitions and changes at home

Moving to a new home

Before the move

- ☐ Visit the new home with your child:
  - ☐ If your child has an over-reactive sensory system, choose a calm time for a private visit
- ☐ Take pictures of the new home:
  - ☐ Either your child or you can snap the shots
  - ☐ Make sure to get pictures of everything inside and outside
- ☐ Make a picture book

- [ ] Review the picture book regularly
- [ ] Create a visual table or story indicating what will be the same and what will be different about the homes

During the move

- [ ] Stagger the timeframe:
    - [ ] If possible, make other plans for your child during the time the boxes are moved into the new home to allow your child to avoid the chaos
- [ ] Plan the transition period:
    - [ ] Plan for your child to be in another environment supported by a schedule and behavioral expectations for each context
    - [ ] Provide a schedule with behavioral expectations if your child is present for the moving of boxes
    - [ ] Use a calendar showing the countdown to the move
- [ ] If possible, present the house to your child in order, clean, and organized when he moves in
- [ ] If your child gets upset:
    - [ ] Use managing crises and emotions tools
    - [ ] Teach how thoughts and emotions are connected to transitions
- [ ] Positively reinforce your child's transition-related successes

Welcoming a new sibling

Before the birth

- [ ] Read books to your child about new siblings coming home
- [ ] Show the child pre-natal pictures
- [ ] Make a calendar showing the countdown to the birth (estimated)
- [ ] Create a visual table or story indicating what will be the same and what will be different about having a new baby in the house

In the hospital

- [ ] Take pictures of the new-born baby and show your child before he meets the baby
- [ ] Have your child visit the hospital to meet the baby

When the baby comes home

- [ ] If you think it will help your child, plan for your child to be in another environment supported by a schedule and behavioral expectations for each context
- [ ] If your child is present for the baby's entry into the home:
    - [ ] Introduce her to your child during a calm period
    - [ ] Provide a schedule with behavioral expectations

- ☐ If your child gets upset:
  - ☐ Use managing crises and emotions tools
  - ☐ Teach how thoughts and emotions are connected to transitions
- ☐ Positively reinforce your child's transition-related successes

Getting a new pet

Before getting the pet

- ☐ Read books to your child about new pets coming home
- ☐ Use pictures:
  - ☐ Show your child pictures that the breeder, shelter, or owner can provide
- ☐ Involve your child in choosing the pet's name
- ☐ Have your child visit the pet's birth home to meet the animal
- ☐ Make a list of items to purchase for the new pet
- ☐ Allow your child to be part of the buying process
- ☐ Talk with your child about what his job can be when the pet arrives
- ☐ Create a visual table or story indicating what will be the same and what will be different about having a new pet in the house
- ☐ Make a calendar showing the countdown to the pet's arrival

When the pet arrives

- ☐ If you think it will help your child, plan for him to be in another environment supported by a schedule and behavioral expectations for each context
- ☐ If your child is present for the pet's entry into the home:
  - ☐ Introduce her to your child during a calm period
  - ☐ Provide a schedule with behavioral expectations
- ☐ If your child gets upset:
  - ☐ Use managing crises and emotions tools
  - ☐ Teach how thoughts and emotions are connected to transitions
- ☐ Positively reinforce your child's transition-related successes

(DEVELOPED WITH INPUT FROM DYMENT, J.H.)

Having new people come into your home

- ☐ Who is coming over?
- ☐ Why are they coming?
- ☐ What is their role in your home?
- ☐ What is your child's role when they are at your home?
- ☐ How long will they stay? Make a calendar showing the countdown to the visit and how long the visitor will stay if longer than a day
- ☐ What is the plan?

- ☐ Provide a schedule with behavioral expectations for the visit
- ☐ If possible, use pictures:
  - ☐ Person or people coming
  - ☐ Any activities your child might do with the person
- ☐ If the visitor's transition into or out of the house will be chaotic, try to stagger your child's introduction to the interaction until after the chaos has settled
- ☐ If your child gets upset:
  - ☐ Use managing crises and emotions tools
  - ☐ Teach how thoughts and emotions are connected to transitions
- ☐ Positively reinforce your child's transition-related successes

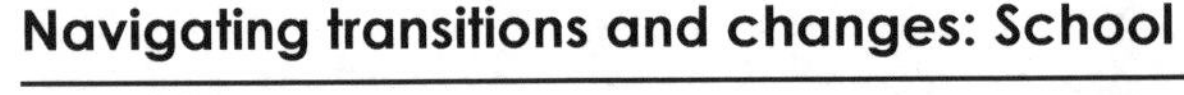

Navigating transitions and changes: School

Your child will be most successful when you support his transitions and changes at the school. You and teachers will lay the foundation for success at school when you develop transitions and changes tools to support your child.

Teachers may discuss some aspects of transitions and changes, and may assume that students are already aware of others. Regardless of whether teachers talk about transitions and changes, you should cover them in an explicit, visual format in order to ensure that your child with AS understands and is prepared.

- Talk to teachers about transitions and changes.
- Use the list and examples provided in this section as a springboard to think about transitions and changes tools that would support your child at school.
- Once you create school transitions and changes tools unique to your child's needs and situation, preview them with your child and have a copy available for review.
- When you create your transitions and changes toolbox, put one tool per page with succinct, simple, accessible information or instructions. Less writing on each page helps the child with AS avoid visual overload.

Tools for navigating transitions and changes in school may include:

- ☐ Welcome to ______ grade
- ☐ I am good at following routines
- ☐ Change is hard, but sometimes there are good things about change
- ☐ My success in ______ grade

- ☐ What will be the same next year?
- ☐ What will be different next year?
- ☐ My aide's plan for next year
- ☐ Transition from homeroom to changing classrooms and new-looking learning center
- ☐ Note sent home about the week's schedule changes and Plan B choices
- ☐ Teacher going on maternity or paternity leave
- ☐ Change in schedule—testing
- ☐ Change in schedule—activity change
- ☐ Schedule addition
- ☐ Weekly reinforcement letter
- ☐ Agenda-setting e-mail for transition meetings

The tool "Information about ________ (name of Science, English Language Arts, Social Studies, Science, Math, Health, Music, Art, Foreign Language Teacher)" found in the Important adults: School section of Parents Take Charge in Chapter 7 is also an excellent transition tool.

The Social Stories™, notes, and tables below serve as examples of school transition support tools, which you can consider a springboard to making your own. Work with your child's special educator and/or teachers to develop transition support tools unique to your child's needs and situation. Feel free to:

- use the space provided in the template checklists you have downloaded to add points to the Social Stories™, notes, and tables
- or create entirely new transitions and changes tools that would support your child.

Work with your child's special educator and team to identify specific points that Social Stories™ or other tools could address to reduce transition stress and support your child's end and beginning-of-year transitions. Special educators and parents can preview and review the stories at the end of the year and the beginning of the following year to fully support every stage of the transition.

Examples: Navigating transitions and changes at school

Welcome to ________ grade

This Social Story™ is intended to preview with a child before he starts a new grade. It is specifically designed for a looping class (a class that stays together for two years with the same students, classroom, and teachers), but you can alter it to reflect a change to a new class.

Hi! My name is _______ and I am a student at ______ School.

In September I will be a _____ grader. Some things about _____ grade will be the same as they were in _____ grade. Some things will be new and different.

I will have the same teachers in _____ grade as I did in _____ grade: ________, ________, and ________. My teachers care about me and are happy to have me again in _________ classroom.

A lot of the kids in my ______ grade class will also be in my ______ grade class. One of my classmates, _______, left and will be at private school. _______ was not in my fourth grade class but will be in our classroom this year. I know _______ from _____ grade.

Something that will be different is our class schedule. We will have our specials at different times and days than last year.

Our lunch and recess times will also be different. Our class will have recess from 10:50–11:10 and lunch from 11:10–11:30. We will share a recess and lunch time with the sixth graders.

This year's classroom will be set up very similarly to last year's classroom. There will still be table spots, a meeting area, a computer table, a library, and a Safe Spot.

I will already know lots of the routines and expectations in ______ grade when I get to school. There will also be new activities and things to learn!

(BLUMENFELD, E., USED WITH PERMISSION)

I am good at following routines

This story is meant to re-orient the child to the second year of his looping class (a class that stays together for two years with the same students, classroom, and teachers) but can be altered if the class does not loop. Special educators and parents can preview this Social Story™ before a new school year.

Hi! My name is _______ and I'm going to be a ______ grader at _______ School.

I will have the same teachers and mostly the same classmates in ______ grade as I had last year in _______ grade. Many of the routines in class will also be the same. In ______ grade, I learned the routines and expectations, and I was really good at following them.

When I arrive at school in the morning, it is expected that I hang my things on the hook outside of class, greet my teachers, and go to the

Safe Spot to review the schedule for the day. If there is time, a teacher will read a book to me.

I know that when the class gathers at the meeting area, it is my job to sit with the group and participate until the red timer goes off. Sometimes, if I feel like I need a break before the timer goes off, I know that I can ask a teacher for a quick break.

If I need to go get a snack or water, or go to the bathroom, all I have to do is ask a teacher and they will say, "Okay." This routine is important because teachers need to know where students are all the time for safety.

If I ever need a break outside of the classroom, I can go to the Break Spot. This is a place where I can relax and calm down. Sometimes I know when I need to go there, and other times one of my teachers might tell me that I need to go there for a break. The Break Spot is a place where I can have some space to kick a ball, lay down, and have a teacher read to me.

During the day, I earn stars for following directions, keeping a safe body, and being a student. Most days last year, I would earn lots of stars every day. Some days I even earned all of the stars I possibly could. I am good at following directions, keeping a safe body, and being a student.

I am an important member of ______ grade. I am good at following the routines of the class, and doing my best in school. My teachers are happy to have me back this year!

(BLUMENFELD, E., USED WITH PERMISSION)

Change is hard, but sometimes there are good things about change

The purpose of this story is to help a child feel less anxious about change. This tool can be particularly useful during the end and beginning of school transitions.

My name is _______ and I'm a smart, creative ______ grade student at _______ School.

There are many things that I'm good at and are easy for me:

- ☐ I'm a talented write
- ☐ I have a gift for creating interesting and realistic characters
- ☐ I have excellent manners
- ☐ I work hard at being a student

Like everyone, some things are hard for me. One of these things is handling change.

There are times that change can be good. There are also times that I handle change well.

Some changes are good:

- ☐ I did not have a dog before, but now I have _______ (dog's name).
- ☐ Monday night I had no homework.
- ☐ Because of my standardized test, my day was shortened on Wednesday and Thursday.

Change can be hard, but sometimes it turns out to be good and I can handle it.

(BLUMENFELD, E., USED WITH PERMISSION)

My success in _____ grade

Special educators, aides, or parents can use this story at the end of the school year to promote closure and decrease stress for the following year.

My name is _______ and I am a student at _______ School.

This past year, I was a ______ grader in ______ classroom. I worked hard and learned a lot in my class. I also got to know my classmates and teachers well. As a ______ grader, I will still see some of my classmates and old teachers.

As a student this year, I worked on writing, drawing, reading, math, science, social tips, and lots of other stuff. I am really good at writing stories. Sometimes I even read my stories to my teachers and classmates. They clapped at the end and asked me questions about my stories. My teachers were proud of me for sharing my stories.

I also did a few research projects and made a few movies that I also shared with the class. I researched puffins, cup stacking, and Mark Twain with _______ (student), and then we presented about our research. People were impressed with our work. I also made movies about SpongeBob and Men in Black 3. My teachers and classmates enjoyed these projects and movies.

A goal that I made for myself in the fall of ______ grade was to be more involved with the class. I worked so hard on this goal! I joined the class for almost all science lessons, book clubs, social studies lessons, social tips, and morning meetings. That is a lot of time with the group. My teachers and parents noticed how hard I worked on this and they are proud of me. My classmates were also happy to have me in the group more often.

My teachers were really proud of me for the work that I did in my class. They think that I am an important member of the class and they know I'll do great in ______ grade!

(BLUMENFELD, E., USED WITH PERMISSION)

What will be the same next year?

Special educators, aides, and parents can use this story at the end of the school year to let the child know everything that will remain the same in the face of a change to a new classroom, new teachers, and different students. The tool can help to alleviate transition stress. Parents can review again with their child over the summer.

In September I will be a _____ grader. Some things about ______ grade will be similar to how they were in _______ grade. Some things will be new and different.

Some of my past teachers will still be at ________ School and I will see them in the building. ______, _______, and _______ will all still be at school. Many of the adults from school that I know will still be here next year, like ______, ______, ______, _______, _______, _______, ________, _______, and ______.

I will also still have ______ for art, _______ for music, and ______ for P.E. These teachers care about me and are happy to have me again in class.

Some of the kids from my ______ grade class will also be in my ______ grade class. We will spend the entire day together. When we switch classes, I will still be with all the same kids throughout the day.

Next year I will still have a daily schedule that has things on it like: morning meeting, math, science, social studies, specials, and time to myself. I'll also still work to earn stars and breaks.

These are all things that will be the same about next year. During a time when things are changing, knowing that some things will still be the same can be a comfort to me. I've been working so hard at dealing with change, my teachers know that I'll be able to handle this.

(BLUMENFELD, E., USED WITH PERMISSION)

You can customize this template by inputting the class names that your child is taking such as ELA, Science, History, and Math. Once customized, print the tool and laminate. School staff can post sticky notes on a laminated sheet of paper with homework for ELA in the ELA box, homework for Science in the Science box, etc. This will give your child a visual overview of what homework he has to complete each night. If it is easier, you can simply use copies of the sheet (unlaminated) and write the homework assignments into the squares.

What will be the same next year?

Grade _____ (number)	**Grade ______ (number)**
☐ My teachers are:	☐ My teachers are:
☐ __________ (teacher name)	☐ ___________ (teacher name)
☐ __________ (teacher name)	☐ ___________ (teacher name)
☐ __________ (teacher name)	☐ ___________ (teacher name)
☐ __________ (teacher name)	☐ ___________ (teacher name)
☐ __________ (teacher name)	☐ ___________ (teacher name)
☐ ________ (aide name) meets me at the door at 7:45am	☐ ________ (aide name) will meet me at the door at 7:45am
☐ I have community service with _______________ (speech and language pathologist name)	☐ I have community service with _______________ (speech and language pathologist name)
☐ I have special interest time	☐ I will have special interest time
☐ I invite friends during lunch to play board games with ___________ (speech and language pathologist name)	☐ I will invite friends during lunch to play board games with ___________ (speech and language pathologist name)
☐ I eat lunch with __________ (peer name) once a week	☐ I will eat lunch with ___________ (peer name) once a week
☐ My advisory teacher is ________ (teacher name)	☐ My advisory teacher will be __________ (teacher name)

(HAQ, M., USED WITH PERMISSION)

What will be different next year?

Special educators, aides, and parents can use this story at the end of the year to explicitly let the child know what will be different the following year. Parents can review again with their child over the summer.

In September I will be a ______ grader. Some things about ______ grade will be similar to how they were in ______ grade. Some things will be new and different. I don't like changes, but I am doing a great job trying to get ready for this change and my teachers are proud of my efforts.

One thing that will be a little different is my class schedule. We will have our specials on different times and days than last year. We will also switch classes for different subjects. Even though these things will be different, I'll still have my own schedule to follow throughout the day. I will still come in a few minutes early to go over the schedule for the day, so I know what to expect.

In my new classroom, there will be some things that will be similar to my classroom now. There will be a meeting area, a computer table, a library, and a Safe Spot. I will still have my own seat, and it will either be at a table spot or a desk.

I already know that a lot of my old teachers and adults that I know at ______ School will be here next year. I will see them in the hallways, in the office, in specials, and around the building. I will also be meeting my new teachers. A few of my new teachers are: _______, ________, and ________. ________ (special educator) has pictures of them and stories about them to tell me so I can get to know more about them before school starts.

Change can be hard but can also be good. I have changed from one grade to another every year. I have experience with this! I have changed grades from kindergarten, to first, to second, to third, to fourth, and to fifth grades! I have also changed classrooms and teachers when I went from kindergarten to first grade, first to second, and third to fourth grade. I can do this! And if I need help, I will still have my parents and old and new teachers to help me.

(BLUMENFELD, E., USED WITH PERMISSION)

Your child's special educator can customize this template to show your child what will be different at school the following year. This information will support your child in feeling calmer about and more prepared for the transition from one school year to the next. You can preview this information with the child at the end of the year, during the summer, and before school starts the following year.

What will be different next year?

Grade _____ (number)	**Grade ______ (number)**
☐ Ms. ___________ (teacher name) is my _____ (number) grade learning center teacher	☐ Ms. ____________ (teacher name) will be my _____ (number) grade learning center teacher
☐ My _____ (number) grade art teacher is _____________ (teacher name)	☐ My new art teacher is _____________ (teacher name) in _____ (number) grade
☐ In _____ (number) grade, I have chorus with _______________ (teacher name)	☐ I will have music technology with ___________ (teacher name) in _____ (number) grade
☐ I have newspaper in _____ (number) grade	☐ In _____ (number) grade, I will not have newspaper
☐ I have advisory two times a week in _____ (number) grade	☐ In _____ (number) grade, I will have advisory three times a week

(HAQ, M., USED WITH PERMISSION)

My aide's plan for next year

Special educators, aides, and parents can use this story at the end of the year to inform the child about his aide's plans for the following year.

My name is ______ and I'm a smart, flexible, hard-working student in ______ grade.

For the last two years, _____ (aide) has been one of my teachers. He is a great teacher, and he really understands me.

______ (aide) does a lot of work with me, and he tries to help me be a more independent student.

Next school year, _______ (aide) is not sure where he will be working. He might be working at our school, but he might not. _______ (aide) is going to be training to be an early elementary classroom teacher, so he needs to get a job that will be working with students in fifth grade or below.

It will be really hard to say good-bye to _______ (aide). The good things that I can try to focus on are that I can stay in touch with ______ (aide) no matter what happens. If he is not working at school next year, we can stay in touch through e-mail. If he is still working at school next year, I will be able to see him around school, in the hallways or in the building.

______ (aide) really cares about me and is so proud of all the goals I've met in ______ and ______ grades. He knows that I am going to be a successful ______ grader because of my creativity, good sense of humor, and hard work.

If I have questions for ______ (aide) about his plans for next year, I can ask him or write them down.

(BLUMENFELD, E., USED WITH PERMISSION)

Transition from homeroom to changing classes and new-looking learning center

Teachers teach in their own classrooms and teach different subjects in grade ______. Teachers organize their classrooms in their own way. They decide how the room and space will look and how furniture will be arranged. I will get an opportunity to preview each teacher's room with ____________ (teacher name) before school begins.

____________ (special educator name) teaches in the learning center and organizes it to help her students learn. She prefers a calm and compact space because she thinks that environment supports quiet learning, attentive listening, and privacy. This atmosphere can help students feel safe.

Grade ______ (number) learning center has been divided into two rooms. A partition now divides the room. Some things will stay the same:

☐ My Safe Spot

☐ My desk

☐ ___________ (special educator name)'s desk

☐ The computer and telephone are in the same location

☐ I will have my special interest time in the learning center

☐ I will have my special interest project with _______ (peer name) in the learning center

☐ I can take a break in the learning center when I need to regroup my thinking and sensory system

Some things will be different:

☐ The space is smaller

☐ Fewer tables

☐ Fewer students will use the space

☐ The space will be quieter

☐ The space has a designated study area:

  ☐ Located near the closet when I enter the room

  ☐ Has a table and chairs

  ☐ This means more space to learn

I will be able to tour my new classrooms and learning center with __________ (teacher name) before school starts. If I feel uncomfortable because my classrooms and learning center look and feel different, it is okay. Sometimes it takes a few days to get used to a change. I can remind myself of all of the things that will be the same. Also, _____________ (teacher) will help me with the change before school starts and _____________ (special educator) and ___________ (aide) will help me when I start school.

(HAQ, M., USED WITH PERMISSION)

Note sent home about the week's schedule changes and Plan B choices

Hi ________ (your child's name),

I hope you are enjoying your weekend. I wanted to give you a heads up on a few schedule changes for this week. I know changes can be frustrating, but I hope the preview and Plan B choices will help.

Changes

Wednesday

I have a workshop on Wednesday so I will not be at school. All teachers have to go to workshops so that we learn new teaching strategies. This will affect your:

- lunch group with the boys
    - community service.

Also, ________ (guidance counselor) will be talking to ______ graders about choosing electives for next year. I think you had said that you were interested in art/drawing classes.

Thursday (potential change)
________ (guidance counselor) may need to meet with ______ graders again on Thursday from noonish to 12:30. ___________ (guidance counselor) has a deadline to get all of you to have your electives picked so he does not have much of a choice. This could impact lunch with _______ on Thursday.

Problem-solve these changes

- Lunch group with the boys—You can still have lunch with __________ (peer name) and _______ (peer name) until noonish. Then, you can walk down with them to _________ (teacher name)'s room for _________ (guidance counselor name)'s discussion. I will leave two games for you and the boys to play. You can also just hang out and talk with them. ___________ (aide name) will be on the other side eating his lunch if there is an issue, which I don't anticipate.
- Community service—You can use the computer in the learning center to search for videos, clips, and episodes to show ____________ (class name). If there is anyone working you will need to wear headphones. I will leave you a handout to fill out with what you want to show them and two to three questions you will ask them about the video. You told me last week that you have observed that we have not chosen a video that all of the class really enjoyed; it seems to be fifty-fifty. By having this time to plan and now knowing what some of them like and do not like, you can achieve that goal of sharing a video that the majority of the class will really like. You can then go down to the office and put the completed handout in my mailbox so that I can pick it up on Thursday; that way I can start watching and approving your picks.
- A Plan B for having your lunch with ________ (peer name) possibly interrupted or cancelled is to ask her if she wants to have lunch with you Monday or Tuesday. This way you still get to hang out with ________ (peer name), and you won't get as frustrated if she or you or both of you need to go to Thursday's presentation.

I understand that these schedule changes are frustrating. I hope that by having this heads up, you can use the Plan B choices for the changes that come up. This may be a good learning experience for you. You have shared with me that you don't always have strategies to deal with being frustrated with change so I hope these can be helpful for you so that the positives trump the negatives. I will check in with you tomorrow, Monday, if you have any questions or if you just want to chat about these changes.

Enjoy the rest of the weekend!

(GUERRA, L.A., USED WITH PERMISSION)

Teacher going on maternity or paternity leave

__________ (teacher name) is going to be out because ______ (he or she) is taking a ______ (number) week __________ (paternity or maternity) leave to spend time with (his/or her) ________ (wife or husband) and new baby. A ________ (paternity or maternity) leave is when the _______ (dad or mom) gets to take time off from work so that ____ (he or she) can help take care of ______ (his or her) new baby. This may not be easy for me because _________ (teacher name) is a great ________ (subject name) teacher. I may miss having ______ (him or her) as a teacher. Change is not always easy, but I can try to remember that it is important for __________ (teacher name) to spend time with ______ (his or her) new baby and help ______ (his or her) ______ (wife or husband).

I will have a substitute teacher for my __________ (subject) class. The substitute is someone I know, ___________ (substitute teacher name). Because I already know ___________ (substitute teacher name), it may be an easier change to deal with. ________ (substitute teacher name) loves _________ (subject) just like _________ (teacher name) does. ________ (he or she) is excited about teaching my classmates and me.

Just like every other class, I am expected to keep my body and brain in the group.

(HAQ, M., USED WITH PERMISSION)

Change in schedule—testing

Dear __________ (your child's name),

All grade _____ (number) students in ________ (location) will be taking __________ (specific test name) tomorrow on _________ (date).

You have been working hard for the past ______ (number) weeks just like your friends in the learning center. This means that you are prepared and ready to take the test. I'm very proud of your hard work. You are a smart student!

I want you to know that tomorrow:

- ☐ You will take the test in ____________ (teacher name)'s room
- ☐ _______ (aide name) will work with you
- ☐ You will have all the required materials with you in ___________ (teacher name)'s room
- ☐ I will give you a _______ (test name) bag, which will have __________ (test name) reference sheet, pencils, eraser, and sharpener
- ☐ You will take your book, drawing paper/pen, and lunch bag with you
- ☐ After you finish _______ (test name) you may come back to the learning center

Everyone has to follow rules during __________ (test name). I want you to know that you can take breaks during ____________ (test name).

There are ______ (number) kinds of breaks:

- ☐ Snack break
- ☐ Reading break
- ☐ Walking break
- ☐ Drawing break

Let ______________ (aide name) know when you need a break.

Your job as a student during ___________ (test name) is:

- ☐ Keep brain and body in one place
- ☐ Listen slowly and carefully to the questions when _______ (aide name) reads to you
- ☐ Highlight important facts/connections
- ☐ Use "elimination strategy" when answering multiple choice questions
- ☐ Plan your open response answer and show all your work

I know all grade ______ (number) students have to answer two or three open response questions tomorrow. Remember that some questions may not be fun to solve, but you still have to give your best effort and answer the questions. If you are confused or don't know the answe,r that does not mean that you are not smart. You are taking ______________ (test name), to help _______________ (special educator name) __________ (aide name), and ____________ (teacher name) teach you better!

I know you'll do great tomorrow because you have worked very hard! I'm proud of you! ___________ (aide name) and ______________ (teacher name) are proud of you too. I'll see you tomorrow. Good luck!

Sincerely,

_________________ (special educator name)

(HAQ, M., USED WITH PERMISSION)

Change in schedule—activity change

Hi __________ (your child's name),

I hope you are having a great night. I wanted to let you know that tomorrow is an early release day for the younger grades. Because of this we will not ______________________ (activity your child will not do). Instead, you and I can ______________________ (new activity plan). ______________ (school activity) and _____________ (school activity) will not be affected.

Have a great evening,
_________________ (teacher name)

(GUERRA, L.A., USED WITH PERMISSION)

Schedule addition

Hi ______________ (your child's name),

I hope you had a great weekend. I wanted to let you know about a small schedule addition. For the next ________ (number) ____________ (specific day of the week), right after _____________ (school activity) you will be working with me for about ___________ (number) minutes. We will be going down to my room to do mini-lessons. What will these mini-lessons be about? Well, we will be talking about a few of the "hidden rules" of girl–boy relationships. It is part of my job to teach social skills, and when you are a teen there are many different "hidden rules" you need to be aware of to help with your social skills. We will meet in ____________ (room name). Your _____________ (specific day) schedule will probably say "hidden rules" work with _____________ (speech and language pathologist name) for the next _____ (number) weeks. These mini-lessons will start this week on ___________ (specific day).

Thanks,
________________ (speech and language pathologist name)

(GUERRA, L.A., USED WITH PERMISSION)

Weekly reinforcement letter

Your child's special educators or your school staff contact can write a positive reinforcement note for your child to help with transitions back to school after the weekend. The note can highlight your child's successes from the previous week and preview anything coming up the following week. You can read the note to your child the day before your child returns to school.

Dear ________,

I hope you're having a relaxing weekend with family!

I noticed this week you tried very hard as a grade ______ (number) student. Trying makes you smart and successful.

I was very pleased to see this week you worked very hard in all your classes:

- In social studies you were a participating member in your reading group. I saw you reading with _____ (peer name) and _____ (peer name). Your brain and body were in one place. You were following "buddy reading" rules. You made connections and jotted down important facts. I was extremely impressed with how you handled a "not so fun" class discussion on Friday. _______ (teacher) shared some unpleasant information in connection to ______________ (topic). I noted it was difficult to listen but you tackled the moment maturely. You exercised mindfulness and stayed in class. You are learning and trying very hard to deal with "not-so-fun" topics. Trying makes you smart!

- In math you worked on two open-response word problems on Thursday with ______ (peer name). That was incredible! You worked very hard with a calm body and mind. Also I noted your work on measuring the area of irregular shapes and finding shapes inside shapes on Thursday! That makes you smart and successful! I'm glad to hear from ______ that you like math.

- In science on Friday you worked diligently with _______ (peer name) and ______ (peer name) on the poster. Your brain and body were in one place in science. I noticed you talked to your group members and shared jobs just like your friends. This makes you smart and successful!

- In ELA you showed perseverance and patience on Thursday and Friday! The room was very loud and testing practice is not your favorite, but you kept going. You completed multiple-choice questions and worked on the graphic organizer. That's smart! I am enjoying working with you and ______ (peer name).

- It is important to take your binder to class. I notice you are carrying your social studies and science binder to class. That is very smart!

This makes you independent and organized. Your job as a grade ______ (number) student is to carry your binder to class. Taking a binder to class shows that you are ready to learn. Also, your binder helps you to stay organized in class. I am very impressed to see that you follow your checklist to gather materials before science and social studies. That is smart and organized!

You are making valuable gains! I know Ms. ________ (teacher name), Mr. ______ (teacher name), and Mr. ______ (teacher name) are proud of you. I'm very proud of you and looking forward to working with you next week.

Warmly,
Ms./Mr. ___________

(HAQ, M., USED WITH PERMISSION)

Agenda-setting e-mail for transition meetings

Call a meeting in the spring of every year to create a transition plan for the following school year. Once you establish the meeting:

- Use the example of an agenda-setting e-mail for transition meetings to help you write a transition meeting e-mail to the liaison, special educator, educational consultant, and anyone else that would benefit from knowing what the parents would like to cover.
- Bring copies of your guide to the meeting to educate the new members of your child's team.

Dear ______ (liaison, special educator, educational consultant, and anyone else),

We look forward to our meeting on _____ (date) at ______ (time). We have invited ______ (professional). We would like to cover the following points:

- Review school guide
- Crisis response plan for next year
- Relationship building support for child with AS
- Homework—accommodations
- Executive functioning support
- Parent meeting with special educator before school begins

- Teaching styles of educators and how that will work with child
- Constellation of students
- Summer plans for child with AS
- Classroom teachers, special educator, and aide (if new)—best way to connect with the child
- AS training for teachers and aide—with parents/guardians, educational consultant, and former special educator
- Physical configuration of room—Safe Spot
- Relationship building between teachers/aide and child over summer
- Special educator home visit with information about the new year and the first day of school
- Academic plan
- Parent contact for following year

Thank you very much.

Sincerely,

________________ (parents or guardians)

Navigating transitions and changes: Community

Your child will be most successful when you explicitly teach her how to cope with transitions and changes for various contexts in the community.

Adults with whom your child interacts may discuss some transition and change skills that your child can develop. In many situations, this will not happen. You should be sure to develop strategies for coping with transitions and changes in an explicit, visual format in order to ensure that your child with AS understands.

- You can develop tools for navigating transitions and changes on your own.
- Others, you may want to develop in conjunction with individuals who support your child in the community.
- Use the list and examples provided in this section as a springboard to think about strategies for navigating transitions and changes

that would support your child in every context in which she participates in the community.

- Once you develop strategies for navigating transitions and changes unique to your child's needs and situation, preview the transitions and changes with your child and have the tool available for review until she copes with the transition or change.
- When you create your navigating transitions and changes toolbox, put one tool per page with succinct, simple, accessible instructions. Less writing per page helps the child with AS avoid visual overload.

Tools for navigating transitions and changes in the community may include:

☐ Travel tool

☐ All tools from the Navigating transitions and changes: School section above. These can be altered and used to support transitions in the community. If you have the necessary information, you can alter them yourself. If not, you can work with the pertinent adult in the community to customize the tool

The tool below serves as an example of tools for navigating transitions and changes in the community, which you can consider a springboard to make your own tools. Feel free to:

- use the space provided in the template checklists you have downloaded to add points to the strategies for navigating transitions and changes
- or create entirely new tools for navigating transitions and changes that would support your child.

Example: Navigating transitions and changes in the community

Travel tool

Use this tool to help your child cope with the numerous transitions and changes he will face when traveling.

☐ Buy or create a large calendar book:

 ☐ One page devoted to each day of the year

 ☐ One-hour segments

 ☐ Space around the border or top

☐ Make the design fun (optional):

 ☐ Choose a favorite color

 ☐ Decorate it

- ☐ Create a schedule:
  - ☐ Fill in every schedule-related segment that you know upfront
  - ☐ Add to the schedule as you learn more
- ☐ Add pictures to the schedule pages:
  - ☐ People and animals that you will see
  - ☐ Place
  - ☐ Activities
- ☐ Write explicit behavioral expectations for each event in the margin next to each scheduled event
- ☐ Offer a Plan B for events that will be difficult for your child
- ☐ Preview:
  - ☐ The entire calendar for the trip several times before leaving
  - ☐ While on the trip, preview each new day the night before
- ☐ Explain your child's needs to families and friends

(RICHARDSON, S., GUIDANCE, BUT I DEVELOPED THE TOOL)

How to use the toolbox

Now that you have created your navigating transitions and changes toolbox, you will be able to:

- decrease stress and confusion for your child by clarifying and helping him or her understand and process transitions and changes in every environment in which he or she interacts
- implement structure for home education and have guidelines for a unified approach to parenting
- create more productive and pleasant relationships between your child and their teachers and service providers now that transition and change support for their environments are explicit
- help your child generalize skills by using the same strategies in multiple environments.

Chapter 10

Promoting Independence

My husband and I envision Alexander, in the future, holding a job and living in an apartment by himself. We would like to help him learn the tools necessary to live independently and start to work to make this future a reality. For example, he will need to be able to cook, go grocery shopping, clean, do laundry, and so on. I believe that it is essential for us to start teaching these skills now to prepare Alexander for independent living.

We work towards this goal in lots of different ways. During the summer, we created a "home camp" because Alexander had a difficult time participating in and tolerating the noise, interpersonal dynamics, and chaos of typical camps. We developed the curriculum by thinking of what we wanted to teach him and how we could make the learning fun and accessible. We realized this was a perfect opportunity to focus on independence skills. One summer we decided to teach Alexander how to shop for groceries, follow a recipe, and cook meals.

One day a week, we chose the recipes for the food he wanted to cook, and he made the food on the following day. We broke the process down into manageable pieces: choose a recipe that sounds delicious, write down the necessary ingredients, go to the farmers' market, go to the grocery store to purchase the remaining items, cook, and clean. We handled the preparatory steps every Tuesday and cooked and cleaned up every Wednesday. We used cookbooks that demonstrated every step of the recipe preparation process with color photos. Visuals and checklists really helped. We all enjoyed the feasts on Wednesday afternoons.

Now Alexander has the skills and confidence to cook simple recipes by himself. For example, he can make fried eggs, pancakes, and a cake. He needs moderate support, such as verbal guidance, for preparing and cooking somewhat more complicated dishes like corned beef hash. When Alexander wants to prepare more than one complex dish at a time, I take the lead with the executive functioning tasks, write checklists detailing Alexander's food preparation steps, and do much of the food preparation myself.

Parents' role in helping their child with AS build independence

As the case manager, your role is to teach your child the independence skill-building process and specific independence skills at home, and to coordinate the independence skill-building effort at school and in the community. This will call for knowledge, tools, and communication. This chapter and your guide will facilitate this process.

In this chapter, you will learn about:

- having the vision for independence for every environment in mind and helping your child develop skills to work towards that vision
- engaging your child in making independence skills-building a goal
- educating your child about the independence-building process trajectory
- providing varying levels of supports needed in different situations and environments
- teaching independence skills
- targeting one independence skill at a time.
- reflecting with your child after he practices independence skills and providing positive reinforcement
- recognizing independence levels
- making interdependence the objective
- coordinating with your child's support team to teach independence at home, at school, and in the community.

Promoting independence across environments

Have a vision and start working towards it now

You can greatly increase your child's potential for reaching independence if you consciously begin the process of working towards it early. Think about the vision you and your child have for her life at home, at school, in her career, and in the community. For example, would you like her to have the skills to be able to live by herself? Do you want her to be able to go to college or graduate school? Do you want her to be able to hold a job? Do you want her to be able to interact independently within her community by managing tasks such as buying bread at the bakery, pumping gas, managing ATM visits, navigating public transportation, and buying plywood from a home improvement store? Do you want her to develop healthy and satisfying relationships? You can certainly tweak your vision as you learn more about your child and she expresses her own goals and dreams. But it is important to start with this vision and coordinate efforts with your child's support team to build the skills to reach the vision as early as possible.

Engage your child in making independence skills-building a goal

You can promote independence at home, at school, and in the community by engaging your child in the goal of being independent. Often children believe that becoming independent will make their lives more difficult. They often think that independence means being all alone and taking on more work. You can have ongoing conversations about the practical reasons behind why being independent is beneficial. For example, you can point out that independence allows you more flexibility to participate in different environments without needing adult support. If your child's special interest is anime, perhaps you can explain to him that being more independent means that he can join an anime club. Also, being independent can build confidence. Following the Michelle Garcia Winner Social Thinking® model, the child will have good thoughts about himself when he experiences success with independence.

Educate your child about the independence-building process trajectory

Children with AS need direct instruction about how independence skills are learned. They often think that if they are taught something once, then they should be able to master it immediately. Neurotypical children grasp this independence-building process more intrinsically than children with AS. They understand that developing a skill is difficult at the beginning, but it gets easier. They realize that they need to practice to own the skill. For example, learning to ride a bike takes practice. The process starts with riding a bike that has training wheels. After the child becomes comfortable with this, parents remove the training wheels and hold the bike as the child gets used to the new experience. With practice the child learns to ride on his own. Independence does not mean that you can start riding a bike without training wheels from the beginning. You should tell your child that he will begin the process of learning each new skill needing considerable support and progress to needing no support or knowing when to get help.

The independence skills-building process follows the same general trajectory as what is described above in every environment (see the "Learning zones" tool in the Promoting independence: School section of Parents Take Charge). The idea is to start with explicit education and full support and fade the support with time as the child becomes more and more competent. Keep track of the pieces of the process your child can do on his own and fade support based on your observations and his feedback.

Provide different levels of support in different environments and situations

Different environments require varying levels of adult support for independence based on factors such as the child's sensory struggles, interests, and levels of anxiety. For example, an individual who struggles with sensory issues and whose special interest is James Bond will likely need less support in a James Bond movie play date at home than he will need in a loud, crowded restaurant. At the James Bond movie play date, the child might be ready for the adults to fade the supports. In more challenging environments, adults may need to implement heavier supports that they might have thought the child no longer needed. We want you to keep in mind that even though there is an independence skill-development trajectory, your child will likely need different support levels in different contexts.

How to teach independence skills

Independence is an abstract goal. As we've explained previously, children with AS grasp concrete goals more easily than abstract ones. For this reason, we as parents and case managers need to explicitly teach children with AS what independence looks like in a variety of different situations and environments. Help your child to make strides towards independence by breaking the process down into manageable steps. Start with working on one independence skill such as showering, and add another such as loading the dishwasher only when your child becomes competent with the first one and continue to practice both.

We will discuss showering and loading the dishwasher to give you a couple of examples of the process for specific skills, but you can apply the same process to whatever skills you and your child decide are most relevant. Once you determine which independence skill will be most useful for your child right now, create a visual checklist detailing each essential step the child must take to achieve the goal of performing the task independently. We provide many checklists for independence skills that you can either use as is or edit to better meet your child's needs in the Parents Take Charge section of this chapter.

Showering

At some point during early childhood, the bathing process transitions from a parent being entirely involved to the child performing the task independently. When this change took place for us, we had a visual schedule that alerted Alexander to take a shower right after dinner every night. Alexander was used to bathing every night at this time, and the transition from dependence on me to independence seemed relatively seamless.

Then I started to notice that even though he showered every night, his hair wasn't clean. Finally it occurred to me to ask him how he washed his hair and body in the shower. He said that he let water run over him. I realized that he didn't know what to do on his own. Even though we had bathed him for many years by lathering soap and washing his body and hair, he didn't pick up that he needed to do the same thing for himself. Only after I explicitly wrote down the steps for showering and posted the steps in the bathroom did his hair and body get washed. Don't get me wrong—it was not an overnight success. It required months of constant reminders and reinforcement.

Now Alexander knows how to wash his hair, but he doesn't always remember to do it. Getting him to remember to wash his hair regularly without reminders from us will be our next step in the process for building this independence skill. If you practice other skills with your child, such as brushing hair and brushing teeth, you may find that the process follows a similar pattern.

Loading the dishwasher

Cleaning up required detailed instruction as well. We started with the general request for Alexander to load the dishwasher. After finding dishes in the dishwasher in a jumbled mess, dirty and piled on top of each other, we realized that we had to break the process down into specific steps:

- Scrape food without water.
- Position the glasses and mugs neatly in the top rack:
    - » glasses along the sides
    - » small saucers and cups in the middle.

- Put the plates neatly in their slots on the bottom rack.
    - Place utensils in the basket.
    - Do not load:
        - » light plastics
        - » anything made of wood.

Alexander now knows how to load the dishwasher. The step that we are currently working on with him is getting him to remember to place his dishes in the dishwasher right after he uses them rather than letting a pile of dishes build up in the sink first. Keep in mind that as your child is learning any independence skill, he or she will likely need thorough and detailed step-by-step instructions to build competence.

Reflect with your child after he practices the independence skills and provide positive reinforcement

You should make sure that your child understands the independence tools and that they are working well for him. Ask him what worked when using the tool and what you and he could change to make it better. Getting your child's feedback about the tools will help keep him engaged and connected to the process, and to develop his independence skills more effectively (Dyment, J.H., personal communication, 2015).

As we have mentioned, children with AS frequently receive negative feedback for mistakes they make in their lives. Your child will benefit from adults teaching him what worked, did not work, and why. At home, at school, and in the community, your child will learn how to be independent when he receives positive feedback for the things he does well (see the "Ways I show independence and maturity during the school day" tool in the Parents Take Charge section of this chapter). You and other adults can help your child grasp what did not work and why by providing explicit, non-judgmental education about what he is doing ineffectively and how to put the correction in place.

Positive reinforcement can help teach a skill. For example, if you want to teach a child how to use a vacuum cleaner and he does not see the value and purpose, you can both explicitly teach the value and purpose and positively reinforce him to use it. Adults might establish a reward system for correct vacuum cleaner usage.

The idea is that with time the child will see the benefit of using the strategy. When the child sees the connection between the use of the skill and positive outcomes, the process becomes self-perpetuating. For example, Alexander will learn how helpful and organizing having a clean home is for him, and he will recognize that he feels less anxious when his space is in order. This recognition positively reinforces the process.

Preview independence skills that your child will need to master later in life

While skills such as showering and loading the dishwasher are age-appropriate to teach using explicit checklists, you will want to preview other skills, through discussion and exposure, that your child will need to master at a later life stage. For example, you might want your child to develop the skills to make his dentist's and doctor's appointments independently when he is an adolescent. You could preview this skill by telling him what you are going to do and how you are going to do it. Then, you could model the skill by making the phone calls to set up appointments in front of your child.

Recognize independence levels

Independence means that your child achieves an independence skill without an adult-enforced system in place to make it happen. For example, if a child plays nicely with his friend for an hour as a result of his parents' promise of a trip to a pizza restaurant if he can accomplish that goal, then that does not mean that the child is independent with the skill. He has not internalized it because he needs adult support to achieve it.

In a sports environment, a child may like to correct people about how to throw the ball the right way. His parents' vision will be that the child participates in sports environments without needing to correct others. They can make this an independence skills goal and explicitly teach the child how to interact without correcting others. Parents can monitor and give their child feedback to support him in developing this skill. Even if the child complies with this structure, he has not necessarily integrated this independence skill. Once the child can go to any environment and know to not correct people, he has internalized the skill and become independent with it.

Interdependence is the ultimate objective

Though we provide many examples of developing independence skills throughout this chapter, real independence means learning to be interdependent. While independence implies that the child must do everything on his own, interdependence means that people rely on each other. We want to support our children in building their independence skills so they can become generally self-reliant, but we also want them to develop their social and advocacy skills to get help from others when they need it.

Ultimately we want the child with AS to be able to identify his strengths and recognize his weaknesses, which will inform what he can and cannot do just as typically developing individuals do. For example, if a roof leaks and the individual with AS doesn't know how to fix roofs, he will know to enlist the help of a skilled friend or professional. On the other hand, if an individual with AS lives on his own and has developed cooking skills, then he can prepare his meals independently. The objective of interdependence is for the individual to know how to get the right help from the right person at the right time if he doesn't have the skills to handle a task.

Promoting independence at home

Following the template for every environment, you can think about the home-related daily living skills that your child will need to reach your vision for him in his home as an adult and start work on their development. For example, if you and he would like for him to be able to live independently, he will need to know the specifics of how to cook, clean his house, clean his body, dress appropriately, and take care of himself. You can start this skill development process early by using the tools in the Parents Take Charge section of this chapter.

Continue to stick to the template outlined for every environment at home by:

- engaging your child in making independence skills building a goal for home
- reminding your child about the independence-building process trajectory
- assessing your child's need for support in developing independence skills at home
- teaching your child the daily living skills, one at a time
- reflecting on how the tools work for your child and provide positive reinforcement

- previewing home-related independence skills your child will need to master later in life
- promoting interdependence at home.

Why teaching independence skills is different for individuals with AS

Scott knows an adult who lives in a residential facility that supports individuals with autism. Although this man is very bright, he was using the same cutting board for cutting both raw chicken and bread. How do most people know that because of bacteria and cross-contamination they should not use the same cutting board for raw chicken and bread? The answer is that typically developing individuals often pick up this information by being in tune during the natural course of events. Typically developing individuals are more likely to be in the kitchen with their family members and learn skills and rules that way.

As we've seen, individuals with AS are not usually engaged in the typical course of events. They are more likely to be absorbed in their special interests or more comfortable using the computer, and may not be inclined to participate in everyday activities at home. If we want our children to be independent, then we have to teach them directly. This doesn't mean that we always have to make them join us, but we do need to be conscious about talking about these types of topics or pointing them out as they arise. For example, if your family is watching a cooking show that provides a teaching opportunity, such as using different cutting boards for raw chicken and bread, then you can use the cue to educate your child. You don't need to comment on every teachable moment, only the ones that are relevant.

Coordinate with your child's support team to teach independence skills at home and at school

It is important to be in communication with school staff about independence-related topics. When you collaborate, you can develop systems that adults at home and at school implement together to help your child develop greater independence. To help you to see concrete results, we suggest that you record data about the independence-developing process. You and your child's school team can gradually teach your child how to develop the skills he needs to progress to the next stage.

Communicate with your child's school to promote work-related independence

As Alexander's homework started to increase in seventh grade, so did our household struggles. He had a difficult time paying attention in class and accessing the curriculum, which impacted homework. It was as if he had never seen the material before. If the process of figuring out the assignment and finding the answers took more than a few steps, he was completely lost.

This quickly led to an unhealthy dynamic. I saw that if I didn't help Alexander, he wouldn't do his homework correctly and would get further and further behind. I felt like I had to teach him the material, which was frustrating and time-consuming for both of us. Homework took two to four hours a night to complete. I didn't want him to fail, but looking back I realize that I was doing too much. It wasn't helping him develop the independence skills that he needed to progress.

After sharing my concerns with Alexander's school team, I started to record data about the homework process, including how long it took and how Alexander fared emotionally. Every day, I made notes about how much time each subject's assignment took to complete, what Alexander did, the exact nature of his struggles if he had any, and the total amount of time that we worked per day. Here is an example of one day's entry:

Friday, January 9

English Language Arts—45 minutes: 15 minutes, writing assignment; 30 minutes, reading.

Social studies—2 hours: Work on review sheet for test [sheet with terms like "13th Amendment"]. He needed to look in his binder and online to find information and write three facts for each term. He also had several essay questions requiring 75-word answers. Alexander could not begin to do this work by himself. The executive functioning demands of looking in two separate places for the answers and writing his response in a third location were too difficult for him. I had to help him find the answers to every question. Even with my 100% help, it took two hours. He was exasperated [and I didn't describe how I felt at this moment].

Science—40 minutes: Study vocab. for Monday's test.

TOTAL: 3 hours and 25 minutes

Every month I presented all of the daily entries and calculated the average time spent on homework every day. We compared the amount of time to prior months. Once I presented this data regularly, and the school could see the exact nature of Alexander's daily struggles, his special educator created a homework system that transformed our experience by organizing his efforts, helping Alexander become more independent, and decreasing his work time.

As part of the new plan, his aide reviewed homework assignments with him at the end of the school day. Together they posted sticky notes on a laminated sheet of paper divided into four squares, with each square representing a subject. This gave him an overview of what he had to do each night. Separately, this special educator had sheets divided by subject, which spelled out step-by-step what he had to do, what materials he needed to complete the work, and a general idea of how the finished product should look. (See the corresponding tool in the Promoting independence: School section of Parents Take Charge.)

At home I would review the instructions for the assignments again with him. Once Alexander said that he could do it on his own, we started to transition to his reading the instructions, getting started on his own, and asking for help when he needed it.

With the new system in place, the team asked that I stop helping Alexander do the assignments. The quality of the work he does independently is an important indicator of his abilities and struggles. Seeing how he does on his own allows his teachers to understand what types of modifications and accommodations are necessary to help him better access the curriculum.

Promoting independence at school

Do you want your child to graduate from high school, go to college, go to graduate school, or hold a job? You can customize the tools in the Parents Take Charge section to help your child build the independence he needs to reach your vision. The tools will teach your child how to manage many tasks independently such as handling homework, taking notes, managing calendars, paying attention in class, bringing proper materials to class, following directions, checking work, and navigating different school contexts including the cafeteria, class periods, and recess. Your child will need to become competent with these skills to progress to the next stage of development.

Communicate with your child's support team at school to promote independence at school

Every stage in your child's life calls for a different set or level of independence skills. As we discussed in Chapter 5, in the early years of elementary school, many children with AS do not understand the roles or expectations of being a student. They need explicit instruction to be independent elementary students. Helping your child build independence in elementary school lays the foundation for transition planning for high school, college, and life after college.

As we mentioned at the beginning of the chapter, you need to start from your and your child's educational and career vision, which will inform which independence skills you need to work on now and in the future. You and your child's support team can coordinate efforts to teach your child the independence skills he needs now and preview the independence skills he will need at the next stage. Independence skills to work towards at school can include going to recess, participating in group work, attending after-school activities, and utilizing less familiar supports in a school such as the librarian, custodian, or administrative assistant, among others that we list throughout the chapter and the Parents Take Charge section.

If your child has an IEP, you and your child's support team will develop a vision for your child together. The "Our Vision for Alexander" Box shares our vision for Alexander as it is described in his IEP.

Our Vision for Alexander

Our hope for Alexander is that he continues to grow as a successful, confident, and independent learner, and that his environment continues to foster high self-advocacy skills and taps into his intellectual potential.

It is the team's vision that Alexander develops increased daily living skills, increased independence, successful academic achievement, satisfying peer relationships, increased self-confidence, general happiness, a solid sense of wellbeing, and feeling as if he is part of the community. We envision that Alexander will develop strategies to independently strengthen his processing, self-regulation, and other skills deficits.

Our vision is that Alexander gains the skills necessary to succeed in college, become independent, and participate effectively with groups to support his ability to ultimately be able to have a career. Alexander has expressed that he wants to become an artist or illustrator.

Keep the independence trajectory consistent across environments. You can communicate with your child's school to make sure that the support team is engaging your child in the independence goal and thinking about independence skill-development the way you do at home: providing instruction and support for the skill and then systematically fading the support until your child is competent with the skills on his own. As we did in the earlier section on independence skills at home, we will provide a couple of specific examples that you can use as models for whatever skills are most relevant to your child.

Going to the school cafeteria

One aspect of school life that Alexander struggles with is going to the cafeteria. He feels overwhelmed and assaulted by the loud and surprising noises and unexpected touch of jostling in the lunch line or sharing crowded tables. He gets angry and feels like he will throw up when he sees chewed food either while someone is chewing or if someone has accidentally or purposely spat it out. If he hears chewing sounds, he gets equally distressed and disgusted. He loses his appetite and often flees the situation.

We realized early on that sending Alexander to the cafeteria didn't work for him. It negatively impacted other students and the rest of Alexander's day. He stopped going and would instead eat in a quiet space such as his classroom. We know that navigating a cafeteria is a skill with which he will eventually need to be able to cope in high school, at sleep-away camp (if he ever goes), at college, and possibly at work. The first step we're taking is to have him go into the cafeteria to pick up a fork that we will purposely not include in his lunch box. The next step will be to have him go into the cafeteria with his aide to purchase one item such as a piece of fruit. Once he becomes competent with that step, he will go into the cafeteria by himself to buy something. We will continue to expose him to the cafeteria in increasing time increments to help him steadily develop this skill. You can apply this gradual approach to other skills, such as going to recess or participating in gym class.

Organization skills at school

Another skill that is important for students and promotes independence is learning how to become and remain organized. When Alexander was in the earlier grades of elementary school, teachers supported this process by labeling where to put belongings. They had designated containers for everything including pens, paper, scissors, sensory tools, completed homework, books, backpacks, and coats. When Alexander moved into sixth grade, he started changing classes. At that point, teachers developed a checklist for the materials that he needed for each class. Once he became competent with the checklists, he became independent with knowing what to bring to class and was able to remember what to bring by himself. Following the process of providing step-by-step instructions and gradually fading support as Alexander gained competence proved successful in helping him to be organized independently.

Promoting independence in the community

How do you envision your child interacting in the community when he is an adult? The process for teaching your child how to reach this vision and to interact independently in the community involves planning, previewing, practicing many times, reflecting with the child about what worked and what did not, and gradually but steadily fading support. The key is to make the process manageable and as enjoyable as possible for the child. You will find tools in the Parents Take Charge section that will lead you and your child through this process to develop independence in multiple community situations including shopping, going to restaurants, going to doctors' offices, using public transportation, and flying. Teaching your child how to feel safe and to keep himself safe in the world is also an important aspect of achieving independence.

Although you may need to engage your child in the goal of developing independence skills in the community, many individuals with AS are eager to participate in the community. Children with AS are particularly motivated to strive for independence when interacting in the community involves their special interest. These cases provide the perfect opportunity to point out the positive aspects of building independence. You can positively reinforce independence skills both by praising your child for his progress and explicitly reminding him of the benefits of gaining independence. Developing independence skills will also build your child's confidence, which will naturally reinforce the process.

Special interests motivate independence skills development: Going to the movies alone

For our family, Alexander's special interest in movies provided the opportunity for him to learn the independence skill of going to the movies alone. For several years Alexander's special interest has been movies, and one of his favorite activities is going to the movies. When Alexander was in fourth grade, he and I visited my mother to help her move. He helped us, but started to get bored. He was certainly not excited about going to buy bathroom supplies for his grandmother's new home. We gave him the option of coming with us to the store or going to the local movie theater and watching a matinee movie by himself. He chose to go to see the movie even though he had never been to a movie theater by himself before. In addition, movies can be loud, and loud, unexpected noises assault his sensory system. His special interest motivated him and trumped his struggles.

I told the movie theater clerk about our situation and the fact that this was Alexander's first time going to a movie alone. He kindly allowed me to walk Alexander to the theater in which his movie was playing and then return a bit early to collect him in the same place. We gave Alexander my mother's cell phone and taught him how to call me in case he needed us. We gave him basic safety instructions. He was so proud of himself when I greeted him after the movie. Though he had explicit instructions and heavy adult support, he took his first step towards developing the independence skill of going to a movie by himself in the community.

Developing independence skills in the community when a special interest is not involved

When Alexander's special interest is not involved, I find that two ingredients for success in developing independence skills are practice and making it fun. Sometimes I think of how I can present a friendly challenge or make the process into a game.

Walking to school

We live about two blocks away from Alexander's school. From the time he was in kindergarten, we often walked to school in the fall and spring. At first, I was in charge of everything, including crossing the street safely. Once Alexander knew the route, I started talking about how to cross the street: go to the crossing place; look one way and then look in the other direction; once you are certain no cars are coming or that the cars have stopped for you, then you can cross the street. After repeating this process many times and knowing that he grasped the concept, I challenged Alexander to lead me across the street. When I was confident that he could cross safely after much practice, I challenged him to walk by himself. With every success, I emphasized how proud I was of him. He was proud of himself too. He now walks to school by himself every day.

Flying alone

Our family has always traveled regularly because we have never lived close to our parents. When we traveled, we talked about every step of the process: we need to check in, go through security, look for our gate, get in line when our zone is called, show our ticket when we approach the agent, find our seat, put our bags away, and so on. After a few years of talking about the process, we started asking Alexander and Will to direct us through the process. We let them take us as far as they could.

One of my favorite experiences of Alexander developing independence skills was learning how to fly from our Boston airport to my in-laws' home in Alabama by himself when he was twelve. Alexander was invited to stay for a week with his grandparents. We booked a flight, and he was ready to try on his own. I wrote out checklists on index cards for every step of the process. (These steps are detailed in one of the tools in the Parents Take Charge section.) The trip went according to the written-out plan, and he was very proud of his accomplishment.

Aim for progress, not perfection

After taking so many trips to buy groceries, Alexander felt confident about going to the store. Recently he took a step towards independence without any help from us. He took some money that he was given as a gift, left the house, and walked to our neighborhood grocery store. He chose the items that he wanted to buy (chips, many chocolate bars, and a soda!) and even picked out something for his brother. He got in line and paid for his food.

In the meantime, Will called me frantically, letting me know what Alexander had done. We live in a relatively urban neighborhood and some of the streets around our house are very busy. Will was scared for Alexander's safety. I drove to the grocery store and found Alexander walking through the parking lot, as calm as could be.

At dinner that night, we talked about the importance of Alexander telling us where he is going and asked him about what he did. He explained his steps and said that he tipped the cashier. He was quite proud of giving the tip, but he had given away close to five dollars of his money to the grocery store clerk. We explained that tips are expected in restaurants, but tipping a cashier is unexpected and unnecessary. He said that he did it because he had seen a cartoon character tip a cashier.

I felt that this experience was a personal victory for Alexander. He was striving for independence and handled most of the steps very well. However, the process also highlighted Alexander's need for explicit instruction for every step towards independence.

Communicate with individuals in the community who interact with your child

The guidance for adults is the same for every environment in which your child interacts. As we've said, you want to begin with your and your child's vision, reinforce the independence skills-development process trajectory, teach the skills and provide adult support, gradually fade the support, and preview the independence skills for the next stage of the child's life.

Start with the vision. For example, if your child struggles with eating new food and does not have allergies, then your vision might be that you would like him to be able to cope gracefully with being served new food in every environment. If you are working on developing this skill at home, you can help generalize this skill development in the community if a family member with whom you have a comfortable relationship invites your child to dinner.

Engage your child in the goal. You can explain to your child the benefits that he will enjoy by being able to cope with any food that people serve. For example, you can tell him that he will interact more successfully in every environment, he will build self-confidence, and others will think positively of him. If he can't tolerate food at other people's homes, then he might miss out on going to dinner with friends.

Reinforce the skill-development process trajectory. Discuss your vision with both your family member and your child. Identify and communicate the level of adult support that your child will need at your relative's home. For example, maybe he can try one unfamiliar side dish and you can send food for the rest of the meal. If he is beyond that stage, perhaps the relative can try serving all-new food.

Explicitly teach the independence skills. For example, if your child will go to the relative's house and try a side dish, then you can teach him to take a small bite of the food. If he likes it, he can eat more and compliment the host. If he doesn't like it, he should remember that it is only a small bite, swallow it, and stay calm. He shouldn't make a face or disapproving sound and shouldn't talk about not liking the food. He can then continue to eat the other foods that he likes instead.

You can share what you are teaching the child with your family member and ask her to acknowledge your child for trying and let you know about any successes. This feedback will inform next steps in the skill-development process trajectory.

This skill-development strategy will work best if you target one independence skill at a time and save the most difficult areas to address at home. You can tell the relative about how to make accommodations for your child's trigger areas to increase his chances for success. You can remind your child that, because we are working on independence, the family will serve him one side dish he can try. Then you can explain to your child the specific ways the family will accommodate him. For example, you might tell him that you know social outings are hard for him and that you asked the relative to help him by asking everyone not to touch him and to try to keep the noise level down.

Preview skills that your child will need in the community at a later stage

As we discussed earlier about promoting independence skills across environments, you should preview skills that your child will need in the community later in life. For example, operating an ATM machine is a skill that your child will eventually need to master that you can preview now. When Alexander and I go to ATM machines together and no one else is around, I ask him to press the buttons for me and we discuss what he is doing. He enjoys this, and the process gives him exposure to a task that he will need to complete on his own at a later stage in his life.

Being safe in the community and knowing when to ask for help

Part of gaining independence means learning how to protect yourself from dangerous situations and when to ask for adult intervention. Children with AS are vulnerable in potentially unsafe situations because they struggle with detecting deception, understanding contexts and expectations, and assessing risk. Many neurotypical children have internal alarm systems that are triggered when someone or something seems out of context.

For example, a neurotypical child may naturally feel uncomfortable if a car stops and an unfamiliar adult offers candy and asks the child to get into the car. However, most children with AS have difficulty discerning that they are in an unsafe situation because they do not have a clear sense of what is expected. They can easily fall prey to predators, even ones that are not cleverly deceptive. Due to their gullibility, children with AS will likely take an adult's promise at face value. For example, an unfamiliar adult could easily convince a child with AS to come into his car by saying that he will be safe. The concept that some adults are safe, some are not, and others are safe most of the time confuses children with AS.

Many children with AS have a difficult time perceiving different levels of risk. Risk assessment involves understanding shades of gray. When neurotypical children encounter a group of teenagers, they are better able to tune into the energy and attitude of the crowd, assess the risk, and decide whether to avoid them. In contrast, many children with AS may not notice potential signs of trouble such as erratic behavior, unusual stances, or unexpected volume.

Safety education is challenging because of all the possible scenarios that might occur. In addition, rules can overlap and cause confusion. For example, parents may tell their child with AS not to talk to strangers. However, a problem could arise if the child refuses to speak to a safety official because he is technically a stranger.

Familiarizing children with concentric circles of connections supports them in understanding the context for various interpersonal connections. Each circle represents relationships. Parents can explain what is expected when interacting with each group. For example, sharing secrets or lending money is safe with family and close friends. (Of course, if "Uncle Bob" is a low-life gambler, this exception should be noted!) While unsafe people can be in any relationship circle, the general rule is that children with AS can trust their inner circle and do not have to expect that strangers are dangerous. They simply need to learn the appropriate guidelines for interacting with each group.

Parents can teach their child with AS that communication with trusted people is always good. The tool in the Parents Take Charge section that discusses when to talk with someone who is trustworthy helps highlight experiences that are critical for children with AS to discuss with someone in their inner circle. This guidance serves as another safety strategy because children with AS do not always intuitively know which topics are most important to share with their inner circle. Parents can explicitly educate their child about how to ask for help and under what circumstances he should speak with someone he trusts. Previewing these strategies with the child can help minimize risk and provide greater clarity in confusing situations.

Parents can take a targeted approach to safety education. They can assess where the child is most vulnerable and establish rules to address the riskiest situations. For example, parents may want to teach their child not to get into a car with anyone without prior permission from a trusted adult. Several resources directly address safety issues from different angles, including the Asperger/Autism Network's website www.aane.org, Dennis Debbaudt's website www.autismriskmanagement.com, and the book *A 5 Is Against the Law! Social Boundaries: Straight Up!* (Buron 2007).

Parents can also be instrumental in relieving a child's stress about safety. For example, if a child is afraid of robbers but he lives in a neighborhood that has not had a robbery in years, parents can help him stop perseverating.

Parents can reassure him that his home is safe and can describe exactly what precautions are in place to keep him protected.

Generalizing independence skills across environments

As you have seen throughout this chapter, the process for developing independence skills is the same for every environment in which your child interacts:

- Create your vision for home, school, and the community.
- Engage your child in the goal of developing independence skills.
- Make sure that your child understands that the process takes time and practice and starts with adult support, which will fade with time.
- Explicitly teach the skills and provide support with the idea of reducing the adult support over time.
- Preview skills that the child will need in his next phase in life.
- Reflect with the child after he practices independence skills and provide positive reinforcement.
- Recognize your child's level of independence.
- Strive for interdependence.

You can support generalization by educating the child about the process and communicating with his support team to make sure that the language used is consistent in every environment. Additionally, you can coordinate efforts with his support team in every environment by teaching the same skill at the same time.

In conclusion: Achieving independence

As we mentioned at the beginning of the chapter, the child is best prepared for independent living when parents start this strategic education early and continue to build in new skills over time. By the time the child is ready to leave home, he or she will have a repertoire of skills he or she can perform competently. In a larger sense, all of the tools sections in the book will lead your child to independence. Understanding his or her unique profile, learning behavioral expectations, managing his or her emotions, and so on will all promote his or her future independence.

Parents Take Charge

Creating Your Child's Promoting Independence Toolbox

This section provides a few examples of tools to guide children with AS to perform daily living skills that they will encounter at home, at school, and in the community. The exercises help you break down these skills into manageable parts. Some may seem obvious, but this level of detail is essential for the AS population to grasp how to become competent with everyday tasks. The number of steps listed depends on the skill requirements. For example, only a few instructional steps are needed for taking a shower because it only calls for organization and no social skills are necessary. On the other hand, phone calls require more support because they are social and entail organization and reciprocal conversation. Each breakdown provides instruction for promoting independence through developing these daily living skills, and works as a simple guide for your child and a teaching template and collaboration toolbox for you and the professionals who support him.

Promoting independence: Every environment

As we've discussed previously, independence-skill acquisition often occurs later for children with AS than for typically developing children. Generalizing independence-skills strategies can expedite this process and lead to greater success in every context. Coordinate with your child's support team to use the same strategies in every setting when helping your child develop independence skills.

Independence skills for every environment

- ☐ Create your independence vision for home, school, and the community
- ☐ Engage your child in the goal of developing independence skills
- ☐ Make sure that your child understands that the process takes time and practice and starts with adult support, which will fade with time

- [ ] Explicitly teach the skills and provide support with the idea of reducing the adult support over time
- [ ] Once the child becomes competent with one independence skill, continue practicing it and simultaneously start teaching another independence skill
- [ ] Preview skills that the child will need in his next phase in life
- [ ] Reflect with the child after he practices independence skills and provide positive reinforcement
- [ ] Recognize your child's level of independence
- [ ] Strive for interdependence

Promoting independence: Home

The goal is to define clearly the daily living skills that will lead your child to independence. These tools may vary greatly from child to child, depending on his profile. These exercises will help you to understand and articulate the skills that your child needs to develop to become more independent.

- Use the list and examples provided in this section as a springboard to think about daily living skills that would support your child at home. If you do not see a daily living skill that is important for your child, simply create one using these examples as models.
- Once you create daily living skills tools unique to your child's needs and situation, preview them with your child and have a copy available for review in each situation and environment until he integrates the tool and demonstrates mastery.
- Once you create daily living skills tools unique to your child's needs and situation, parents, babysitters, and anyone else in a home care role can use these tools to teach your child how to master each daily living skill.
- Daily living skills should be introduced one at a time as part of home education.
- Once the child becomes competent with one daily living skill, continue practicing it and start teaching another daily living skill.
- When you create your promoting independence toolbox, put one daily living skill per page with succinct, simple, accessible instructions. Less writing on each page helps the child with AS avoid visual overload.

- Parents can further support the process by using video modeling (video someone executing the steps listed on this page) to both show and describe how to perform the daily living skills.

Skills for daily living in the home may include:

- ☐ Personal hygiene
- ☐ Shower
- ☐ Clean up after shower
- ☐ Brush hair
- ☐ Brush teeth
- ☐ Clean room
- ☐ Clean up after a meal
- ☐ Clean up after an activity
- ☐ Phone calls

The lists below serve as examples of daily living skills, which you can consider a springboard to making your own lists. Feel free to:

- use the space provided in the template checklists you have downloaded to add points to the daily living skills
- or create entirely new daily living skills that would support your child.

Examples: Promoting independence at home

Personal hygiene

- ☐ Personal hygiene means taking care of your body in order to look and feel your best
- ☐ How to have good personal hygiene:
    - ☐ Wash your hands with soap after going to the bathroom
    - ☐ Wash your body with soap in the shower each day
    - ☐ Brush your teeth in the morning and at night
    - ☐ Wear clean clothes
    - ☐ Use a tissue to wipe your nose
    - ☐ Use a napkin to wipe your mouth when you eat

Why is having good personal hygiene important?

- ☐ Good hygiene helps you avoid health risks such as athlete's foot, rashes, infections, cavities, and illnesses
- ☐ You don't want to smell bad
- ☐ People with bad hygiene are more vulnerable to being bullied and disliked
- ☐ People respect and like people with good hygiene

Shower

- ☐ Turn on the water
- ☐ Use soap to wash your body
- ☐ Rinse your face

When you wash your hair

- ☐ Wet all of your hair
- ☐ Put shampoo in your hand
- ☐ Lather all of your hair with shampoo
- ☐ Make sure to wash out all of the shampoo

How to clean up after the shower

Parents can take a picture of how the bathroom looks after cleaning up and insert the image on the page with the instructions.

- ☐ Put your dirty clothes in the hamper
- ☐ Hang your towel back on the rack

Brush hair

Parents can take a picture of how the child's hair looks after brushing and insert the image on the page with the instructions.

- ☐ Look in the mirror
- ☐ Identify your part
- ☐ Brush your hair back on both sides of the part
- ☐ Brush your hair down at the back of your head

Brush teeth

- ☐ Brush your teeth for at least one minute (morning and night)
- ☐ Brush front, back, and chewing surface of every tooth
- ☐ Floss between every tooth
- ☐ Use mouthwash

Why do we brush our teeth?

- ☐ To keep our teeth and gums healthy
- ☐ To make sure we do not have bad breath

Clean room

Parents can take a picture of how the room looks after cleaning and insert the image on the page with the instructions.

- ☐ Make the bed with all pillows and stuffed animals
- ☐ Put pajamas either back in the drawer (if clean) or in the hamper (if dirty)
- ☐ Put everything on the floor back in its original place
- ☐ Neaten the desk

Clean up after a meal

- ☐ Bring plates, bowls, and utensils to the kitchen sink
- ☐ Rinse and get food off
- ☐ Place gently and neatly in the sink or dishwasher

Clean up after an activity

- ☐ Clean up the activity
- ☐ Put everything where it belongs

Phone calls

How to make a call when the person with whom you would like to speak answers

- ☐ Dial the number
- ☐ If someone picks up, you recognize the voice, and it is the person you are calling, then say:
  - ☐ *Hello ______, this is ______ calling*
  - ☐ *How are you?*
  - ☐ *I am calling because:* (explain your purpose for calling)
- ☐ Once you have completed the conversation, say:
  - ☐ *It was nice to talk with you*
  - ☐ *Goodbye* or *I'll talk with you later* or *Have a nice day/night*

How to make a call when someone whom you know answers, but it is not the person with whom you would like to speak

- ☐ Dial the number
- ☐ If someone picks up and you either do not recognize the voice or it is not the person whom you were calling, then say:
  - ☐ *Hello. This is ______ calling*
  - ☐ *May I please speak with ______?*
- ☐ If the person says *I will get him/her*, then say:
  - ☐ *Thank you*
- ☐ When the person gets on the phone, say:
  - ☐ *Hello ______. This is ______ calling*
  - ☐ *How are you?*
  - ☐ *I am calling because:* (explain your purpose for calling)
- ☐ Once you have completed the conversation, say:
  - ☐ *It was nice to talk with you*
  - ☐ *Goodbye* or *I'll talk with you later* or *Have a nice day/night*

How to make a call when someone answers whom you do not know and it is not the person with whom you would like to speak

- ☐ Dial the number
- ☐ If someone picks up and you either do not recognize the voice or it is not the person whom you were calling, then say:
  - ☐ *Hello. This is ______ calling*
  - ☐ *May I please speak with ______?*
- ☐ If the person says, *I'm sorry he or she is not here right now*, say:
  - ☐ *OK. Would you please let him/her know ______ called?*
- ☐ If the person asks you for your number, say:
  - ☐ *My number is ______*
  - ☐ *Thank you*
  - ☐ *Goodbye*

When someone calls our house wanting to speak with someone other than you

- ☐ Pick up the phone and say:
  - ☐ *Hello*
- ☐ If the caller asks for someone other than you and that person is at home and available, then say:
  - ☐ *Just a minute please. I will get him/her*
- ☐ If the person being called is either not home or is unavailable, then say:
  - ☐ *I am sorry. He or she is not here right now*
  - ☐ *May I please take a message?*
- ☐ Then write the full message on a piece of paper with the name of the caller and make sure that the person receives the message when he/she returns

When someone calls our house wanting to speak with you

- ☐ Pick up the phone and say:
  - ☐ *Hello*
- ☐ If the caller asks for you, say:
  - ☐ *This is ______ speaking*
- ☐ When you realize who the caller is, then say (as if you are happy to hear from him/her. If you are not happy to hear from the person, use a neutral tone):
  - ☐ *Hi ______. How are you?*
- ☐ Listen carefully and respond to what the person is saying
- ☐ Add comments or ask questions related to the topic
- ☐ Take turns speaking

- ☐ When the conversation is complete, say:
  - ☐ *Thanks for calling* _______
  - ☐ *It was nice to speak with you*
- ☐ You will know that the conversation is complete when:
  - ☐ The person has what he needs from the conversation and says *Thank you*
  - ☐ The talking slows down and the topic is finished
  - ☐ The other person says that he/she needs to go

Promoting independence: School

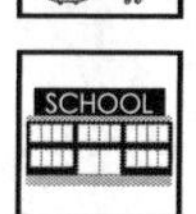

Your child will be most successful when you explicitly teach him the independence skills he needs to be a student and preview independence skills that he will need in the next phase. For example, if your child is in elementary school, then you can preview middle-school independence skills. You and teachers will lay the foundation for success at school when you explain these independence skills for your child.

Teachers may discuss some independence skills during the school day, and may assume that students are already aware of others. Regardless of whether teachers talk about independence skills, you should cover them in an explicit, visual format in order to ensure that your child with AS understands.

- Talk to teachers about helping your child develop independence skills.
- Share the independence skills strategies (in Promoting independence: Every environment) with your child's teachers.
- Use the list and examples provided in this section as a springboard to think about independence skills that would support your child at school.
- Once you create independence skills for school unique to your child's needs and situation, preview them with your child and have a copy available for review until she integrates the skills and demonstrates mastery.
- When you create your independence skills toolbox, put one independence skill per page with succinct, simple, accessible

instructions. Less writing per page helps the child with AS avoid visual overload.

Skills for independence in school may include:

- ☐ Learning zones
- ☐ Handling homework
- ☐ Taking notes
- ☐ Managing calendars
- ☐ Bringing proper materials to class
- ☐ Following directions
- ☐ Attending in class
- ☐ Checking work—self-edit
- ☐ The math working process
- ☐ Negotiating the cafeteria
- ☐ Navigating recess
- ☐ Center time
- ☐ Class maps
- ☐ Ways I show independence and maturity during the school day
- ☐ I am good at following "The Blue Rug Rule"
- ☐ Fading support

Also see "Educational interventions organized by impairment" in the Parents Take Charge section of Chapter 4.

The tools below serve as examples of tools to support students develop independence skills at school, which you can consider a springboard to making your own lists. Feel free to:

- use the space provided in the template checklists you have downloaded to add points to the tools
- or create entirely new tools to support independence skill-development at school.

Examples: Promoting independence at school

Learning zones

This tool explicitly teaches students about the independence trajectory related to learning. The first chart is an example. You can customize the blank chart in the templates you have downloaded.

	Learning	Practicing	Showing what I know
What is the purpose of this zone?	☐ Be introduced to new ideas and information ☐ Get to know more about these ideas and information ☐ Ask questions	☐ Try it out ☐ Get feedback ☐ Get new ideas from teachers and peers and adjust my work ☐ Ask questions ☐ Many mistakes are expected. Mistakes help us learn when we are in this zone!	☐ Use what I know ☐ Teach others what I know ☐ We try to make as few mistakes as possible in this zone, but most people still make one or two
When do students in _______ class use this zone?	☐ During math instruction at the rug ☐ When learning new things at the rug ☐ When learning new strategies in reading and writing	☐ When working in my lab book ☐ When writing first drafts and editing during Writer's Workshop ☐ When working on my To-Do list ☐ When working in groups or partners ☐ When doing homework (IXL, Razkids, or any other homework teachers assign) ☐ When using computer programs like IXL or Razkids in school ☐ When practicing typing	☐ When completing math assessments ☐ When presenting work alone, in groups, or with partners ☐ When writing final drafts
When do scientists use this zone?	☐ When doing research ☐ When learning from other scientists and their experiments ☐ When reading information about specific topics	☐ When forming hypotheses ☐ When completing experiments ☐ When asking other scientists, teachers, and peers questions they have ☐ When asking for help from other scientists, teachers, or peers	☐ When presenting their findings to other scientists ☐ When developing new medicines and treatments, based on their findings ☐ When talking to the public or writing about their findings

(DYMENT, J.H., USED WITH PERMISSION)

	Learning	Practicing	Showing what I know
What is the purpose of this zone?	☐ ☐ ☐ ☐	☐ ☐ ☐ ☐	☐ ☐ ☐ ☐
When do students in ________ class use this zone?	☐ ☐ ☐ ☐	☐ ☐ ☐ ☐	☐ ☐ ☐ ☐
When do students in ________ class use this zone?	☐ ☐ ☐ ☐	☐ ☐ ☐ ☐	☐ ☐ ☐ ☐

(DYMENT, J.H., USED WITH PERMISSION)

Handling homework

This tool is used at home and at school. Print two poster-sized copies of this template and post at home and at school. Print a paper-sized copy and laminate it; the child will keep this in his homework folder. Get red, blue, green, and purple sticky note pads. If social studies is the class name written in red, then write the social studies assignment on the red sticky sheet. For example, the social studies assignment might be to complete review sheet. Review the homework assignment at school. Start with the sticky notes on the laminated poster and, as part of the review, have the child move the sticky sheets to the appropriate boxes. Once the child gets home, move the sticky sheets from the paper-sized laminated homework sheet to the poster-sized one at home. This will help your child grasp the big picture of what homework he must complete each day. As your child masters this process, let him write the assignments himself and oversee the process.

You can customize this template by inputting the class names that your child is taking such as ELA, Science, History, and Math. Once customized, print the tool and laminate. School staff can post sticky notes on a laminated sheet of paper with homework for ELA in the ELA box, homework for Science in the Science box, etc. This will give your child a visual overview of what homework he has to complete each night. If it is easier, you can simply use copies of the sheet (unlaminated) and write the homework assignments into the squares.

Class name	**Class name**
Class name	**Class name**

(HAQ, M., USED WITH PERMISSION)

Homework assignments—organization support (1)

Page 1

What do I have to do for ____________ (class name)?

(HAQ, M., USED WITH PERMISSION)

Page 2

What do I need to get started?

- ☐ Go to the teacher web page for more directions:
  - ☐ Web address: ______________________
- ☐ Look at handouts:
  - ☐ Handout called: ______________________
  - ☐ You can find it: ______________________ (location)

☐ Search website(s):

- ☐ Web address:
- ☐ Web address:
- ☐ Web address:

☐ Textbook:

- ☐ Title: ______________________
- ☐ You can find it: __________________ (location)

☐ Other

- ☐

(HAQ, M., USED WITH PERMISSION)

Page 3

What does it look like? (Use the space on the page to show visually how the finished assignment should look.)

(HAQ, M., USED WITH PERMISSION)

Homework assignments—organization support (2)

Date: ____________________

Subject	Assignment	Materials I will need: B=book, WS=worksheet, BI=binder	Due date
Homeroom			
ELA			
Math			
Science			
Social studies			
Other			

*When you get an assignment, put it into your homework binder.
*Bring home your homework binder **every day**!

(DYMENT, J.H., USED WITH PERMISSION)

Taking notes

Hi-tech note-taking

- ☐ Use an app called AudioNote, which allows you to:
  - ☐ Record the teacher talking
  - ☐ Type
  - ☐ Take pictures of any visual teacher provides
- ☐ Depending on your child's independence and executive functioning skills, start with teacher's involvement

(DYMENT, J.H., USED WITH PERMISSION)

Low-tech note-taking

- ☐ Print out teacher's PowerPoint for class ahead of class
- ☐ Use slides to follow discussion
- ☐ Write down notes next to slides

(DYMENT, J.H., USED WITH PERMISSION)

Managing calendars

- ☐ Use iCal for kids
- ☐ Sit down with the child twice a week
- ☐ Update the child's calendar together
- ☐ Input upcoming events and assignments such as:
  - ☐ Science project with mini-deadlines
  - ☐ Field trips
  - ☐ Assemblies

(DYMENT, J.H., USED WITH PERMISSION)

Bringing proper materials to class

Color-coding strategy

- ☐ Sit down with the class schedule and the child
- ☐ Focus on one day's schedule, such as Monday
- ☐ Discuss what materials the child will need when moving from first to second period:
  - ☐ Ask the child
  - ☐ Usually the child knows, when calm
- ☐ Make a list of material needed for the second period class
- ☐ Highlight the list in red
- ☐ Apply to every day of week that the child transitions into that particular class
- ☐ If red is social studies, then the child will always know what to bring to social studies such as:

- ☐ Social studies notebook
- ☐ Social studies textbook
- ☐ Pen

☐ In the initial conversation, create one supply list and hang on to it so the child can refer back to it until he integrates the information

☐ In subsequent conversations, create supply lists for other classes and color code with different colors

☐ Refer to color-coded lists when gathering supplies

(DYMENT, J.H., USED WITH PERMISSION)

Having a model of the finished product strategy

☐ If the child is very visual and artistic, ask him what it looks like when he enters social studies

☐ Ask him to draw what it looks like when he enters social studies

☐ Allow him to think it through

☐ Let the child use the model that he created as a tool to check when preparing to go to social studies

☐ Repeat this process for every class

(DYMENT, J.H., USED WITH PERMISSION)

Checklist strategy

☐ Depending on the child's level of independence, either:

- ☐ Provide a teacher-created checklist of supplies the child needs to gather for each class
- ☐ Ask the child to come up with the list of supplies he needs to gather for each class and create the checklist

☐ Allow the child to refer to the checklist when gathering supplies for classes

(DYMENT, J.H., USED WITH PERMISSION)

Following directions

Independence with following directions is difficult to assess. You need to consider many things such as making sure the child heard the directions, processed the directions, and knows what they mean.

You can support independence with following directions by:

☐ Making directions visual

☐ Providing directions in checklist format

☐ Writing the directions on the board

☐ Making sure directions are on the assignment

☐ Repeating directions verbally

☐ Once you isolate what is making following directions difficult and address that, then peers and natural consequences of not following directions can be a tool

☐ If a child has been given directions several times and in several formats and still has a question about directions, then you can ask him how he will figure out the answer. Even if processing is difficult, the child needs to practice the tool to develop independence

(DYMENT, J.H., USED WITH PERMISSION)

Attending in class

- ☐ Preview class material
- ☐ Review class material
- ☐ Note-taking strategies can help:
  - ☐ AudioNote
  - ☐ PowerPoint
- ☐ Provide PowerPoint, but leave out some words—the child must follow to fill in words
- ☐ Reflect with the child on how he attended in class—this process allows the child to get to know their own strengths and weaknesses
- ☐ Provide tools of what to do if he misses something in class:
  - ☐ Talk to a friend
  - ☐ Ask teachers
  - ☐ Copy notes
  - ☐ Look at his notes
  - ☐ Go after school for extra help
  - ☐ If the lesson has a handout, read it to see if it provides what he missed
  - ☐ Do a little extra research
  - ☐ Look around the room for clues
  - ☐ Start the work and see how it goes. If stuck, ask teacher and peers

(DYMENT, J.H., USED WITH PERMISSION)

Checking work—self-edit

You can support independence with checking work by providing a checklist for writing.

	Checklist items	**Check when complete**
Punctuation	I read my written piece aloud to check for periods, question marks, exclamation marks, commas, and quotation marks	
Capital letters	I checked for capitals at the beginning of sentences	
Sentences	☐ My sentences are complete ☐ I don't have any run-on sentences	☐ ☐ ☐
Spelling	I checked spelling and fixed the words that did not look right	
Introduction	My introduction paragraph has 3–4 complete sentences	

Conclusion	My conclusion paragraph has 3–4 complete sentences
Main idea and details	My first main idea has two supporting details
Main idea and details	My second main idea has two supporting details

(HAQ, M., AND GUERRA, L.A., USED WITH PERMISSION)

The math working process

Doing math work is a process. Sometimes it is a short process and sometimes it is a long process. Usually mathematicians learn more when the process takes longer. The goal of a mathematician is to learn as much as possible. This is the working process that mathematicians use:

1 Read the entire problem carefully.

2 Think about **what you know**, **what information it gives you,** and **what you need to do** to solve the problem.

3 Try to solve the problem.

If the solution is reasonable and accurate, mathematicians...	If the solution is not reasonable or not accurate, mathematicians...
1. Check it over to make sure it is their best work 2. Move on to the next problem	1. Re-read the problem carefully 2. Check to see if they typed or wrote down the information correctly 3. Ask for help so they can learn something new 4. Try to solve the problem again with the new information

(DYMENT, J.H., USED WITH PERMISSION)

Negotiating the cafeteria

Negotiating the cafeteria can be challenging for many reasons.

- ☐ Isolate the challenge:
    - ☐ Sensory challenges
    - ☐ Social issues
    - ☐ Boredom
    - ☐ Unstructured time

- ☐ Map out the time in ten-minute increments to find out where the issue occurs:
  - ☐ First ten minutes:
    - ☐ Get in line
    - ☐ Buy lunch
    - ☐ Pay for it
  - ☐ Second ten minutes:
    - ☐ Find a spot to sit down
    - ☐ Eat
  - ☐ Third ten minutes:
    - ☐ Bored
- ☐ Create intervention with the child such as the following:
  - ☐ If downtime after eating is challenging, bring a pack of cards, or book (hopefully social)
  - ☐ In the last ten minutes when you struggle, take a three-minute walk or choose to go to the bathroom at that time
  - ☐ If noise is a problem, bring earbuds
  - ☐ If unexpected touch is the challenge, advocate for yourself and request a different seating option either on the edge or near a corner

(DYMENT, J.H., USED WITH PERMISSION)

Navigating recess—create a recess book for the class

If willing, your child's special educator can create this book to help your child and his classmates know how to navigate recess. If your child's special educator is too busy and you think this tool would support your child, then you might consider offering to create it if you have the time. If you create it, you can speak with your child's special educator to get the information necessary to develop the book such as activities available for recess, how to play, game rules, tips, a list of who enjoys which activity, and problem-solving suggestions.

Two pages are devoted to each activity such as four square, basketball, tether ball, swing on the tire swing, pirates and knights, hopscotch, soccer, climbing structure, house, princess, and hunting for crystals.

- ☐ **Four Square**
  - ☐ Object: To bounce the ball in somebody else's square
  - ☐ How to play:
    - ☐ Four people play this game at a time
    - ☐ If it is your turn, stand inside a square

- ☐ If it is not your turn, wait in line
    - ☐ The person in square 4 starts with the ball and tries to bounce it into another person's square
    - ☐ If the ball bounces inside your square and then out, then you have to move to square 1
  - ☐ Rules
    - ☐ Everybody who wants to, gets to play
    - ☐ Do not slam the ball
    - ☐ Keep the ball close to the game if possible
    - ☐ If you get out, wait in line for your next turn
  - ☐ List the children who enjoy the activity
  - ☐ You can include a picture of a four square court
- ☐ **Basketball**
  - ☐ Object: To throw the ball through the basketball net
  - ☐ How to play
    - ☐ Children split up into two teams
    - ☐ If you have the ball, pass to someone on your team or try to throw the ball into the basket
    - ☐ When you don't have the ball, you can say, "Pass to me!"
    - ☐ If the other team has the ball, try to block their shot without touching them
  - ☐ Rules
    - ☐ Everybody who wants to, gets to play
    - ☐ No hitting or pushing
    - ☐ Keep the ball close to the court
  - ☐ Tip: Sometimes when playing basketball you might get bumped accidentally. If this happens, take a deep breath and decide if you still want to play
  - ☐ List the children who enjoy the activity
  - ☐ You can include a picture of a basketball court
- ☐ **Tether Ball**
  - ☐ Object: To wrap the ball around the pole
  - ☐ How to play:
    - ☐ Children stand around the pole
    - ☐ When the ball comes your way, reach out and swat the ball around the pole
  - ☐ Rules
    - ☐ Everybody gets a turn
    - ☐ Swat the ball carefully and try to make sure nobody gets hit with it

- ☐ List the children who enjoy the activity
- ☐ You can include a picture of a tether ball pole

☐ **Hunting for Crystals**

- ☐ Object: To find rocks and crystals
- ☐ How to play
    - ☐ First, look around to make sure you are in a Safe Spot—a spot where no other games are going on. (For example, it would not be safe to play this game in the middle of a soccer field!)
    - ☐ Look for shiny rocks
- ☐ Rules
    - ☐ If you find glass or something you are not sure is safe, do not touch it. Tell a teacher
    - ☐ If you find a rock that is bigger than your hand, do not move it
- ☐ Tip: Sometimes when you are looking for rocks, you may not notice someone coming towards you with a ball. If you get bumped, take a deep breath and decide if you want to look for rocks somewhere else
- ☐ List the children who enjoy the activity
- ☐ You can include a picture of the area where children hunt for crystals

☐ **Climbing Structure**

- ☐ There are many things you can do on the structure
    - ☐ Go down the slide (tube slide or roller slide)
        - ☐ One person on the slide at a time
        - ☐ Only go down the slide, not up
        - ☐ Go down the slide on your bottom, feet first
    - ☐ Climb the wall
    - ☐ Go on the monkey bars
    - ☐ Use the tire swing
        - ☐ Three people at a time on the tire swing
        - ☐ Feet go inside the hole of the tire
        - ☐ Everybody gets a turn
    - ☐ Climb on the red web
    - ☐ Step or climb on the mushrooms
    - ☐ Slide down the pole
        - ☐ Only slide down the pole—do not climb up
        - ☐ One person on the pole at a time
- ☐ List the children who enjoy the activity

The last page is a recess problem-solving page that the class brainstorms:

- ☐ Children brainstorm solutions for problems that they usually go to teachers for at recess

(DYMENT, J.H., USED WITH PERMISSION)

Center time [free time in the classroom for younger students]—Uh, oh! What do I do...?

- ☐ What do I do if I can't find someone to play with me?
    - ☐ Look at the board to see who is in the same center
    - ☐ Ask someone in the same center, "Do you want to __________?"
    - ☐ Ask another person
    - ☐ Ask a teacher
- ☐ What do I do if I'm not sure which center to choose?
    - ☐ Think about what I have done before and what I liked
    - ☐ Look at the board and see which center my friend chose. Do that for today so that I can play with my friend
    - ☐ Narrow my choices down to my "top two." Then decide
- ☐ What do I do if I don't know the rules to the center or game?
    - ☐ Ask someone I am playing with
    - ☐ Read the directions, if I am playing a board game
    - ☐ Ask a teacher
- ☐ What do I do if nobody wants to play in the same center as I do?
    - ☐ Choose a different center for today and ask someone to do it with me tomorrow
    - ☐ Stay at that center on my own today and ask someone to do it with me tomorrow
    - ☐ Ask a teacher if they are available to do it with me today
- ☐ What do I do if I am not getting along with the people in my center?
    - ☐ Try to compromise
    - ☐ Listen to each other
    - ☐ Bring my materials to a different part of the room
    - ☐ Choose a different center
- ☐ What do I do if the person I am playing with doesn't know the rules?
    - ☐ Explain the rules to them in a calm, quiet voice
    - ☐ Read the directions with them
    - ☐ Remind them of the rules
    - ☐ Ask a teacher for help

- ☐ What do I do if somebody breaks the rules?
  - ☐ Give a friendly reminder about what the rule is
  - ☐ Be flexible and move on
  - ☐ Let a teacher know. It is the teacher's job to help kids follow rules

(DYMENT, J.H., USED WITH PERMISSION)

Class maps

The purpose of this tool is to help your child understand what happens in each section of class and identify areas that the child handles well and areas where the child struggles. You can put interventions in place when you understand what is causing the issue. You can create your own class map for any class in which your child interacts.

Science

	What happens?	Ideas I have about this
First ten minutes	☐ Getting organized	
Middle of class	☐ Lesson (writing in lab book) ☐ This changes the most ☐ I sometimes doodle during this time, but I am listening ☐ Watch science videos ☐ Do experiments ☐ Read articles ☐ Work in groups	☐ Towards the later end of the middle of class, I start to get tired and somewhat distracted
Last ten minutes	☐ Go over homework ☐ Finish up the work ☐ Sometimes begin to get organized for the next class	

Math

	What happens?	Ideas I have about this
First ten minutes	☐ Some kids work on the "do now" ☐ I get organized during this time. (The "do now" is for kids who are already organized) ☐ Go over the answers of last night's homework ☐ Write down tonight's homework (sometimes)	☐ It takes me the longest to get organized for math, compared to the other subjects

Middle of class	☐ Learn new things ☐ Might take notes ☐ Class lesson ☐ Work/practice in groups, pairs, or on my own	☐ Classwork would be a good time to use the restroom or take a break because I'm not missing new things or important homework. (I won't miss as much) ☐ Towards the "later middle" of class is when I get tired. It's harder to stay focused
Last ten minutes	☐ Finish up the lesson ☐ Go over tonight's homework ☐ Put papers in my binder (classwork section, notes section, etc.)	☐ Sometimes I am waiting for class to end by this time

English in Language Arts

	What happens?	Ideas I have about this
First ten minutes	☐ I get organized ☐ Chat with friends ☐ Wait for the teacher ☐ Teacher usually begins a lesson	
Middle of class	☐ Teacher might continue the lesson ☐ We might work on our own (reading, practicing, writing) ☐ Class discussion	
Last ten minutes	☐ Go over homework (sometimes) ☐ Finish up the lesson	

Class name: ______________________

	What happens?	Ideas I have about this
First ten minutes	☐	☐ ☐
Middle of class	☐	☐ ☐
Last ten minutes	☐	☐ ☐

Ideas

- ☐ The beginning and end of class are used a lot for organization. This is important for me
- ☐ If I am late to class or I take a long time to get organized, I might miss some of the lesson
- ☐ Classwork or practice time is usually a good time to take a break or use the restroom. I will get less practice, but at least I won't miss important lessons or organizational information

Follow-up questions

- ☐ What does it look like to "get organized"?
- ☐ If "getting organized" takes longer than ten minutes, what can you do to make sure you don't miss the lesson?

(DYMENT, J.H., USED WITH PERMISSION)

Ways I show independence and maturity during the school day

This tool can be used with a child to positively reinforce the ways that the child is showing independence.

Morning work

- ☐ I unpack my things without reminders
- ☐ I chat with my friends when I arrive
- ☐ I hand in my homework every day, on my own
- ☐ I complete my morning work on my own

Math

- ☐ I listen to the lesson and participate
- ☐ I put my book on the pile when I'm done

Book groups

- ☐ I meet with my book group, when I need to
- ☐ I complete my book group work
- ☐ I read aloud when it is my turn
- ☐ I listen while others are reading

Specials

- ☐ I follow directions in specials
- ☐ I play safely during P.E.
- ☐ I walk to Ms. ____________ on my own
- ☐ I invite a friend to lunch group, when it is my turn
- ☐ I work hard with Ms. ____________

Recess

- ☐ I follow the safety rules of recess
- ☐ I join new games if I am interested
- ☐ I include everybody

Writing

- ☐ I follow the writing process!
- ☐ I work carefully on my handwriting
- ☐ I write complete sentences and use punctuation
- ☐ I think of topics on my own

Other

- ☐ When I am using the restroom or running an errand for a teacher, I walk in the hallways by myself
- ☐ I walk out to the car at the end of the day, on my own
- ☐ I do my homework at home, every night
- ☐ I go to extended day
- ☐ I give compliments to friends
- ☐ I ask for breaks when I need them

Goals that I have

____

____

____

(DYMENT, J.H., USED WITH PERMISSION)

I am good at following "The Blue Rug Rule"

This tool can positively reinforce a child for becoming independent with a rule.

Hi. My name is ____________ and I am a ________ grader in ____________ (name of class).

About a month ago, my teachers told me about "The Blue Rug Rule."

This rule says it is my job to stay at the rug until the red on the visual timer is up.

When the red on the visual timer is up, I am allowed to take a break in the Safe Spot and I don't need to tell a teacher before I go.

I have become very good at this!

My teachers are very proud of me for following "The Blue Rug Rule."

(DYMENT, J.H., USED WITH PERMISSION)

Fading support

Safe Spot and change

This Social Story™ is about fading support gradually. In this case, the change is from a very enclosed Safe Spot to a more open Safe Spot. You can use stories like this to support the process of fading support as your child becomes more independent.

I have two Safe Spots in my school. Both Safe Spots are enclosed and have a desk and chair. My Safe Spot is my private space that helps me to stay calm and think clearly. In grade six, I sometimes work at my Safe Spot, but most of the time I do my work in the classrooms with my classmates. I am getting better at working with my friends outside the Safe Spot. This shows that I am learning how to manage change better and stay calmer. My teachers understand me and know when I hit my limit. All my teachers know how to support me to become an independent, mature, and successful student.

When I was younger, I needed the Safe Spot to keep me calm and help me learn. In grade six, _________ (teacher) and _________ (teacher) support me to become more independent, mature, and a successful middle-school student. Now I can stay calm and think clearly in class with my classmates. I can manage change more. And, I can learn and work better with someone else or in a group. I am becoming an active, independent, participating member in class with my friends. This makes me successful!

Now I am showing that I can be an independent, mature, and successful grade _______ (number) student, which means that I may need a Safe Spot but it can look different. It can look like a middle-school Safe Spot. My middle-school Safe Spot will still have a desk and chair, but it will have two walls rather than three walls. My Safe Spot is open and still my private space. My open Safe Spot will also help me learn and stay calm.

_____________ (teacher) will support me to adjust to my new-looking Safe Spot in the learning center. She knows that I am ready for this change and that I will do my best to be successful.

(HAQ, M., USED WITH PERMISSION)

Desk and classroom

This Social Story™ is about fading support gradually. In this case, the change is from having the child sit at a separate Safe Spot to learn to the child sitting at a desk with peers to learn. You can use stories like this to support the process of fading support as your child becomes more independent.

Students go to school to learn about the world and to become successful individuals. A student's job is to learn and a teacher's job is to teach. Learning happens in the classroom. Most of the time learning happens sitting at the desk with classmates or sometimes sitting in a circle on the rug. Teachers need to make sure they are doing a good job and students are learning. Therefore, teachers need to assign seats to students to make sure they are learning with their classmates.

There are advantages of sitting in a desk cluster with classmates. Learning becomes interactive, which means you discuss and have conversations when you are learning and trying to understand something new. When you sit with your classmates, you show that you want to learn just like your friends. Also, sitting with your classmates means that you are interested and part of the learning community.

Sometimes it is fun to sit with friends and sometimes it is not. If deskmates are loud, it is difficult to focus. If deskmates are not doing their job, then it is frustrating to work with them. But this does not always happen. Most of the time deskmates are cooperative, reliable, and helpful. Learning can become interesting and fun.

Sitting with my deskmates is something that I am going to try just like my _______ grade friends. If I sit with my friends in class, __________ (aide's name) will still help me. Every ______ grade student at __________ (school) learns sitting at a desk cluster.

If I learn and work with my ________ grade friends, it could be more interesting and I will be part of my learning community. There are some activities that are more fun in a group such as spending time together as a family at ______________ (favorite location) and spending time as a family _________________ (doing favorite group activity). Sitting with my classmates is helpful for me and for my teachers.

My job is to sit with my classmates in class. I will try my best, keep my thoughts, focus, and body in one place, and work smart just like my ______ grade classmates. This is how learning is done in __________ grade. This is how I sit in class.

(HAQ, M., USED WITH PERMISSION)

Promoting independence: Community

Your child will be most successful when you explicitly teach her the independence skills for various contexts in the community.

Adults with whom your child interacts may discuss some independence skills that your child can develop. In many situations, this will not happen. You should be sure to go over independence skills in an explicit, visual format in order to ensure that your child with AS understands.

- You can develop tools for independence skill-building on your own.
- Others, you may want to develop in conjunction with individuals who support your child in the community.
- Use the list and examples provided in this section as a springboard to think about independence skills that would support your child in every context in which she participates in the community.
- Once you develop independence skills tools unique to your child's needs and situation, preview them with your child and have a copy available for review until she integrates the skills and demonstrates mastery.
- When you create your independence skills toolbox, put one expectation per page with succinct, simple, accessible instructions. Less writing per page helps the child with AS avoid visual overload.

Skills for independence in the community may include:

- ☐ Going shopping
- ☐ Going out to eat
- ☐ Going to doctors' offices
- ☐ Going to community offices
- ☐ Using public transportation
- ☐ Flying

The lists and explanations below serve as examples of tools for supporting independence in the community, which you can consider a springboard to make your own lists. Feel free to:

- use the space provided in the template checklists you have downloaded to add points to the independence skills
- or create entirely new tools for developing independence skills that would support your child.

Examples: Promoting independence in the community

Going shopping

This process is similar for any shopping outing including going to drug stores, clothing stores, bakeries, office supply stores, hardware stores, plant stores, and so on. This method will help your child develop the foundational skills of shopping independently. You can promote independence in younger years by controlling the environment more. If possible, start by being selective about where and when you go. The goal is to make the process manageable and fun.

- ☐ Keep a grocery list at home
  - ☐ When your child is younger, discuss adding items to the list and let him see the process
  - ☐ As your child becomes more independent, ask him to add items to the list
  - ☐ If you want to go hi-tech, input your grocery list into an app and the app will sort your list by aisle of your grocery store
- ☐ Plan ahead
  - ☐ Determine potential issues and develop a plan proactively. For example:
    - ☐ If it gets loud, you can put on music with headphones
    - ☐ If you get cold, you can put on a sweater
    - ☐ If you get bored waiting in line, you can play with a toy, listen to music, etc.
    - ☐ If the lights hurt your eyes, you can wear a hat or sunglasses
  - ☐ Collect and bring supplies to support the plan:
    - ☐ Music player
    - ☐ Headphones
    - ☐ Sweater
    - ☐ Toy
    - ☐ Sunglasses
    - ☐ Hat
  - ☐ As your child develops independence, let him develop his own plan for dealing with potential issues
- ☐ Identify skills you are teaching and focus on one at a time on subsequent trips. Once the child is competent with one skill, keep practicing it and add another
  - ☐ Navigating a grocery store
  - ☐ Asking for help
  - ☐ Checking out
  - ☐ Waiting in line
  - ☐ Paying
- ☐ Preview what you will do at the grocery store with your child
  - ☐ We have ten items to purchase—show grocery list
  - ☐ We will walk through the aisles and pick out the items
  - ☐ Once we have every item, we will:
    - ☐ Wait in the check-out line
    - ☐ Load our groceries onto the counter
    - ☐ Pay for the groceries
  - ☐ Then, we will leave

- ☐ Go grocery shopping with your child
  - ☐ Begin the education process by bringing your child with you to the store during less busy shopping times (if possible)
  - ☐ Talk about what you are purchasing and where it is located with your child
  - ☐ Turn learning about the grocery store into a game and make it fun:
    - ☐ Ask your child to lead you to his favorite food
    - ☐ If your child is visual and artistic, you can ask him to draw a map of the grocery store
    - ☐ Use the app that sorted your list by aisle—map out your route
  - ☐ As the child develops more independence and it feels safe to you, allow him to pick out an item in a different aisle by himself
  - ☐ Continue to gradually and steadily increase the responsibility your child takes for the process and decrease your support
- ☐ Ask for help
  - ☐ Let him witness you asking for help when you do not know where to find something
  - ☐ As your child develops more independence, coach him to ask a grocery store staff person where to find an item
  - ☐ Continue to gradually and steadily increase the responsibility your child takes for the process and decrease your support
- ☐ Check-out
  - ☐ Discuss how to choose which counter to use:
    - ☐ Choose the line with fewest people and least food on the counter
    - ☐ Do not go to a line marked "closed"
  - ☐ Discuss how to wait in line:
    - ☐ Go to the back of the line
    - ☐ Bring something to do during the downtime
    - ☐ Create something to do in the moment if you did not bring anything
    - ☐ Stand quietly
    - ☐ Respond politely if someone speaks to you
    - ☐ Allow enough space, but not too much space, between you and the people in front of and behind of you
    - ☐ Stay alert so you know when to move as other people leave
  - ☐ Let your child be part of putting the divider on the counter and placing items from the grocery cart
- ☐ Pay for items
  - ☐ When your child is old enough to understand, start educating him about paying with cash, check, or credit cards
  - ☐ Talk through the payment process as you do it:
    - ☐ Have money ready

- ☐ If using a credit card:
  - ☐ Swipe the card when the cashier says it is time
  - ☐ Put the card away safely after you swipe
  - ☐ Sign the receipt, if there is one
- ☐ If you have coupons, educate your child about how to use them
- ☐ As your child develops more independence, allow him to take over part of the process for you
- ☐ Teach your child that he does not need to tip the cashier!

- ☐ Reflect with your child—how did it go?
  - ☐ What went well?
  - ☐ What could we do differently the next time?
- ☐ Implement changes on the next trip based on what might not have gone well

(TOOL DEVELOPED WITH INPUT FROM DYMENT, J.H.)

Going out to eat

This method will help your child develop the foundational skills for going out to eat independently. You can promote independence in younger years by controlling the environment more. If possible, start by being selective about where and when you go. Gradually and steadily increase the child's responsibility and decrease your support. The goal is to make the process manageable and fun.

- ☐ Make a reservation—let your child hear you make it
  - ☐ As your child develops independence, let him practice making reservations either by phone or online
- ☐ Plan ahead
  - ☐ Determine potential issues and develop a plan proactively:
    - ☐ If it gets loud, you can put on music with headphones while waiting to be seated
    - ☐ If you get cold, you can put on a sweater
    - ☐ If you get bored at the table before the food arrives, we can play hangman, play cards, or talk
    - ☐ If the lights hurt your eyes, you can wear a hat or sunglasses
  - ☐ Collect and bring supplies to support the plan:
    - ☐ Music player
    - ☐ Headphones
    - ☐ Sweater
    - ☐ Paper and pens for hangman
    - ☐ Cards

        - ☐ Sunglasses
        - ☐ Hat
    - ☐ As your child develops independence, let him develop his own plan for dealing with potential issues and bring the needed items
- ☐ Identify skills you are teaching and focus on one at a time on subsequent trips. Once your child is competent with one skill, keep practicing it and add another
    - ☐ Learning how to wait
    - ☐ Ordering food and drink
    - ☐ Practicing good manners at a restaurant
    - ☐ Asking for help
    - ☐ Holding a conversation while eating
    - ☐ Asking politely for the check
    - ☐ Paying the check
    - ☐ Making reservations
- ☐ Preview going out to eat
    - ☐ Our family going out to ____________ (restaurant name)
    - ☐ We will drive to the restaurant at _________ (time)
    - ☐ The drive will take ______ (number) minutes
    - ☐ We will park in the restaurant parking lot
    - ☐ We will walk into the restaurant
    - ☐ Because we have a reservation, we will tell them our last name
    - ☐ When our table is ready, the hostess will walk us to our chairs
        - ☐ Sometimes restaurants are not ready and we might have to wait
        - ☐ If you have to wait you can:
            - ☐ Talk with the group
            - ☐ Read a book
            - ☐ Put on headphones and listen to music
    - ☐ Once we sit down, the hostess will give us menus
    - ☐ Soon the hostess will ask for our drink order. If the restaurant has it, you can order one of the following:
        - ☐ Water
        - ☐ Lemonade
        - ☐ Orange juice
    - ☐ Put your napkin in your lap
    - ☐ We will look at the menu and choose our food:
        - ☐ You can choose what you want, if you know
        - ☐ If you need help, you can ask me or our server

- [ ] Once we order the food, we will have some time to wait while the chef prepares the food. During this time we can:
  - [ ] Talk
  - [ ] Play hangman
  - [ ] Play cards
- [ ] Once our food arrives, we need to put games away and eat
  - [ ] We will have a conversation during this time
  - [ ] Remember your manners:
    - [ ] Left hand in lap
    - [ ] Chew with your mouth closed
    - [ ] Sit up straight with feet on the floor
    - [ ] Cut food or ask for help
    - [ ] Say please and thank you to the server
    - [ ] Listen as people speak
    - [ ] Take turns talking
- [ ] Once everyone finishes eating
  - [ ] We might talk for a few more minutes to finish our conversation
  - [ ] We will ask for the check
  - [ ] We will pay for the meal
  - [ ] Say thank you
- [ ] Then, we will leave

- [ ] Go to the restaurant with your child
  - [ ] Begin the education process by bringing your child with you on a short restaurant outing during a less busy time (if possible)
  - [ ] Use your preview checklist to keep track of where you are in the process
  - [ ] Make going to a restaurant fun:
    - [ ] Play games with your child
    - [ ] Talk about his favorite subject
  - [ ] Continue to gradually and steadily increase the responsibility your child takes for the process and decrease your support
- [ ] Ask for help
  - [ ] Let him witness you asking for help when you have a question about the menu or need to go to the restroom
  - [ ] As your child develops more independence, coach him to ask a server or hostess to help him
  - [ ] Continue to gradually and steadily increase the responsibility your child takes for the process and decrease your support

- ☐ Reflect with your child—how did it go?
  - ☐ What went well?
  - ☐ What could we do differently the next time?
- ☐ Implement changes on the next trip based on what might not have gone well

(TOOL DEVELOPED WITH INPUT FROM DYMENT, J.H.)

Going to doctors' offices

This process is similar for any doctor's office outing including going to the dentist, specialist doctor, or therapists. This method will help your child develop the foundational skills of going to doctors' offices independently. You can promote independence in younger years by controlling the environment more. If possible, start by being selective about where and when you go. Gradually and steadily increase the child's responsibility and decrease your support. The goal is to make the process manageable and as fun as possible.

- ☐ Make an appointment—let your child hear you make it
  - ☐ As your child develops independence skills, let him practice making appointments
- ☐ Plan ahead
  - ☐ Determine potential issues and develop a plan proactively. For example:
    - ☐ If it gets loud, you can put on music with headphones while waiting to be seated
    - ☐ If you get cold, you can put on a sweater
    - ☐ If you get bored, you can read a book, listen to music, use the activity bag (see Chapter 5), or do homework
    - ☐ If the lights hurt your eyes, you can wear a hat or sunglasses
  - ☐ Collect and bring supplies to support the plan:
    - ☐ Music player
    - ☐ Headphones
    - ☐ Sweater
    - ☐ Book
    - ☐ Activity bag (see Chapter 5)
    - ☐ Homework
    - ☐ Sunglasses
    - ☐ Hat
  - ☐ As your child develops independence, let him develop his own plan for dealing with potential issues and collect the items

- ☐ Identify skills you are teaching and focus on one at a time on subsequent trips. Once your child is competent with one skill, keep practicing it and add another
  - ☐ Learning how to wait
  - ☐ Checking in and providing what receptionist needs
  - ☐ Asking for help
  - ☐ Doing what the nurses and doctors need you to do
- ☐ Preview going to the doctor's office
  - ☐ You are going to your doctor's office __________ (date) at _______ (time)
  - ☐ We will drive to the doctor's office at _________ (time)
  - ☐ The drive will take ______ (number) minutes
  - ☐ We will park in the parking lot
  - ☐ We will walk into the doctor's office and check in with the receptionist. We might have to wait in line. If we have to wait you can:
    - ☐ Put headphones on and listen to music
    - ☐ Sit down in a chair and read your book
  - ☐ We might need to answer some questions that the receptionist asks and we will give the receptionist:
    - ☐ Our insurance card
    - ☐ Our co-pay [health-care insurance fee]
  - ☐ Once we complete with the receptionist, we will walk to the waiting room of the doctor's office. We will have to wait. During this time you can:
    - ☐ Use anything in your activity bag
    - ☐ Do your homework
  - ☐ Once the nurse calls us, she will probably:
    - ☐ Take your weight and height
    - ☐ Walk us to a room
  - ☐ We will have to wait in the room for the doctor. During that time you can:
    - ☐ Use the activity bag
    - ☐ Do your homework
  - ☐ When the doctor arrives, he will:
    - ☐ Ask us questions
    - ☐ Examine you
  - ☐ Once he completes his work, we can leave
- ☐ Go to the doctor's office with your child
  - ☐ Begin the education process by bringing your child during a less busy time (if possible)
  - ☐ Use your preview checklist to keep track of where you are in the process

- ☐ Make going to the doctor's office fun:
  - ☐ Take a special outing after the appointment such as getting a favorite food item or doing a favorite activity
  - ☐ Play games with your child during downtime
  - ☐ Talk about his favorite topic
- ☐ Continue to gradually and steadily increase the responsibility your child takes for the process and decrease your support

☐ Ask for help

- ☐ Let your child witness you asking for help when you have a question
- ☐ As your child develops more independence, coach him to ask for help
- ☐ Continue to gradually and steadily increase the responsibility your child takes for the process and decrease your support

☐ Reflect with your child—how did it go?

- ☐ What went well?
- ☐ What could we do differently the next time?

☐ Implement changes on the next trip based on what might not have gone well

(TOOL DEVELOPED WITH INPUT FROM DYMENT, J.H.)

Going to community offices (such as post office or bank)

This method will help your child develop the foundational skills of going to community offices independently. You can promote independence in younger years by controlling the environment more. If possible, start by being selective about where and when you go. Gradually and steadily increase the child's responsibility and decrease your support. The goal is to make the process manageable and as fun as possible.

☐ Plan ahead

- ☐ Determine potential issues and develop a plan proactively. For example:
  - ☐ If it gets loud, you can put on music with headphones while waiting to be seated
  - ☐ If you get cold, you can put on a sweater
  - ☐ If you get bored, you can listen to music or talk with me
  - ☐ If the lights hurt your eyes, you can wear a hat or sunglasses
- ☐ Collect and bring supplies to support the plan:
  - ☐ Music player
  - ☐ Headphones
  - ☐ Sweater
  - ☐ Sunglasses
  - ☐ Hat
- ☐ As your child develops independence, let him develop his own plan for dealing with potential issues and collect the items

- ☐ Identify skills you are teaching and focus on one at a time on subsequent trips. Once your child is competent with one skill, keep practicing it and add another
    - ☐ Learning how to wait in line
    - ☐ Mailing a package
    - ☐ Buying stamps
    - ☐ Interacting with post office clerk
    - ☐ Asking for help
    - ☐ Paying
- ☐ Preview going to the post office
    - ☐ You are going to your post office today at _______ (time)
    - ☐ We will drive to the post office at _________ (time)
    - ☐ The drive will take ______ (number) minutes
    - ☐ We will park on the street next to the post office
    - ☐ We will walk into the post office and check in with the clerk. We might have to wait in line. If we have to wait you can:
        - ☐ Put headphones on and listen to music
    - ☐ We will ask her to:
        - ☐ Mail a package
        - ☐ Purchase stamps
    - ☐ The post office clerk will:
        - ☐ Weigh our package
        - ☐ Give us the stamps
        - ☐ Tell us how much money we owe
    - ☐ We will pay the money
        - ☐ When your child is old enough to understand, start educating him about paying with cash, check, or credit cards
        - ☐ Talk through the payment process as you do it:
            - ☐ Have money ready
            - ☐ If using a credit card:
                - ☐ Swipe the card when the cashier says it is time
                - ☐ Put the card away safely after you swipe
                - ☐ Sign the receipt, if there is one
        - ☐ Once we pay, we can leave
- ☐ Go to the post office with your child
    - ☐ Begin the education process by bringing your child during a less busy time (if possible)
    - ☐ Use your preview checklist to keep track of where you are in the process

☐ Make going to the post office fun:

- ☐ Take a special outing after the appointment such as getting a favorite food item or doing a favorite activity
- ☐ Play games with your child during downtime
- ☐ Talk about his favorite topic

☐ Continue to gradually and steadily increase the responsibility your child takes for the process and decrease your support

☐ Ask for help

- ☐ Let him witness you asking for help when you have a question
- ☐ As your child develops more independence, coach him to ask for help
- ☐ Continue to gradually and steadily increase the responsibility your child takes for the process and decrease your support

☐ Reflect with your child—how did it go?

- ☐ What went well?
- ☐ What could we do differently the next time?

☐ Implement changes on the next trip based on what might not have gone well

(TOOL DEVELOPED WITH INPUT FROM DYMENT, J.H.)

Using public transportation

This method will help your child develop the foundational skills of taking public transportation independently. You can promote independence in younger years by controlling the environment more. If possible, start by being selective about where and when you go. Gradually and steadily increase the child's responsibility and decrease your support. The goal is to make the process manageable and fun.

☐ Plan ahead

- ☐ Determine potential issues and develop a plan proactively. For example:
  - ☐ If it gets loud, you can put on music with headphones while waiting to be seated
  - ☐ If you get cold, you can put on a sweater
  - ☐ If you get bored, you can listen to music or talk with me
  - ☐ If the lights hurt your eyes, you can wear a hat or sunglasses
- ☐ Collect and bring supplies to support the plan:
  - ☐ Music player
  - ☐ Headphones
  - ☐ Sweater
  - ☐ Sunglasses
  - ☐ Hat
- ☐ As your child develops independence, let him develop his own plan for dealing with potential issues and collect the items

- ☐ Identify skills you are teaching and focus on one at a time on subsequent trips. Once your child is competent with one skill, keep practicing it and add another
  - ☐ Purchasing a ticket
  - ☐ Using a map
  - ☐ Sitting or standing on public transportation
  - ☐ Learning how to wait in line
  - ☐ Dealing with downtime
  - ☐ Purchasing a ticket either with an agent or through a machine
  - ☐ Asking for help
  - ☐ Knowing when to get off
- ☐ Preview the trip with your child
  - ☐ We are going to the science museum today
  - ☐ We will take the subway
  - ☐ Show the route to your child visually
    - ☐ Use a map
    - ☐ Written steps for taking the subway:
      - ☐ We will walk to the _______ (stop name) stop from our house
      - ☐ Pay for our tickets
      - ☐ Get on subway at _________ (stop name) stop going _________ (direction)
      - ☐ Take the subway one stop
      - ☐ Get off at ___________ (stop name) stop
  - ☐ When we are on the subway the plan for sitting or standing is:
    - ☐ Plan A: find a seat together
    - ☐ Plan B: if there is only one available seat, you will sit and I will stand close to you
    - ☐ Plan C: if there is no room, then we will both stand next to each other and hold onto a bar for support
    - ☐ Sit or stand quietly
    - ☐ Respond politely if someone talks to you
    - ☐ Bring something to do during the downtime
    - ☐ Create something to do in the moment if you did not bring anything
    - ☐ Stay alert so you know when to get off
  - ☐ We will know that it is time to get off the subway when:
    - ☐ The subway attendant announces the stop
    - ☐ The train stops
    - ☐ The doors open
  - ☐ We will calmly walk off the train

- [ ] Buy tickets
    - [ ] Discuss how to choose which ticket counter or machine to use:
        - [ ] Choose the line with fewest people
        - [ ] Do not go to a line marked "closed"
    - [ ] Discuss how to wait in line:
        - [ ] Go to the back of the line
        - [ ] Bring something to do during the downtime
        - [ ] Create something to do in the moment if you did not bring anything
        - [ ] Stand quietly
        - [ ] Respond politely if someone speaks to you
        - [ ] Allow enough space, but not too much space, between you and the people in front of and behind you
        - [ ] Stay alert so you know when to move as other people leave
    - [ ] When your child is old enough to understand, start educating him about paying with cash, check, or credit cards
    - [ ] Talk through the payment process as you do it:
        - [ ] Have money ready
        - [ ] If using a credit card:
            - [ ] Swipe the card when the cashier says it is time
            - [ ] Put the card away safely after you swipe
            - [ ] Sign the receipt, if there is one
        - [ ] If you use a machine, discuss every step
        - [ ] As your child develops more independence, allow him to take over part of the process for you
        - [ ] Teach your child that he does not need to tip the cashier!
- [ ] Ride on public transportation with your child
    - [ ] Begin the education process by bringing your child with you on a short trip (one stop) during a less busy time (if possible)
    - [ ] Use your preview checklist to keep track of where you are in the process
    - [ ] Make riding on public transportation fun:
        - [ ] Play games with your child
        - [ ] If your child is visual and artistic, you can ask him to draw a map of public transportation route lines
    - [ ] As your child develops more independence and it feels safe to you, allow him to lead you through part of the process
    - [ ] Continue to gradually and steadily increase the responsibility your child takes for the process and decrease your support

- ☐ Ask for help
  - ☐ Let him witness you asking for help when you are confused or do not know where to go
  - ☐ As your child develops more independence, coach him to ask a public transportation attendant to help him
  - ☐ Continue to gradually and steadily increase the responsibility your child takes for the process and decrease your support
- ☐ Reflect with your child—how did it go?
  - ☐ What went well?
  - ☐ What could we do differently the next time?
- ☐ Implement changes on the next trip based on what might not have gone well

(TOOL DEVELOPED WITH INPUT FROM DYMENT, J.H.)

Flying

This tool can serve as both a preview and a checklist for your child throughout the process. This is an example of the type of tool you can offer your child when he is independent enough to do an activity by himself. Preview the tool and give it to him to use when he flies independently.

Getting started

- ☐ _______ will bring you to the airport
- ☐ You will go with _______ to the airline counter and check in
- ☐ Go through security:
  - ☐ Take electronic items out of your bags and place them in a plastic bin
  - ☐ Take off your shoes, place them in a plastic bin, and put the bin on the conveyor belt
  - ☐ Put your bags on the conveyor belt
  - ☐ Watch your belongings go through the security machine
  - ☐ Pick up all of your belongings at the other side of the conveyor belt once you go through security
- ☐ Walk to the gate with _________
- ☐ Check in at the gate
- ☐ When the airline agent tells you it is time, get on the plane with your bags

First leg of trip: _______ to _______

- ☐ The airline agent will:
  - ☐ Tell you when to board the plane
  - ☐ Help you find your seat

- ☐ When on the plane, store your bags
  - ☐ Backpack—under the chair in front of you
  - ☐ Suitcase—in the overhead bin
- ☐ Sit down and buckle your seat belt
- ☐ Things you can do when seated:
  - ☐ Read
  - ☐ Eat
  - ☐ Work on art
  - ☐ Make lists
  - ☐ Sit quietly
  - ☐ Watch an in-flight movie
  - ☐ Use electronics (when they announce that it is okay):
    - ☐ Watch movies
    - ☐ Listen to music
- ☐ When the flight attendant announces that it is time to discontinue use of electronics:
  - ☐ Turn off electronics
  - ☐ Store in your backpack
- ☐ When the flight attendant announces that you can unbuckle your seat belt:
  - ☐ Unbuckle your seat belt
  - ☐ Collect your bags
- ☐ The airline agent will:
  - ☐ Meet you at your seat
  - ☐ Walk with you to your next gate for the second flight

Second leg of trip: __________ to __________

- ☐ The airline agent will:
  - ☐ Tell you when to board the plane
  - ☐ Help you find your seat
- ☐ When on the plane, store bags
  - ☐ Backpack—under the chair in front of you
  - ☐ Suitcase—in the overhead bin
- ☐ Sit down and buckle your seat belt
- ☐ Things you can do when seated:
  - ☐ Read
  - ☐ Eat

- ☐ Work on art
- ☐ Make lists
- ☐ Sit quietly
- ☐ Watch an in-flight movie
- ☐ Use electronics (when they announce that it is okay):
  - ☐ Watch movies
  - ☐ Listen to music

☐ When the flight attendant announces that it is time to discontinue use of electronics:

- ☐ Turn off electronics
- ☐ Store in your backpack

☐ When the flight attendant announces that you can unbuckle your seat belt:

- ☐ Unbuckle your seat belt
- ☐ Collect your bags

☐ The airline agent will:

- ☐ Meet you at your seat
- ☐ Walk with you to your gate

☐ ________ (person's name) will meet you at the gate!

Safety education

The goal is to define clearly the safety education points that you would like to teach your child to help him learn to keep himself safe in the world. These topics may vary from family to family. These exercises will help you to understand and articulate the safety education important for your child.

- Use the list and examples provided in this section as a springboard to think about safety education topics that would support your child over the next year and later in his or her life. If you do not see a safety education tool that is important to your family, simply create one using these examples as models.
- Once you create safety education tools unique to your child's needs and situation, preview them with your child and have a copy available for review in each situation and environment until he or she integrates the concepts and demonstrates mastery.
- Once you create safety education tools unique to your child's needs and situation, parents, babysitters, and anyone else in a

home care role can use these tools to teach your child how to be safe.

- Safety education topics should be introduced one at a time as part of home education.
- Once the child becomes competent with one safety education topic, continue practicing it and start teaching another one.
- When you create your independence toolbox regarding safety education, put one expectation per page with succinct, simple, accessible instructions. Less writing on each page helps the child with AS avoid visual overload.

The lists and explanations below serve as examples of tools for safety education, which you can consider a springboard to make your own lists. Use the space provided in the template checklists you have downloaded to add points to the safety education tools, or create entirely new tools for safety education that would support your child.

Safety education topics may include:

- ☐ Concentric circles of relationships
- ☐ When to talk with someone you trust
- ☐ What to turn to others for
- ☐ Steps for asking for help

Examples: Safety education

Concentric circles of relationships

Review this concentric circles of relationships visual with your child and explain the expected behavior when interacting with each group: family and close friends, friends, familiar people (teachers and known neighbors), acquaintances, and strangers.

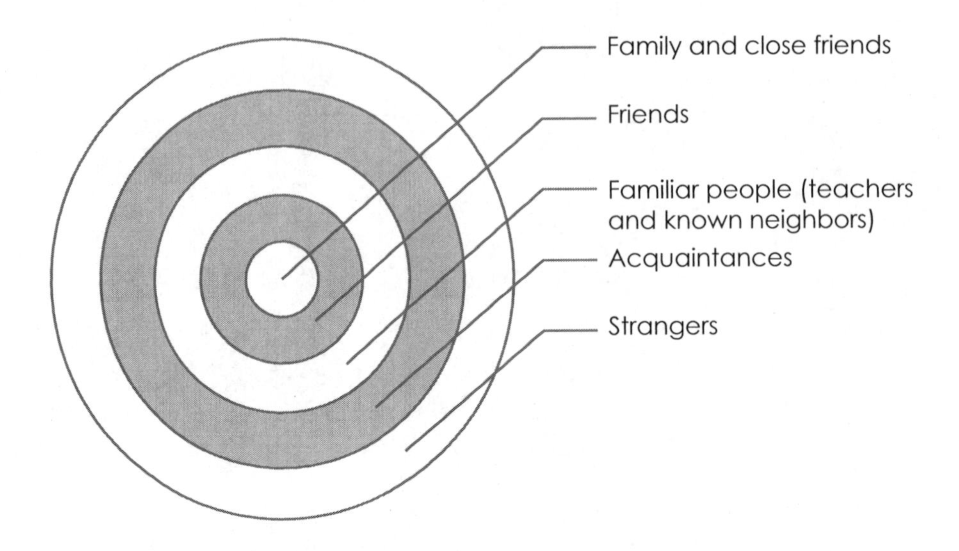

When to talk with someone you trust

Tell someone you trust when:

- ☐ Something bad happens to you, or if you aren't sure if what's happened to you is a bad thing
- ☐ Something good happens to you, or if you aren't sure whether what's happened to you is good
- ☐ A stranger or acquaintance is asking you to engage in social or sexual activity
- ☐ Something happens to you that confuses you or makes you feel bad
- ☐ You experience new, intense, or special feelings such as worry, fear, confusion, excitement, or romantic interest
- ☐ You are feeling really great or when you are feeling really awful

(ZAKS 2006, P.264)

When to turn to others

- ☐ *Relationships*—What is happening?
  - ☐ Are you happy?
  - ☐ Is something not going the way you want it to?
- ☐ *School, camp, or extra-curricular activities*—What is happening?
  - ☐ Are things going well?
  - ☐ Are you having any difficulties?
- ☐ *Emotionally*—How are you feeling and what is happening?
  - ☐ Are you satisfied with your life?
  - ☐ Are you feeling lonely, bored, or frustrated?

- ☐ Things that confuse you
- ☐ Things that you enjoy
- ☐ Problems you are working on or trying to get beyond

(ZAKS 2006, P.265)

Steps for asking for help

1. Approach somebody you trust to ask for help.
2. Tell the trusted person what happened.
3. Ask questions.
4. Listen for advice.
5. Ask more questions if you have any.
6. Come to a conclusion with the help of the trusted adult.
7. Make a decision for the future with the help of a trusted adult.

(ZAKS 2006, P.267)

How to use the toolbox

Now that you have created your promoting independence toolbox, you will be able to:

- decrease stress and increase confidence for your child by clarifying and teaching daily living skills necessary to function independently in every environment in which he or she interacts
- implement structure for home education and have guidelines for a unified approach to parenting
- improve efficiency at school and in the community now that he or she can operate more independently
- help your child generalize skills by using the same strategies in multiple environments.

Chapter 11

Pulling It Together

As we said at the beginning of Chapter 3 and have emphasized throughout the book, AS presents differently in every person. Adults at home, at school, and in the community embarking on new relationships with children with AS often know nothing about their unique profiles. Without explicit education, children with AS often do not themselves understand their unique profiles and needs. For this reason, having professionals with prior experience working with individuals with AS on your team is useful but often not sufficient. This is where your role as case manager begins.

This chapter teaches you how to pull everything in this book together to make a difference for your child and the people with whom he interacts. It includes strategies for how to use the text and your guide, as well as how to share the guide with others.

Using your guide to support your child

By working through each chapter, you have learned to embrace the case manager role, collaborate effectively, and help your child with AS succeed at home, at school, and in the community. This book has taught you how to develop your guide to use as your AS-friendly case management tool.

The text in this book and your guide will help you support your child by educating him and the people that interact with him about his unique profile and needs, clarifying environments, establishing strategies for crises and struggles, and working towards your vision for your child's independence at home, at school, and in the community. The impact of this support and your collaboration efforts is far-reaching. When your child feels understood, calm, and secure in all environments, your family, your child's classmates, group members, teammates, teachers, service providers, and anyone else that interacts with him regularly will benefit.

Step One: Understand your child's unique profile

Everything begins with your child's unique profile. You and your child can advocate most effectively, and you and the professionals at school and in the community can determine best strategies and interventions, when everyone understands your child's unique profile. After determining the specifics of your child's unique profile in Chapter 3, you can revisit this chapter annually and add any new data from assessment results. On the whole, though, this toolbox will probably remain relatively static and is an excellent part of the guide to share with everyone.

Step Two: Lay the foundation for successful collaboration and communication

As we have emphasized throughout this book, you are your child's case manager and the leader of her team. Spend time on the collaboration and communication chapter to figure out how to lay the groundwork for getting the team to work together to support your child. One of the most significant contributions that you can make is to develop and nurture a strong connection with the professionals that support your child. Building these relationships on trust and honest communication will contribute significantly to helping your child thrive in all environments.

Step Three: Clarify environments for your child

Your child will be able to participate more effectively in life at home, at school, and in the community when he understands what is happening, when and why it is happening, what is expected of him, and what the roles of the key players are. The chapters about routines and schedules, behavioral expectations, and important adults will help you explicitly and proactively clarify every environment. You can use the tools from these chapters to educate your child using an AS-friendly, simple, and visual format. These tools can help to structure and organize environments that are often perceived as confusing and chaotic by many children with AS.

Routines and schedules

To set up environments to support your child's needs, make sure that the adults in every environment understand that your child will be most successful when routines and schedules are provided and previewed, and when any changes to the routines and schedules are previewed, too. You will want to develop and revise these tools every new school year, when entering new professional domains, and when routines and schedules change.

Behavioral expectations

Similar to the strategy for implementing routines and schedules, you will want to make sure that adults at home, at school, and in the community understand that your child will be most successful when he understands the behavioral expectations for every context in which he interacts. You will want to develop and revise these tools every new school year, when entering every new professional domain, and when behavioral expectations change.

Important adults

As we've seen, important adults at home, at school, and in the community can impact your child's life significantly. You will get the best results when these adults understand your child and your child understands them and his role when interacting with them. Given the child's social and communication differences, it is possible for misunderstandings and misperceptions to arise in these relationships. The text and tools in this chapter will help you to bridge any gaps and support your child's relationships with important adults in all environments. You can introduce these tools as you introduce your child to new important adults at home, at school, and in the community.

Step Four: Establish strategies for crises and be prepared to address them in the moment

Adults at home, at school, and in the community can better support children with AS, create more harmonious environments for everyone, and avoid traumatic incidents when they are prepared in advance for crises and challenges such as transitions and can respond in the moment. The text and tools in the managing crises and emotions and navigating transitions and changes chapters will help support this process. Your child will manage challenging situations more effectively when adults use consistent strategies and preview these tools with him in every environment.

Managing crises and emotions

Once you agree upon the strategies for managing crises and emotions by developing the crisis response plan, the tools that you need to use will depend on the ebb and flow of your child's personal growth. You and important adults at home, at school, and in the community will likely develop social and behavioral goals to address the crises and emotions that occur in each environment. Adults should understand your child's struggles and intervene when they arise. You should plan to select, modify, and replace tools based on their effectiveness and your child's progress.

Navigating transitions and changes

As we discussed, transitions and changes are hallmark challenges for children with AS. There are a great variety of transitions and changes, and they can occur second to second, day to day, year to year, or only occasionally. Use the tools in this chapter as transitions arise. Some tools might apply on a daily basis, the way that the tools for managing crises and emotions do. Others, such as the transition tools provided to help you prepare for transitioning to the next school year, you will develop once a year, like you do the tools for routines and schedules.

Step Five: Lead your child to independence

As parents and case managers, we are always keeping in mind the big picture, or our vision, for every environment. Our ultimate goal is to help our children with AS to become independent. The tools in Chapter 10 on promoting independence are specifically designed to foster independence, but all of the tools in the book are meant to achieve that end. With each tool, the goal is to fade support as your child achieves greater independence.

Share your guide

Now that you have a foundation of knowledge about AS, have determined how AS uniquely impacts your child, and know what you can do to help your child, you can share your guide. Given that your guide is an instruction booklet for your child, a toolbox and teaching template for his teachers and support team, and a case management road map for you, you will share it in different ways.

Learn how to use your guide as an instruction booklet for your child

Your guide offers a variety of tools that you can use with your child in different ways. You will revisit the unique profile toolbox many times as part of an ongoing profile education process. Use the collaboration and communication toolbox to teach your child AS-friendly strategies that work for him. Preview routines and schedules with your child and keep them visible in every environment. Remember to preview changes, if possible. Introduce tools in your behavioral expectations and independence toolboxes one at a time in every environment. Start with the tools that will have the greatest positive impact for your child. Once your child becomes competent with one tool, you can continue practicing it and introduce another one. You can choose tools from the managing crises and emotions and navigating transitions and changes toolboxes to support your child's greatest struggles. Remember to preview these tools before a crisis, upset, or transition so he knows what to expect.

All of these tools will help lead your child to greater independence. As your child develops, you will slowly transfer the case manager role responsibilities over to her. Her role in helping to develop the guide and to share the information with others will gradually increase from nearly none to a significant amount. The more she is involved in sharing information about herself, the more she will understand the need to help others know her. In other words, as your child's self-awareness—her understanding of her particular profile and struggles—grows, so will her ability to advocate for herself. The vision is that you will teach your child to increasingly share the case management role when she is in high school, and she will assume the case management role as a young adult and beyond. You are now in the process of setting your child up for this independence.

Provide adults with a customized, AS-friendly toolbox and teaching template

Once you develop your guide, you will have a comprehensive and integrated treatment plan that is flexible. Adults at home, at school, and in the community can use this guide as their own toolbox to know how best to support and interact with your child and why. They can also use it to help teach your child, using the same strategies and language across environments, about his unique profile and AS-friendly strategies that work for him. They can clarify their respective environments, proactively put strategies in place for crises, upsets, and challenges, and play an essential role in helping to lead your child to greater independence.

The key is to determine what tools or toolboxes to share with which adult. Which parts of the guide you share with adults at home, at school, and in the community depends on the level and type of involvement the adult has with your child. For example, you will likely share your entire guide with your spouse and childcare professionals at home, your child's special educator at school, and his therapist in the community. Adults that have a moderate level of interaction with your child such as general educators and service providers at school and in the community may need just the unique profile toolbox, the collaboration and communication toolbox, and a few tools that you know will particularly support your child in those specific interactions. For adults that have much less involvement with your child such as an athletic coach, you may only provide the unique profile toolbox. If you are uncertain about what to share with professionals at school, you can identify a person on the school team who can help you make decisions about what to share with whom.

Just as the guide itself is a dynamic document that you can update as your child grows and changes, the process of using the tools is also dynamic. This book provides a comprehensive set of tools to use with your child from kindergarten through eighth grade. You will initially make choices about which tools to share with which adults. While you will likely share the unique profile toolbox with everyone and AS-friendly strategies from the collaboration and communication chapter with most, you will likely swap other tools in and out as your child progresses. You will continue to choose tools to respond to new issues, growth, or circumstances.

The tools and strategies we've presented in this book are based on years of collaborating with a solid team. Your child's teachers may have their own ideas, want to use these tools as a jumping-off point for developing their own tools or strategies, or simply use the tools as they are. Just as many of our tools were contributed by educators and service professionals who have worked with Alexander and our family over the past decade, so your child's teachers and support team may add their own tools to your guide. Your AS-friendly toolbox will serve as a foundation for the collaboration process.

It is important for you to recognize and communicate to other important adults that tools from different chapters often work together to fully address your child's needs and issues. For example, your child may have a meltdown due to an unexpected transition or change that impacts his schedule. In this instance, you may use tools from the transitions chapter, the managing crises and emotions chapter, and the routines and schedules chapters concurrently. Similarly, if your child struggles with a teacher, you may choose tools and strategies from the important adults chapter and review the text for the collaboration and communication chapter.

The process

Once you complete your guide, you can share all of it or parts of it with the professionals at school and in the community. We recommend meeting in person to present the guide and provide an overview, leaving a copy of the guide for the professionals in each environment to explore in depth, and letting them know that you are available to answer any questions or to discuss further.

Working with a child with AS is often complex. To be clear that your goal is to make things simpler and easier, you want to present the guide in a manner that is accessible and helpful. You can explain that the intention of sharing the guide is to:

- provide a resource and toolbox to make their job easier
- save professionals time and effort by answering many of the typical questions that arise when working with a new child, such as "Why is he doing this?" and "What just happened?"
- help organize professionals' thinking and planning about the child
- begin the relationship between professional and home in a proactive way by providing material for dialogue and shared language.

You can let professionals know that they can refer to the guide proactively, in advance, and in the moment of trying to understand what caused a problem or what could have been done differently. Given the breadth of information covered in the guide, you can expect that professionals will read and integrate the information over time.

The way that professionals receive the guide will depend largely on your communication and attitude. Unlike an IEP, your guide is not legally binding. Remember that you are making a request that the adults modify their behavior with your child to help him be more successful. You can help them make the connection that the tools in your guide will support them and your child, and that your child will interact more effectively and access more of their environment, and remain calmer, if they follow these suggestions. Check in and ask if they are agreeable and equipped to carry them out. If so, you are off to a great start. Showing them your appreciation will likely keep things moving in the right direction and make your advocacy efforts more successful in the long run.

Use your guide as a case management road map

Once you develop your guide, you will have all you need to become a skilled case manager. You can do this! You can use the tools in your guide to support yourself, your child, and everyone that interacts with him at home, at school, and in the community. In every environment, keep the guide accessible for your child and the pertinent adults.

At home, you can use your guide to:

- organize yourself to be a case manager
- educate your child about his unique profile and needs and how to interact effectively at home, remain calm, and become more independent
- align your parenting approach. Divorce rates are high for parents of children with special needs. You can alleviate many stressors by getting on the same page, being more consistent parents, and creating a more harmonious home environment
- teach siblings about your child with AS. They will also benefit from many of the tools
- train childcare professionals
- share important information with family and close friends.

At school and in the community, you can use your guide to:

- collaborate with your child's team
- educate your child's team about your child's unique profile and needs
- provide your child's team with an AS-friendly toolbox, customized to your child's profile and needs
- help your child understand himself and the environments in which he interacts, remain calm, and become more independent.

A message from the authors

We understand that parenting a child with AS is complex, and we designed this book to help you make your life and your child's life easier and more harmonious. Our goal has been to join you and walk with you through the process of supporting yourself, your child, and the people who interact with her.

We know that we have covered a lot of ground and provided a lot of information. We also recognize that the process of creating and sharing your guide and toolbox requires an initial investment of time and effort, but we believe in the long run it will save you and others a lot of time and heartache. The templates available to download from www.jkp.com/go/elwoodandmcleod will help you develop your customized guide easily and quickly.

Use this book as a resource to decrease your stress and increase your effectiveness. As we said in the introduction, approach it in any way that makes most sense to you and for your life. Just as you individualize the guide to reflect your child's unique profile and needs, feel free to customize your approach. In my experience, being able to think comprehensively about Alexander and his needs by using most of the tools has proven useful. After developing your guide, you may take a different tack and want to start simply with one, two, or three tools that have a powerful effect and slowly add more as they make sense for your child. You want to be sure that the process is manageable for you, your child, and his team. You have the ability to positively impact many lives in your case manager role. May the guide and toolbox you've created serve as a road map for a successful journey.

Conclusion

Since I introduced our guide, Alexander's experience and the experiences of people that interact with him have improved significantly. Interacting with Alexander is still different from interacting with typically developing children, but now the adults in his life understand his unique presentation in the world and why he sometimes acts in unexpected ways. Rather than judging his behavior as "bad" and feeling frustrated, they can now recognize his actions as predictable aspects of his profile. They can anticipate his triggers and help him manage them. For example, most teachers preview fire alarms with him now because they know the noise will upset him. One teacher wrote out an action plan showing him how to proceed when the alarm sounded. The staff also made headphones available to lessen the impact of the loud ringing. Using the guide, they can respond quickly with interventions that guide Alexander to peace and success. Most adults that he interacts with now respect him for working so hard, feel empathy for the complexity of his struggles, and experience less distress when working with him. Many enjoy him and develop a close bond with him.

As I have shared with you throughout this book, prior to creating the guide, Alexander's new teachers and professionals in the community entered a minefield when the school year or a new activity started. I watched the disruption and chaos helplessly as it took several months for the school staff to really get to know Alexander's profile. Everyone was doing the best they could at the time, including Alexander, but the experience was miserable for all of us. I now have the tools and knowledge to join the educators and professionals during the learning curve, and we proceed through the minefield together. My guide is our map, which I can use to help lead them away from the landmines that are part of his profile. The learning curve is now much shorter. Teachers and professionals can focus on their expertise rather than reacting to explosions, and can spend their time finding ways to take Alexander's growth to a new level.

We have been fortunate to encounter teachers and other professionals who have been willing and able to work with Alexander using the tools and strategies we've developed. Alexander's fourth and fifth grade special educator collaborated with me to build part of my school guide and carefully reviewed the other information I provided in the guide. She became an influential advocate and trusted partner in helping Alexander thrive. She used the guides in weekly school team meetings, as a resource for herself both proactively and in the moment, and to train the new staff.

Before Alexander's sixth grade year, I reviewed copies of his guide with his new teachers. His new special educator and I collaborated well and worked from a common understanding from the start. Alexander regularly communicated that he liked school that year, which was a happy new experience for all of us. Issues still arose, but we were able to address them before they spiraled out of control. We used strategies and tools that have proven to work well for Alexander over time. In addition, his special educator created new tools, which we added to our guide. One of her many strengths is positive reinforcement. Alexander deeply appreciated her weekly notes, which acknowledged him for all of the things he did well during the week (see the weekly reinforcement letter in the Parents Take Charge section of Chapter 9). Her positive words helped ease the transition to each new week and build their relationship, and her support motivated him to try harder.

I introduced an abridged version of Alexander's school guide to his school team during his transition meeting for seventh grade. They were very receptive to the information, understanding it would help them and him succeed. They hadn't received anything like our guide before and expressed how helpful they found it.

Alexander senses this shift and feels understood and respected. The positive reinforcement that he receives boosts his self-confidence. He remains calm more often, which allows him greater access to his social and academic curricula. He is happy and thriving, and every environment in which he interacts benefits.

In addition to teachers and professionals, Alexander himself contributes to the positive trajectory. He understands himself and his home, school, and community much better as a result of the guide, and his self-awareness helps him advocate for himself. For example, he fully grasps that his sensory system may cause him problems many times every day, and he uses his strategies to cope with these problems successfully. If the noise in a classroom or at home escalates to a point that is too loud for him, he often remembers to ask for a break to leave the room before he gets too frustrated. He also knows that schedules support him in every environment. If he feels confused about what is happening during an activity or a particular school day, he asks for a schedule. He now realizes that if he has a meltdown then other people will likely have negative thoughts about him. He doesn't want to embarrass himself.

Home, school, and the community no longer baffle Alexander. He has learned many of the rules and expectations for different environments. He now knows or is told what it takes to be a family member at home, a student at school, and a participant in the community in all aspects of his day. If he forgets, his teachers, professionals, and I use written reminders. We preview and review expectations with him before new events. Alexander has come to grasp, for example, that he needs to have nice manners at the dinner table, interact with his principal in a different way than he interacts with his peers, and participate according to his psychologist's behavioral expectations in her office. He wants so badly to do well. His perseverance inspires me.

All of us, including Alexander, continue to make mistakes. Struggles arise, but we have not had a crisis since I introduced the guide. We continue to learn every day. Alexander grows and changes, and we recognize that our strategies must evolve with him. The difference is that the fear and inadequacy that we felt has largely transformed into confidence. We are operating from a much stronger position, and his support team and I now use the same strategies and speak the same language.

Learning to support Alexander has been the foundation of our success. I understand his profile. I enjoy collaborating with the members of his team. I am his case manager, and I fully embrace my role. My advocacy efforts are now helping him reach his full potential at home, at school, and in the community. We will always experience highs and lows, but I know how to support Alexander and the value of communicating effective strategies to everyone who works with him. As we collectively uncover more successful tools and techniques, I will continue to add them to my guide. My guide is my evolving case management tool that provides me with a road map, his support team with a toolbox and teaching template, and Alexander with an instruction booklet for how to be a family member, student, and community participant. We have a strategic plan.

As I have shared with you, this journey has been humbling and at times difficult, with unexpected twists and turns. However, I've also received many deep and meaningful rewards for which I am grateful. Every struggle taught me something valuable. Every player contributed positively to our lives, even when situations or interactions were uncomfortable. The struggles ignited my creativity and forced me to grow and find solutions. In addition to learning how to support Alexander, I have learned the importance of remembering to savor his growth and successes, have a sense of humor, and nurture myself. Alexander's unique expression of life inspires me to be the best person I can be so that I can connect with him in a meaningful way and help him realize peace, happiness, and independence. I recognize that he does best when I can love and accept unconditionally, be open-minded, be honest, have compassion and empathy, and be patient. His words or actions will quickly remind me when I do not achieve this standard. I receive this reminder as a beautiful, daily gift because I feel best when I achieve this standard, too.

I have deep respect for what Alexander and other individuals with AS go through every day. I recognize how hard Alexander works to navigate a world that often feels confusing, overwhelming, and assaulting to his sensory system. Individuals with AS must expend an incredible amount of energy even before the typical demands of life begin. I feel great fulfillment that my guide can help Alexander with his struggles. I am hopeful that your guide will help your child, too.

Many members of our family, the school staff, and the community have risen far above and beyond the call of duty to support Alexander and our family. I will always remember those generous contributors with appreciation. I learned a tremendous amount through the strengths of every individual with whom I have collaborated. These important adults each uniquely touched my life and helped take Alexander to new heights in his growth.

I hope my experience helps you to recognize that you are not alone. There are solutions, and some of the most difficult times lead to unexpected, deep satisfaction and life gains. For me, finding solutions to Alexander's problems felt similar to creating art. As I created and shared my guide with others, something transformative occurred. I felt a deep sense of personal satisfaction. After feeling lost and helpless for so long, I began to feel stimulated and purposeful. I finally knew that I could make a difference. You can make a difference, too. I hope you can use my struggles to overcome your own more quickly. I hope that the insights from the experiences I shared and the expertise Scott provides might serve you in the way that I so desperately wanted when I started this journey. We wrote this book to provide you with all of the information and tools that took me years of struggle, schooling, and collaborating with Alexander's special educators, professionals, and Scott to understand. We want you to start your journey prepared.

I encourage you to embrace your role. We know you didn't ask for it and that it can be challenging. However, if you rise to the challenge, then you, your child, and every person with whom he or she interacts will benefit. You will start him or her on a path leading towards self-awareness, independence, harmony, and social and academic achievement.

It is difficult to put into words the depth of gratitude that I feel towards Alexander. Just by being himself, he has helped me evolve as a person, inspired me spiritually and intellectually, and introduced many people, topics, and ideas into my life that I might have never known. Being his mother has been an adventure, and, though we have encountered both treacherous and awe-inspiring terrain, I find adventures highly stimulating. I thank him from the bottom of my heart for adding such richness and color to my life and for allowing me to share our personal journey with you.

References

Abele, E., and Montgomery, B. (October 2, 2010) *Training in the Social Use of Language.* Presentation at Antioch University for PYI 542.

American Psychiatric Association (2013) *Diagnostic and Statistical Manual of Mental Disorders, DSM-5.* Arlington, VA: APA. Available at http://dsm.psychiatryonline.org.

Attwood, T., Henault, I., and Dubin, N. (2014) *The Autism Spectrum, Sexuality and the Law: What Every Parent and Professional Needs to Know.* London: Jessica Kingsley Publishers.

Braaten, E., and Felopulos, G. (2004) *Straight Talk about Psychological Testing for Kids.* New York and London: Guilford Press.

Buron, K.D. (2007) *A 5 Is Against the Law! Social Boundaries: Straight Up! An Honest Guide for Teens and Young Adults.* Shawnee Mission, KS: Autism Asperger Publishing Company.

Buron, K.D., and Curtis, M. (2003) *The Incredible 5-Point Scale: Assisting Students with Autism Spectrum Disorders in Understanding Social Interactions and Controlling Their Emotional Responses.* Shawnee Mission, KS: Autism Asperger Publishing Company.

Cronin, M. (January 9, 2011) *Educational Interventions for Children with Asperger's Syndrome and High Functioning Autism II.* Presentation at Antioch University for FYI 539B.

Epstein, L., and Mardon, S. (2007) *The Harvard Medical School Guide to a Good Night's Sleep.* New York: McGraw-Hill.

Freedman, S. (2010) *Developing College Skills in Students with Autism and Asperger's Syndrome* (First edition). London: Jessica Kingsley Publishers.

Friedberg, R.D., and McClure, J.M. (2002) *Clinical Practice of Cognitive Therapy with Children and Adolescents: The Nuts and Bolts.* New York and London: Guilford Press.

Gray, C. & White, A.L. (2002). *My Social Stories Book.* London: Jessica Kingsley Publishers.

Gray, C. (2010) *The New Social Stories Book, Revised and Expanded 10th Anniversary Edition: Over 150 Social Stories that Teach Everyday Social Skills to Children with Autism or Asperger Syndrome, and their Peers.* Arlington, TX: Future Horizons.

Hane, R.E.J., Sibley, K., Shore, S.M., Meyer, R.N., Schwarz, P., and Willey, L.H. (2004) *Ask and Tell: Self-Advocacy and Disclosure for People on the Autism Spectrum.* Shawnee Mission, KS: Autism Asperger Publishing Company.

Korin, E. (May 1, 2011) *Working With Teens and Adults on the Autism Spectrum.* Presentation for Antioch University for PYI 537BS.

Kranowitz, C. (2010) *The Goodenoughs Get in Sync: 5 Family Members Overcome Their Special Sensory Issues.* Arlington, TX: Sensory World.

Kuypers, L. (2011) *The Zones of Regulation: A Curriculum Designed to Foster Self-Regulation and Emotional Control.* San Jose, CA: Social Thinking Publishing.

Miller, L.J. (2006) *Sensational Kids: Hope and Help for Children with Sensory Processing Disorder.* New York: Penguin Group (USA).

Myles, B.S., and Simpson, R.L. (2001) 'Understanding the hidden curriculum: an essential social skill for children and youth with Asperger Syndrome.' *Intervention in School and Clinic 36*, 5, 279–286.

Myles, B.S., and Southwick, J. (2005) *Asperger Syndrome and Difficult Moments: Practical Solutions for Tantrums, Rage, and Meltdowns.* Shawnee Mission, KS: Autism Asperger Publishing Company.

Myles, B.S., Trautman, M.L., and Schelvan, R.L. (2004) *The Hidden Curriculum: Practical Solutions for Understanding Unstated Rules in Social Situations.* Shawnee Mission, KS: Autism Asperger Publishing Company.

Prutting, C.A., and Kirchner, D.M. (1987) 'A clinical appraisal of the pragmatic aspects of language.' *Journal of Speech and Hearing Disorders 52*, 2, 105–119.

Stoner, J., Bock, S.J., Thompson, J.R., Angell, M.E., Heyl, B.S., and Crowley, E.P. (2005) 'Welcome to our world: parents' perceptions of interactions between parents of young children with ASD and educational professionals.' *Focus on Autism and Other Disabilities 20*, 1, 39–51.

Williams, M.S., and Shellenberger, S. (1996) *"How Does Your Engine Run?" A Leader's Guide to The Alert Program for Self-Regulation.* Albuquerque, NM: TherapyWorks.

Winner, M.G. (2005) *Think Social! A Social Thinking Curriculum for School-Age Students for Teaching Social Thinking and Related Skills to Students with High Functioning Autism, PDD-NOS, Asperger Syndrome, Nonverbal Learning Disability, ADHD* (First edition). San Jose, CA: Think Social Publishing.

Winner, M.G. (2007) *Thinking about YOU Thinking about ME: Teaching Perspective Taking and Social Thinking to Persons with Social Cognitive Learning Challenges.* San Jose, CA: Think Social Publishing.

Yack, E., Aquilla, P., and Sutton, S. (2003) *Building Bridges Through Sensory Integration: Therapy for Children with Autism and Other Pervasive Developmental Disorders.* Las Vegas, NV: Sensory Resources.

Zaks, Z. (2006) *Life and Love: Positive Strategies for Autistic Adults.* Shawnee Mission, KS: Autism Asperger Publishing Company.

Recommended Resources

Books

Attwood, T. (2007) *The Complete Guide to Asperger's Syndrome.* London: Jessica Kingsley Publishers.

Buron, K.D., and Curtis, M. (2003) *The Incredible 5-Point Scale: Assisting Students with Autism Spectrum Disorders in Understanding Social Interactions and Controlling Their Emotional Responses.* Shawnee Mission, KS: Autism Asperger Publishing Company.

Dater, B. (2014) *Parenting without Panic: A Pocket Support Group for Parents of Children and Teens on the Autism Spectrum.* London: Jessica Kingsley Publishers.

Epstein, L., and Mardon, S. (2007) *The Harvard Medical School Guide to a Good Night's Sleep.* New York: McGraw-Hill.

Freedman, S. (2010) *Developing College Skills in Students with Autism and Asperger's Syndrome* (First edition). London: Jessica Kingsley Publishers.

Gray, C. (2010) *The New Social Stories Book, Revised and Expanded 10th Anniversary Edition: Over 150 Social Stories that Teach Everyday Social Skills to Children with Autism or Asperger Syndrome, and their Peers.* Arlington, TX: Future Horizons.

Klin, A., Volkmar, F., and Sparrow, S. (2000) *Asperger Syndrome* (First edition). New York and London: Guilford Press.

Kranowitz, C. (2010) *The Goodenoughs Get in Sync: 5 Family Members Overcome Their Special Sensory Issues.* Arlington, TX: Sensory World.

Miller, L. J. (2006) *Sensational Kids: Hope and Help for Children with Sensory Processing Disorder.* New York: Penguin Group (USA).

Myles, B.S., and Southwick, J. (2005) *Asperger Syndrome and Difficult Moments: Practical Solutions for Tantrums, Rage, and Meltdowns.* Shawnee Mission, KS: Autism Asperger Publishing Company.

Myles, B.S., Trautman, M.L., and Schelvan, R.L. (2004) *The Hidden Curriculum: Practical Solutions for Understanding Unstated Rules in Social Situations.* Shawnee Mission, KS: Autism Asperger Publishing Company.

Schilling, C. (2010) *The Best Kind of Different: Our Family's Journey with Asperger's Syndrome.* New York: HarperCollins.

Winner, M.G. (2005) *Think Social! A Social Thinking Curriculum for School-Age Students for Teaching Social Thinking and Related Skills to Students with High Functioning Autism, PDD-NOS, Asperger Syndrome, Nonverbal Learning Disability, ADHD* (First edition). San Jose, CA: Think Social Publishing.

Yack, E., Aquilla, P., and Sutton, S. (2003) *Building Bridges Through Sensory Integration: Therapy for Children with Autism and Other Pervasive Developmental Disorders.* Las Vegas, NV: Sensory Resources.

Websites

MGH Aspire
www.mghaspire.org

Lurie Center for Autism
www.luriecenter.org

Asperger/Autism Network
www.aane.org

Social Thinking
www.socialthinking.com

The Gray Center for Social Learning and Understanding
www.CarolGraySocialStories.com

Autism Risk & Safety Management
www.autismriskmanagement.com

DVD

Mind Reading: An Interactive Guide by Simon Baron-Cohen
www.jkp.com/mindreading

List of Tools

List of Social Stories™

Chapter 10: Promoting Independence

Index

Sub-headings in *italics* indicate tables.

  preview information about new adults with your child 183

S